OLD TESTAMENT STUDIES

Edited by

David J. Reimer

OLD TESTAMENT STUDIES

The mid-twentieth century was a period of great confidence in the study of the Hebrew Bible: many historical and literary questions appeared to be settled, and a constructive theological programme was well underway. Now, at the turn of the century, the picture is very different. Conflicting positions are taken on historical issues; scholars disagree not only on how to pose the questions, but also on what to admit as evidence. Sharply divergent methods are used in ever more popular literary studies of the Bible. Theological ferment persists, but is the Bible's theological vision coherent, or otherwise?

The Old Testament Studies series provides an outlet for thoughtful debate in the fundamental areas of biblical history, theology and literature. Martin Hengel is well known for his seminal work on early Judaism and nascent Christianity. In this volume he turns his attention to the Septuagint—the first bible of the church, yet a product of Greek-speaking Judaism. Hengel probes into the historical and theological puzzles posed by the Septuagint opening a window on the formation of canon and attitudes to scripture in the Christian tradition, and on the relationship between Judaism and Christianity in the early centuries of the era.

THE SEPTUAGINT
AS CHRISTIAN SCRIPTURE

THE SEPTUAGINT AS CHRISTIAN SCRIPTURE

Its Prehistory and the Problem of Its Canon

Martin Hengel

with the assistance of Roland Deines

Introduction by
Robert Hanhart

Translated by
Mark E. Biddle

T&T CLARK
EDINBURGH & NEW YORK

T&T CLARK LTD

A Continuum imprint

59 George Street
Edinburgh EH2 2LQ
Scotland

www.tandtclark.co.uk

370 Lexington Avenue
New York 10017–6503
USA

www.continuumbooks.com

First published 2002

ISBN 0 567 08737 9

British Library Cataloguing-in-Publication Data
A catalogue record for this book is available from the British Library

Typeset by Waverley Typesetters, Galashiels
Printed and bound in Great Britain by MPG Books Ltd, Bodmin, Cornwall

In honour of my colleague
Luise Abramowski

CONTENTS

Preface   xi

Select Bibliography   xv

Introduction: Problems in the History of the LXX Text from
Its Beginnings to Origen   1
by Robert Hanhart

I. A Difficult Subject   19

**II. The LXX as a Collection of Writings Claimed by
Christians**   25

  1. The Translation Legend in Judaism and the Number
of the Translators   25

  2. Justin   26
    (a) The Legend in the Apology *and* Dialogue   26
    (b) Justin's 'Old Testament Library'   28
    (c) The Dispute about the Translation of Isaiah 7:14   29
    *(d) The Appeal to the Seventy and the Charge of
    Falsifying Scripture*   31
    (e) The 'Generous' Treatment of Minor Variants   33
    *(f) Justin's Appeal to the Seventy in his Discussion
    with Jews in Rome*   34

  3. The Seventy in Later 'Dialogues'   35

  4. The Translation Legend in the Early Fathers after Justin   36
    (a) Persistent Problems   36
    (b) Pseudo-Justin's Cohortatio ad Graecos   37
    (c) Irenaeus   38
    (d) Clement and Tertullian   40
    (e) Summary   40

  5. The Form of the Christian LXX   41

  6. The Jewish Reaction   43

  7. The Question of the Hebrew 'Originals'   47

  8. Augustine's Attempt at Compromise   51

  9. The Problem of the *Book of Enoch*   54

**III. The Later Consolidation of the Christian 'Septuagint
Canon'**   57

1. The First Codices: The Writings Contained in Them
   and Their Order   57

2. The Earliest Canon Lists   60

3. The 'Second Class' Character of the Writings Not
   Contained in the 'Hebrew Canon'   66

4. The Rejection of Authentic 'Apocrypha'   70

IV. The Origin of the Jewish LXX   75

1. The Translation of the Torah and Its Enduring
   Significance   75

2. The Translation of Other Writings   80
   (a) Dependence on Palestinian Judaism   80
   *(b) The Translation and Origin of Individual
   Writings*   83
   (c) The Writings Not Found in the 'Hebrew Canon'   91

3. The Canon in the Jewish Diaspora   96
   (a) The Prologue of Jesus ben Sirach   96
   (b) Philo's Therapeutae   98
   (c) Josephus: Ap 1:37–43   99

**V. The Origin of the 'Christian Septuagint' and Its
Additional Writings**   105

1. Early Christianity   105

2. The Problem of the Inclusion of the Writings Not
   Contained in the 'Hebrew Canon'   112
   (a) Writings Outside the 'Hebrew Canon'   113
   *(b) Independent Documents outside the 'Hebrew
   Canon'*   114
   *(c) The Dissemination and Prevalence of These Writings
   in the Church*   122

Index of Biblical and Extra-Biblical Citations   129

Index of Authors   143

Index of Subjects   147

PREFACE

With the Septuagint, it is the same as in Goethe's lines:

Poems are painted window panes!
From the market one looks into the church,
Where all is dark and sombre . . .

A considerable number of theologians regard the Septuagint as Goethe views the poems in 'der Herr Philister': they know it, if at all, merely from the outside, and are therefore able to do little with it. At best, it has a subservient function, for example in aiding the establishment of the text of the Hebrew Bible, as proof of quotations and allusions, and also for New Testament lexicography. Due to the overwhelming orientation toward the original Hebrew text of the Old Testament and the Greek text of the New Testament, larger related passages in the Septuagint, let alone one or more books, are seldom read with the aim of ascertaining their style, translation technique and historical locus. Rather, the Septuagint is used as a reference work for individual verses and sections. This view 'from the market into the church' where 'all [seems] dark and sombre' distorts our understanding of its intrinsic historical and theological value. The Septuagint is not only a unique linguistic monument without analogy in the Greek literature of antiquity (no other work of this scale was translated into Greek from a foreign language), but it also constitutes the first complete and pre-Christian 'commentary' to the Old Testament. For every translation is an interpretation, and the LXX, as the first rendering of the writings of the Hebrew Bible into the Greek lingua franca, is this in an especial way. It was both the bible of primitive Christianity and the early church until well into the second century, and later it was the 'Old Testament' of the Greek church. Also, it fundamentally formed the theological language of oldest Christianity and, moreover, assisted in changing and leaving its mark on the spiritual world of late Antiquity.

This relative neglect of the Septuagint has many different causes. First of all, some are external, in that there is still no handy bilingual Hebrew-Greek version which would make constant comparison possible, inviting intensive and continuous reading. Further, the excellent Göttingen edition is still unfinished (and the price virtually prohibitive), while Rahlfs's widely disseminated edition is scarcely sufficient for academic purposes because of its too narrow textual basis, all too limited critical apparatus, and, in particular, because the most important references to variants of the later revisions and reworking of the text are virtually completely absent. Thus, the revision of Rahlfs's Psalm edition in the Göttingen Septuagint is an urgent desideratum. Second, the Septuagint is seen as a 'mere' (and thus second-class) 'translation', of interest to only a few specialists of the intertestamental period— although particularly in its latest writings it shows that the 'Old Testament' lasted into the first century AD, that is, until the time of Jesus and early Christianity. It is thus easily overlooked that the Septuagint represents anything but a unity. Rather it stems from 350 years of turbulent history and represents the most important self-witness to Greek-speaking Judaism. The basic study of so-called 'Hellenistic Judaism' of the understanding of early Christianity in the truest sense of the word, should begin with the Septuagint and not with Philo of Alexandria. For Philo, being a Jewish religious philosopher, was rather an outsider; his actual theological achievement lay in the fact that he, as a Platonizing philosopher, extensively interpreted, in several stages, the translation of the Pentateuch by the Seventy.

However, when one does actually enter the 'holy chapel' and 'is greeted', one cannot escape astonishment:

> There at once it's coloured bright,
> History and ornament flashing light,
> Portentous effect of a gentle glow;
> This to God's children applies,
> Flourish and feast your eyes!

This translation contains an immense richness of philological, historical and theological points of view, and one can continually make new discoveries both in it and in the history of its influence on Jews and Christians. Further, the Septuagint is an ecumenical work, even though the object of Judaeo-Christian controversy for two centuries (until the Christians snatched it away from the Jews, who replaced it with Aquila's 'Greek Targum'), not only because it is still the Bible of the Orthodox Church today but also much more because through the so-called apocryphal books it constantly reminds the Christian church of its Jewish roots.

Unlike the New Testament, its fifty-three documents (without the *Psalms of Solomon*) still offer a fallow field in which new discoveries can be made in diverse ways, both from the point of view of the formation of the texts at various times, places and under different influences, and from the point of view of the history of its controversial impact, which is a basic component of church history.

The important introductory essay which Prof. Dr Robert Hanhart, the great Septuagint scholar, contributed to this volume goes back to a Tübingen Oberseminar during the winter term 1990/1. At this Oberseminar I delivered a short version of my book which on the

whole has a long and complicated history. His opinion deviated from
mine on several points, and this makes his contribution especially
valuable. The problems of the Septuagint need open discussion.

A first, much briefer version was presented in 1987 in a series of
papers concerning the development of the canon and the inter-
confessional differences pertinent to the scope of its Old Testament
portion at an annual meeting of the Ecumenical Working Group of
Protestant and Catholic theologians. After thorough editing and
expansion, section II:1–4 (pp. 25–41) of the same paper comprised the
basis for a paper at the second Durham–Tübingen Research Symposium
on Earliest Christianity and Judaism in Durham, England, in September
1989. The leading theme of the symposium was the division between
Jews and Christians in the first and second centuries. It appeared in
1992 in the symposium volume edited by J. D. G. Dunn (*Jews and
Christians: The Parting of the Ways A.D. 70 to 135* [WUNT I/66;
Tübingen, 1992], 39–84) under the title 'Die Septuaginta als von den
Christen beanspruchte Schriftensammlung bei Justin und den Vätern vor
Origenes'. Since the papers of the Ecumenical Working Group are also
now being published, I prepared the whole paper for publication with
the assistance of Dr Roland Deines. Dr Deines has been very helpful in
editing the notes and twice preparing the manuscript in various versions.
The greatly abbreviated summary of my contribution to the collected
volume of the second Durham–Tübingen Symposium is also his work. I
offer him cordial thanks here for his energetic assistance. In the
meanwhile, the papers of the Theological Working Group have also
appeared in print under the title *Verbindliches Zeugnis 1:
Kanon-Schrift-Tradition*, W. Pannenberg and T. Schneider, eds
(Dialogue der Kirchen VII; Freiburg and Göttingen, 1992). My
contribution is printed there on pp. 34–127. Since then, I have reworked
and supplemented it. For their valuable advice, I thank my colleagues
Robert Hanhart, Anna Maria Schwemer and Christoph Markschies.

MARTIN HENGEL

SELECT BIBLIOGRAPHY

An extensive bibliography up to and including 1969 appears in: S. P. Brock, C. T. Frisch and S. Jellicoe, *A Classified Bibliography of the Septuagint* (Leiden, 1973). It is supplemented in the *Bulletin of the International Organization of Septuagint and Cognate Studies* (abbreviated BIOSCS) which has appeared since 1968. E. Tov assembled a specialized bibliography covering lexical and grammatical problems: *A Classified Bibliography of Lexical and Grammatical Studies on the Language of the Septuagint* (Jerusalem, 1982). The following also offer overviews with rich bibliographies: E. Tov, 'Die griechischen Bibelübersetzungen', *ANRW* II 20/1 (Berlin and New York, 1987): 121–89; S. P. Brock, 'Bibelübersetzungen I 2: Die Übersetzungen des Alten Testaments ins Griechische', *TRE* VI (1980), 163–72.

The fundamental literature mentioned below (in alphabetical order) will be cited in the footnotes only by the author's name. In all other references to literature, the bibliographical information will be stated at the first occurrence and thereafter will be indicated only by author's name and, if necessary, short title:

D. BARTHÉLEMY, *Études d'histoire du texte de l'Ancien Testament* (OBO 21; Freiburg and Göttingen, 1978), a collection of essays with many important works on the LXX.

R. BECKWITH, *The Old Testament Canon of the New Testament Church and Its Background in Early Judaism* (London, 1985).

G. J. BROOKE and B. LINDARS, eds, *Septuagint, Scrolls and Cognate Writings* (SBL.SCSS 33; Atlanta, 1992), a collection of essays.

O. EISSFELDT, *Einleitung in das Alte Testament* (4th edn; Tübingen, 1976).

M. HARL, G. DORIVAL and O. MUNNICH, *La Bible Grecque des Septante* (Paris, 1988), an extensive summary of research with a comprehensive bibliography.

S. JELLICOE, *The Septuagint and Modern Study* (Oxford, 1968).

S. JELLICOE and H. M. ORLINSKY, eds, *Studies in the Septuagint: Origins, Recensions, and Interpretation: Selected Essays with a Prolegomenon by S. Jellicoe* (New York, 1974), cited as *Studies*.

J.-D. KAESTLI and O. WERMELINGER, eds, *Le Canon de l'Ancien Testament* (Geneva, 1984), a collection of essays.

F. G. KENYON and A. W. ADAMS, *Der Text der griechischen Bibel* (Göttingen, 1961).

E. SCHÜRER, G. VERMES, F. MILLAR and M. GOODMAN, *The History of the Jewish People in the Age of Jesus Christ*, Vols I–III/2 (Edinburgh, 1973–87), cited as Schürer [rev.].

A. C. SUNDBERG, *The Old Testament in the Early Church* (HTS 20; Cambridge, Mass., and London, 1964).

H. B. SWETE, *An Introduction to the Old Testament in Greek* (Cambridge, 1902 = New York, 1968).

J. ZIEGLER, *Sylloge: Gesammelte Aufsätze zur Septuaginta* (MSU 10; Göttingen, 1971).

INTRODUCTION

Problems in the History of the LXX Text
from Its Beginnings to Origen

ROBERT HANHART

To appear suddenly in an advanced seminar, unfamiliar with its previous proceedings, can easily awaken fear—fear of explicating what is already well known, but even more of contradicting the shared conclusions of seminar members, so that, afterward, they face the task of reconsidering everything. My colleague, Prof. Dr Hengel, who has informed me of the general theme of your seminar and has prepared me intellectually with his extremely rich study of 'The Septuagint as Christian Scripture and the Development of Its Canon', has somewhat mitigated this second fear with his gracious statement that he desired my participation precisely 'because'—I quote—'you see many things differently' (letter of 3 September 1990). One thesis underlying my presentation, entitled 'Problems in the History of the LXX Text from Its Beginnings to Origen', will probably very quickly become apparent to you as such a 'different perspective'. Now the defence of a thesis is not easy in any case—recently I read the following statement in a newspaper: 'Whoever defends a thesis must leave gaps.' The gaps may often be filled by that which questions or even contradicts the thesis. With this reservation and in the hope that, if not the thesis, then a few of the detailed observations may be valuable to you, I dare appear before you; I hope not like a wild boar in the vineyard of the Lord (Ps. 80[LXX 79]:14).

As befits my discipline, I would like to present a few thoughts concerning the history of the LXX text from the time of its origin to the time of its final establishment as 'Holy Scripture' in the Christian church. The beginning is documented by the legend of the pseudepigraphal *Letter of Aristeas*, the end by the philological work of Origen.

Before we turn our attention to what seem to me some of the important aspects of the text's history during this period, permit me briefly to present where I believe the essence of this period can be seen in light of the 'Greek Holy Scriptures'. This attempt may appear as a 'terrible simplification', not only because of the simplification occasioned by brevity, but also because of its obvious theological premises. It may, however, occasion discussion.

To express the significance of the Greek Old Testament for the Judaism of the Hellenistic period and for the primitive Christian church—I follow the definition of Franz Overbeck, although also including the Judaism of the period—it may essentially be defined as the 'Urgeschichte' (primal history). This means that the literary forms of the two communities—regardless of whether 'canonized' or 'extra-canonical'—are fundamentally the genres of canonized witnesses. With reference to the Old Testament, these genres are historiography, prophecy-apocalyptic and wisdom. Exceptions, such as nascent literary commentaries, confirm the rule. Forms of expression that do, indeed, originate in the canonized witness, but that are not characteristic—such as the letter and apologetics—are not literary genres in the precise sense, but came to be recorded literarily as the result of the pressures of circumstance. From the perspective of literary *form* a distinction between canonical and extra-canonical cannot be established.

The problem of the text's history, the subject of my presentation, relates to *canonical* Scripture, canonical for both the Jewish and the Christian communities. At this point I can do no more than outline the conceptual basis for the view of the problems of the history, intellectual history and theology of the canon itself—in the sense of those subtle perceptions for which we are grateful to our colleague Hans Peter Rüger (who unfortunately passed away so young)—which are represented here.

We can see that Hellenistic Judaism had a relatively well defined canon of 'Holy Scripture' already in the second century BC, which thus preceded the witnesses of the New Testament writings; in the definition of what was to be regarded as 'canonical' the foundation is being laid for the later differentiation between 'canonical' and 'apocryphal'.

I see evidence for this position in the prologue of Jesus ben Sirach from the second half of the second pre-Christian century: he assumes as canonical Scripture not only the three divisions transmitted by the Masoretes comprising the νόμος (the תורה), the προφῆται (the נביאים) and the ἄλλα πάτρια βιβλία (10; cf. 1) or the λοιπά τῶν βιβλίων (25; the כתובים), which, including the already composed *Dodekapropheton* (49:10), were available to the grandson and translator in the Praise of the Fathers in his grandfather's book of proverbs (Chap. 44–50). He also distinguishes this literature from the one based on it as commentary, beginning with the work of his grandfather, because of the ἀνάγνωσις and the resulting ἱκανὴ ἕξις (10–12). He repeats the same distinction in reference to the problem of *translation* by basing his excuse for the obscurity of his own translation (οὐ γὰρ ἰσοδυναμεῖ αὐτὰ ἐν ἑαυτοῖς 'Εβραϊστὶ λεγόμενα καὶ ὅταν μεταχθῇ εἰς ἑτέραν γλῶσσαν, 22) on the fact that 'even the law, the prophets, and the other books read in the original (ἐν ἑαυτοῖς λεγόμενα) manifest a significant difference (οὐ μικρὰν ἔχει τὴν διαφοράν, 26)' when compared with the translation.

It seems to me justifiable to conclude that the distinction—in relation both to their character and the quality of their translation—between Law, Prophets and the other Writings, on the one hand, and the literature first exemplified in the work of his grandfather, on the other, was grounded first and foremost in the distinction between 'canonical' and 'apocryphal' already current at the time.

It can therefore be assumed that a differentiation within, 'Holy Scripture' as a whole was already existing in Judaism. I believe that the primitive Christian witnesses attest this differentiation as a 'given': the Palestinian canon in the form preserved in the Masoretic tradition was seen as authentic canon, the other writings transmitted in the Alexandrian canon—both those translated from Hebrew or Aramaic and those originally written in Greek—as 'apocryphal'.

It may seem like an over-statement to use this terminology in relation to this period, although sufficient examples illustrate that external categories may be more appropriate for characterizing a period than those already known. But this distinction brings one close—as early as the pre-Christian era of Judaism—to the solution of a problem that will be significant for the problem of the *Christian* canon. The content of the Alexandrian LXX canon, which does not meet the canonical standard transmitted in Josephus (*c. Ap* I 36–42) according to which the succession of the prophets, determinative of canonicity, ended in the time of Artaxerxes I or Ezra and Nehemiah—the description of the Seleucid religious persecution in 1 and 2 Maccabees, Jesus ben Sirach's mention of the high priest Simon—would have been, from the outset, not only appended to, but considered inferior in terms of authority to the Scriptures of the Palestinian canon. The only question that remains open is whether this distinction was a phenomenon common to Palestinian and Hellenistic Judaism or a point of contention between the two communities: to my knowledge, there are no pre-Christian sources useful in answering that question.

In reference to our problem of the textual history of canonical Scriptures in the Jewish and the Christian traditions, the issue cannot be the conflict evident in both realms surrounding the canonicity of certain writings. Reference to a danger seems justified to me here; namely, that often one does not permit the exception to prove the rule, but makes the exception into the rule and concludes from the existence of such a conflict that an original multiplicity of canonical witnesses was reduced only in later periods. For the question of the textual history of canonical Scripture, the 'Alexandrian canon' may be assumed to be a reliable basis: originating in pre-Christian Judaism—although differing in size in the Christian manuscript tradition—and accepted by the primitive Christian church as 'Holy Scripture'. Within this document, there is only one definitive line which can be drawn, the line separating the materials belonging to both the Palestinian and the Alexandrian canons from those transmitted in the Alexandrian only. Further gradations within the complex so demarcated, especially the special status of the Torah within the canon (which also has particular significance for the history of LXX origins since it constitutes the basis in terms of lexicography and translation technique for the translation of the other Scriptures), cannot be denied. But, since a reciprocal polemic between various theological streams may not, in my opinion, be deduced from the evidence, the fact that Hellenistic Judaism around that time (i.e. in the second half of the second pre-Christian century) possessed documents confirming both the special status of the Torah (the pseudepigraphical *Letter of Aristeas*)[1] and the existence of the Alexandrian canon in its full scope (the Prologue of Jesus ben Sirach)[2] remains for me proof that differentiation within a body of literature recognized as canonical, apart from the dividing lines mentioned, signifies, at most, difference in degree but not in substance.

Beside quotations in writings belonging only to the Alexandrian canon, I believe that the reference to prophetic word as Scripture in the *Damascus Scroll* (to name only one example) supplies the best evidence *in the realm of pre-Christian Judaism* of the Hellenistic period that all the writings of the 'Palestinian canon' transmitted in the Masoretic tradition already possessed the canonical significance of 'Holy Scripture'. According to current historical-critical evidence, this word originated in the Hellenistic period. Deutero-Zechariah's call for the sword to arise against the good shepherd (Zech. 13:7) is linked to the reference to the 'shepherd allegory' (chap. 11): '. . . when the word transpires that was written by the prophet Zechariah: בבוא הדבר אשר כתוב ביד זכירה (הנביא), 'Awake O sword against my shepherds (חרב עורי על־רועי)'. But those who obey him are 'the poor of the flock' (הם עניי הצאן)—11:11).[3] The fact that this document reflects the awareness of a particular trend within Hellenistic Judaism is, with reference to the question of the canonicity of the Palestinian canon, much more likely an argument for an early fixation of acknowledged Scripture than an argument for an isolated recognition.[4] *For the realm of the primitive Christian church*

[1] According to the stylistic arguments of E. Bickermann ('Zur Datierung des Pseudo-Aristeas', ZNW 29 [1930] = Studies in Jewish and Christian History I [Leiden, 1976], 109–36) between 145 and 125 BCE.

[2] After 117 BCE: (Ptolemy Physkon 170–164, 145–117)—arrival in the thirty-eighth year (= 132), translation ἐπὶ τοῦ Εὐεργέτου (27)—after his death.

[3] CD (Text B) XIX: 7–9; cf. 'Die Bedeutung der Septuaginta in neutestamentlicher Zeit', ZThK, 81 (1984): 395–416; esp. 407 n. 32.

[4] The fact that appeal can be made—in a document to be defined as a confessional writing that could by form easily be 'Holy Scripture' and belonging to a remote Jewish community in the Hellenistic period—to an extant witness as 'written word' (דבר כתוב) speaks indeed for the fact that the Judaism of this period as a whole knew the 'Holy Scriptures' as an object of reference, and that only the scope of the writings recognized as 'Holy Scriptures' remains an open question, as is clearly the case for the Samaritans and the Sadducees with respect to their restriction to the Torah.

and its Scripture, I continue to see similar evidence in the manner and fashion in which the New Testament witnesses take up the literature of the Palestinian canon as Scripture. But for this I must refer to observations concerning the 'Significance of the Septuagint in the New Testament Period' which I was able to present seven years ago—also in Tübingen.[5]

Evidence concerning the history of the text must now be considered in the light of these theoretical premises concerning the canon. This evidence, valid both for the Jewish tradition of canonized witnesses and for the Christian tradition based upon it, has been ascertained only recently by discoveries of the last decades, especially with respect to the Jewish tradition. As far as I can see, this evidence places the history of the biblical text during the period of the 'Urgeschichte', both in the Jewish and in the Christian realms, in a new light. As a translation of already canonized writings, the LXX translation itself has canonical significance both for Judaism and for the Christian church. It derives this significance, however, only from the strength of the canonical authority of its Hebrew original. It was for this reason that the Greek translation was from the moment of its origin onward continuously subjected to verification against the original Hebrew text and to recensional correction according to this criterion, as demonstrated by recently discovered translations of Jewish origin from pre-Christian and early Christian times. The definition of this relationship as 'original' and 'copy' is completely justified in this case. What we already knew, through Origen, concerning the Christian church of the late second and third centuries, and through the translations or new editions of Aquila, Theodotion and Symmachus in the second century, in regard to Judaism of Christian time, has now been demonstrated to be equally true for the Judaism of the pre-Christian and pre-Aquilan period. In 1903, Eduard Schwartz saw 'the beginning of a new era of Hexapla research, hopefully in the not too distant future'[6] based on Cardinal Mercati's discovery of fragments of a Psalter Hexapla from the tenth century CE in the Bibliotheca Ambrosiana—the first and only discovery of extensive portions of Origen's Hexapla in the original columnar format; the same is true to an even greater degree for research on the Septuagint in the period before Origen and Aquila based on the discovery of the Greek Minor Prophets scroll from Naḥal Ḥever.[7] The former case concerns only the clarification and deeper understanding of an already known textual history, but the latter concerns the confirmation of a state of affairs without previous

---

[5] Cf. above, p. 4 n. 3.

[6] E. Schwartz, 'Zur Geschichte der Hexapla', *Nachrichten v.d.k. Gesellschaft der Wiss. Zu Göttingen, phil.-hist. Klasse* (Göttingen, 1903 [1904]), 693–700 (= *Gesammelte Schriften* 5 [Berlin, 1963], 183–91). The citation is from p. 190 (= p. 699).

[7] D. Barthélemy, *Les devanciers d'Aquila*, VTSup 10 (Leiden, 1963); E. Tov, ed., *The Greek Minor Prophets Scroll from Naḥal Ḥever*, DJD VIII (Oxford, 1990).

documentary attestation, but at best hypothetically postulated: the pre-decessors of Aquila.

The final establishment of the Scripture as unimpeachable witness of revelation was realized in pre-Christian Judaism through the continuous comparison of the Greek translation to the Hebrew original, the copy to the prototype. The disputed ἀφόμοιον in the Prologue of Jesus ben Sirach may be explained in this way. The first Christian witnesses adopted it in this form. From this perspective, in light of the text form of the Minor Prophets scroll from Naḥal Ḥever, I would explain the divergences transmitted in New Testament material from the LXX form of the text, which stands closer to the Hebrew original, as given in Judaism and not as the result of individual initiative. Via the inter-mediary of the second-century Jewish translators, it was taken up again in the same way in the philological work of Origen—at the point of transition from apologetic to post-apologetic Christian literature, from 'Urgeschichte' to 'Geschichte', from canonical Scripture as a form of expression to commentary—to test agreement with the Hebrew original as a control for the LXX text, now canonically established in the Christian church.

So far as its object is concerned, the periodization resulting from these caesurae relates to an identical phenomenon: the unadulterated preser-vation of the witnesses established as Holy Scripture in view of the relationship between original and translation. In other respects, however, such as their background of intellectual history and of theology, each period differs.

For pre-Christian Judaism, this is a theological and text-historical problem within the community as a whole and is documented as agreement rather than conflict between Palestinian and Hellenistic Judaism.

The primitive Christian church, however, sees itself as concerned with an extant theologumenon that, as such, represents an object open neither to dispute nor discussion. The question of the original form of an Old Testament witness adopted as scriptural evidence comes up nowhere in the New Testament witnesses. Subsequently, in Origen at the end of the 'Urgeschichte', it is the object of discussion along two lines. (1) From an apologetic/polemical perspective it is a dispute with contemporary Judaism concerning a Jewish-Christian battle over the falsification of Scripture that erupted in the period of the Apologists, primarily in Justin. (2) Within the Christian community itself the question concerns canonicity in the translation of statements transmitted by the LXX that do not agree with the Hebrew original.

With respect to the first period, characterized by the continuous correction of the Greek translation of the LXX against the Hebrew original, it may be difficult to deduce theological issues or contro-versies from currently known recensional elements reflecting the

Hebrew original. The tradition is too fragmentary. With respect to the amount of such recensional work reflecting the Hebrew text, the step from the recension perceptible in the few pre-Christian fragments (Papyrus Fouad 266 [Deut.]) to that appearing in the Minor Prophets scroll, the work, although significant, also seems to be only quantitative, and not qualitative. It is only in the Minor Prophets scroll that one might have found clear evidence for corrections of the old LXX-text against the Hebrew original, which are not merely formal, but involving content as well. These parts, however, are lost; but based on the recension principle it may be assumed that these corrections were found there. Seven years ago I pointed out, with reference to cases significant for New Testament scriptural evidence, that, according to the principle of recension observable in the preserved fragments, Old Testament statements such as Zechariah 12:10 (וְהִבִּיטוּ אֵלַי אֵת אֲשֶׁר־דָּקָרוּ, 'They will look on me whom they have pierced') may have been transmitted in the Minor Prophets scroll not in the sense of the old LXX ἐπιβλέψονται πρός με ἀνθ' ὧν κατωρχήσαντο, 'They will look upon me so that they may dance [joyously]'), but in the form corresponding to the Hebrew original transmitted in John 19:37 (ὄψονται εἰς ὃν ἐξεκέντησαν, cf. Rev. 1:7). Similarly, the statement in Isaiah 25:8 (בִּלַּע הַמָּוֶת לָנֶצַח, 'He [YHWH, v. 6] devoured death for ever') may have been transmitted in a hypothetical Greek 'Isaiah scroll' not in the form of the LXX text (κατέπιεν ὁ θάνατος ἰσχύσας, 'he, death, become mighty, has devoured'), but in the sense of a form of the text resembling that cited by Paul as λόγος γεγραμμένος in 1 Corinthians 15:54–55 in combination with Hosea 13:10 ([ὁ κύριος] κατέπιεν τὸν θάνατον εἰς νῖκος),[8] or with Paul and Theodotion (κατεπόθη ὁ θάνατος εἰς νῖκος). These are truly 'substantive corrections'!

In this connection I want to call attention to a phenomenon that I can explain only as the result of the intention of the Jewish tradents of the LXX, now documentarily attested, to revise the translation as the copy against the Hebrew original. I refer to the much discussed fact that all Greek biblical texts of Jewish origin found to date, whether from pre-Christian or Christian times, transmit the name יהוה not in the form κύριος encountered in all the LXX manuscripts of Christian origin, but in some form of the Tetragrammaton. I explain this, as I did before, in terms of the consistent recensional principle of the translation as copy to the original, not in terms of the translators' intention—in other words, in a secondary phase in the history of the text, not in the origin of the Greek edition of Israel's Holy Scripture. The replacement of the sacred name with אדני, undoubtedly first transmitted masoretically, but

---

[8] Cf. α΄ καταποντίσει τὸν θάνατον εἰς νῖκος; σ΄ καταποθῆναι ποιήσει τὸν θάνατον εἰς τέλος (*ZThK* 81 [1984], 404–5).

already presumed in the *Damascus Scroll*,[9] is the precursor and origin of the translation of the name יהוה in the LXX as κύριος, not (*contra* Graf Baudissin) the consequence drawn from it by the Masoretes.[10]

The fact that, in a secondary phase in the text's history, Jewish LXX manuscripts consistently replace κύριος with the Tetragrammaton renders even more improbable Baudissin's thesis of a later rabbinic replacement of the name יהוה with the honorific אדני on the basis of the representation of the name with κύριος in the LXX—a rather unlikely thesis to begin with; for when in the post-apologetic period could the LXX have still possessed such authority for Judaism? The Tetragrammaton in LXX manuscripts could not give rise to the equation of יהוה with אדני. The rabbinic theologumenon would then depend on Christian manuscripts!

The original association, within Judaism, of the epithet אדני with the name יהוה is too close—already in the books of the Torah—to have originated within Hebrew tradition in the theologumenon of the ineffability of the sacred name. The existing, original association is the source of the theologumenon. Furthermore, the designation of Israel's God as κύριος, which is attested in Hellenistic Judaism, the 'apocryphal' writings of the Alexandrian canon: the book of 2 Maccabees, the Wisdom of Solomon, and Philo, is too thoroughly accepted and widespread for its legitimation to have been based on anything other than the canonized writings of the LXX.

This recognition (that the Old Testament divine name of κύριος was a 'given' for the first Christian witnesses through the scriptural witness of Judaism and was not created by Christian witnesses) is of decisive significance for the understanding the New Testament Scriptures. This is as obvious as it is weighty for questions (concerning which I can only learn from the New Testament scholars) arising from it. What is important for our present purpose is the conclusion that from the very beginning on there has been no conflict in the early Christian church to accept the Greek Old Testament in the form in which it already existed in Judaism: as κύριος the God of the Old Testament is the God of the Christian church and—to use a phrase I often heard from Hans Conzelmann—the Father of Jesus Christ.

A Jewish-Christian confrontation concerning the truth and falsification of the common 'Holy Scripture' did, indeed, arise at a certain point in the period we characterize as 'Urgeschichte'. The basis for the conflict is not, however, the translation phenomenon, either in the sense of whether the choice of the Greek equivalent corresponds to the semantics of the Hebrew word in question, as is the case for

---

[9] p. 15:1 (chap. 19:1). L. Rost, *Die Damaskusschrift* (Lietzmanns kleine Texte 167; Berlin, 1933), 26. E. Lohse, *Die Texte aus Qumran* (Munich, 1964), 97.

[10] *Kyrios*, 1929.

the divine epithet κύριος; or in the sense, already enunciated in the Prologue of Jesus ben Sirach, that a translation can never be totally faithful to its original. The point at issue is the bilateral charge of falsification of Scripture by means of tendentious additions or omissions in either the original or the translation. The process of translation at most offers new possibilities for such falsification, in that a translation equivalent may intentionally alter the meaning of the original—as the Christians supposed that the Jewish translators in the second Christian century replaced παρθένος 'virgin' with νεᾶνις 'young woman' in Isaiah 7:14 in reference to the mother of Immanuel, עלמה.[11] The cause of the Jewish-Christian conflict about authenticity and falsification of Scripture is not to be seen in the existing multiplicity of forms of the text. The continuing comparison of the translation as copy with the original, recognized by both sides, allowed for this multiplicity, as the Minor Prophets scroll from the time of Paul indicates. On the basis of this evidence, the widely held thesis that the translation efforts of Aquila, to be dated a few decades later, were prompted by the Jewish-Christian dispute concerning falsification of Scripture must be newly reconsidered. The cause lies deeper, and the multiplicity of Scripture, of which the Greek translation is the most significant phenomenon, was at most the secondary cause, a means and tool in the Jewish-Christian dispute. The cause was not a matter of textual history, but the question of what the text in its existing multiplicity meant. This question must have become a burning issue at the point which—to use the terminology of Franz Overbeck—marked the transition from 'Urgeschichte' to history, from primitive Christian to Christian literature: namely at that point at which the apologetic/polemical dispute between Jewish and Christian communities becomes an acknowledgement—one which continued, from our perspective unfortunately, to be largely polemically motivated—of the coexistence of the two communities.

Origen stands at this dividing line. His work points both backward and forward: backward through its apologetic material—the final form of expression of the 'Urliteratur' and as such the link connecting to Christian literature in the proper sense; forward through its exegetical material and its systematic. The essential prerequisite for the completion of this transition is the ultimate clarification of the question of the final form of the 'Holy Scriptures' common to Jews and Christians. This part of Origen's work, completed in the monumental work of the Hexapla and the Tetrapla, points, according to authentic statements from Origen himself, from this dividing line backward to the apologist past and forward to the Christian literature of the future. For Origen both directions are equally significant. The apologetic aspect of the dispute

[11] Just. *Dial.* 43:8, etc.

with Judaism, now drawing to its end, cannot be more clearly expressed than in the words of his letter to Africanus:[12]

> We take pains not to remain ignorant of that transmitted [forms of the text] among them [the Jews] so that, in the dispute with the Jews, we will not offer something that is not transmitted in their manuscripts, and so that we adduce what is transmitted among them, even if it is not transmitted in our books. For if we are prepared in this way, they will not scorn us.

The significance of the textual form of the Greek Old Testament recognized as canon in the Christian church cannot be more clearly emphasized than when, in the same letter, he calls for the unfailing recognition by the Christian faith of those parts of the LXX translation not transmitted in the Hebrew original. To abandon them would be in effect to abandon the highest content of the Christian faith. For 'Providence, who granted to all the churches of Christ edification in the Holy Scriptures (ἡ πρόνοια ἐν ἁγίαις γραφαῖς δεδωκυῖα πάσαις ταῖς Χριστοῦ ἐκκλησίαις οἰκοδομήν) would not have, then, been concerned with it' (8).

What may be abandoned are not those portions marked in his philological work with an obelus as additions to the Hebrew original; they have been established as 'Holy Scripture', ἁγία γραφή. What may be abandoned are the parts marked with an asterisk, existing only in the Hebrew original, and supplied by Origen from the new translations of the Jewish translators of the second Christian century—as we know from Jerome,[13] and as the tradition confirms, primarily from Theodotion. Here—and here only—the textual value of the material remains an open question:

> Whoever will, may admit them; whoever finds them a stumblingstone, however, may proceed as he will to accept or reject them (καὶ ὁ μὲν βουλόμενος προῆται αὐτά, ᾧ δὲ προσκόπτει τὸ τοιοῦτον ὃ βούλεται περὶ τῆς παραδοχῆς αὐτῶν ἢ μὴ ποιήσῃ; In Matthaeum XV:14 regarding Matt. 19:16–30).[14]

---

[12] Ἀσκοῦμεν δὲ μὴ ἀγνοεῖν καὶ τὰς παρ' ἐκείνοις, ἵνα πρὸς Ἰουδαίους διαλεγόμενοι μὴ προφέρωμεν αὐτοῖς τὰ μὴ κείμενα ἐν τοῖς ἀντιγράφοις αὐτῶν, καὶ ἵνα συγχρησώμεθα τοῖς φερομένοις παρ' ἐκείνοις εἰ καὶ ἐν τοῖς ἡμετέροις οὐ κεῖται βιβλίοις. Τοιαύτης γὰρ οὔσης ἡμῶν τῆς πρὸς αὐτοὺς ἐν ταῖς ζητήσεσι παρασκευῆς, οὐ καταφρονήσουσιν (9).

[13] *Prologus in libro Paralipomenon*, Biblia Sacra iuxta Latinam Vulgatam Versionem VIII (Rome, 1948), 4–5.

[14] The freedom of use relates only to the asterisked portions mentioned immediately above, not to the obelised portions from the old LXX tradition mentioned first. The statement οὐ τολμήσαντες αὐτὰ πάντη περιελεῖν, 'we dared not expunge them fully', can have only categorical significance in view of the affirmation in the letter to Africanus: 'Had we dared, we would have incurred guilt.'

Here, and only here, at the dividing line which can be discerned as unambiguously as this only in Origen's work—still open in its connection back to the apologetic-polemical controversy with contemporary Judaism over the truth and falsification of the word of Scripture, and forward to the final establishment of the text as Holy Scripture, in the Christian church now in the LXX form and including portions different from the Hebrew original—can I beyond any doubt make out the intellectual and theological condition which was to lead to the rift in the Jewish and Christian community over the Old Testament text in the original and its Greek translation, which up to that time had been accepted as their common bible. This rift, on the Jewish side, resulted in the condemnation of the Greek translation *per se*,[15] and on the Christian side—by means of the Philonic interpretation of the *Letter of Aristeas*—in the theory of the divine inspiration of the translation, a theory that justifies the differences.[16]

Here again, we cannot be concerned with the question of the 'canonical-apocryphal', i.e., with the definition of what was recognized by both sides at the time as canonical. This question is freighted with insoluble problems in Origen particularly. His canon catalogue transmitted in Eusebius (*Hist Eccl* VI, 25:2) reaches his intended number of twenty-two books without the Minor Prophets and lists as apocryphal writings, ἔξω δὲ τούτων, only τὰ Μακκαβαϊκά (with the inexplicable Hebrew designation Σαρβηθσαβαναιελ). Yet, research into the history of the text, taking into account the frequent references to apocryphal witnesses in the writings of Origen, has also yielded with relative certainty a hexaplaric or 'Origenic' recension of Jesus ben Sirach,[17] of the Wisdom of Solomon (written originally in Greek),[18] and probably even of the Book of Judith (a hexaplaric school?).[19] We are interested now in the fundamental distinction between original and translation in what is recognized as canonical.

With respect to Origen's work, we are concerned here only with the view to the past that reveals how far, in view of this newly arisen division, he took seriously the (Christian) duty to elucidate in detail the differences in the textual tradition that were the point of contention. He himself, like the Apologists, was not yet able to see these differences in terms of the alternative between original or translation. It is revealing that the *Letter*

---

[15] For citations see *VT* 12 (1962): 139–63, here 144 and 147–9.

[16] The citations are the same as in n. 15.

[17] J. Ziegler, *Septuaginta* XII/2 (Göttingen, 1965), 57–63; cf. *idem*, 'Die hexaplarische Bearbeitung des griechischen Sirach', *BZNF* 4 (1969): 174–85 (= 'Sylloge', *MSU* 10 [1971], 510–28); and *idem*, 'Die Vokabel-Varianten der *O*-Rezension im griechischen Sirach', *FS G. R. Driver* (Oxford, 1963): 172–190 (= 'Sylloge', 615–33).

[18] J. Ziegler, *Septuaginta* XII/1 (Göttingen, 1962), 50–6.

[19] R. Hanhart, *Septuaginta* VIII/4 (Göttingen, 1979): 23–5; *idem*, 'Text und Textgeschichte des Buches Judith', *MSU* 14 (1979): 14–45.

of Aristeas is interpreted as inspiration of the Seventy by Clement of Alexandria, but not by Origen.

The thorough elucidation of the preconditions of the text's history based on the background of Christian-Jewish apologetics seemed to Origen to be the only possible—and, from the Christian standpoint, the only justifiable—basis for dialogue and accord between the Christian church of his time and contemporary Judaism. According to this elucidation, the multiplicity of the old LXX tradition—both with respect to discrepancies in relation to the Hebrew original finally established as canonical, as well as in relation to changes in the Greek resulting from the process of copying from one manuscript to the next—is counter-balanced by the attempt to identify the translation with the original in Jewish translations of the second Christian century.[20]

We have source material revealing the thoroughness and intensity of this work; it is rare in the history of thought that, after centuries have passed, a historiographical tradition from Late Antiquity not only confirms but also explains previously inexplicable statements through newly discovered sources.

I am speaking of the fragments of the tenth-century Psalter Hexapla, discovered in 1896 by cardinal Giovanni Mercati in the Biblioteca Ambrosiana in Milan and published in 1958, one year after his death, which have thrown new light on Origen's textual work as reported by Eusebius.[21]

> Origen was gripped by such a powerful determination to investigate meticu-lously the divine word (τοσαύτη δὲ εἰσήγετο τῷ ᾿Ωριγένει τῶν θείων λόγων ἠκριβωμένη ἐξέτασις) that he (even) learned the Hebrew language and familiarized himself with the writings transmitted among the Jews in their original in the Hebrew script (ὡς καὶ τὴν ῾Εβραΐδα γλῶτταν ἐκμαθεῖν τάς τε παρὰ τοῖς ᾿Ιουδαίοις φερομένας πρωτοτύπους αὐτοῖς ῾Εβραίων στοιχείοις γραφὰς κτῆμα ἴδιον ποιήσασθαι) and that he even sought out and studied the versions of others beside the Seventy who translated the Holy

---

[20] The weight lies on the agreement to be attained by the comparison with the original via the middle term of the new Jewish translations. It is not clear how far he believed it possible to identify an original text along this path on which the transformations of the old LXX tradition arose through the negligence or audacity of the copyists ἡ τῶν ἀντιγράφων διαφορά, εἴτε ἀπὸ ῥαθυμίας τινῶν γραφέων, εἴτε τόλμης τινῶν μοχθηρᾶς, in Matt. XV:14).

[21] *Psalterii Hexapli Reliquiae cura et studio Johannis Card. Mercati editae*, in Biblio-theca Vaticana (Vatican City, 1958); *idem*, 'Osservazioni' (1965); cf. Adrian Schenker, *Hexaplarische Psalmenbruchstücke* (OBO 8; Freiburg/Göttingen, 1975); *idem*, *Psalmen in den Hexapla* (Studi e Testi 295; Vatican City, 1982). Mercati's first report was 'D'un palimpsesto Ambrosiano contenente i Salmi esapli e di un'antica versione latina del commentario perduto di Teodoro di Mopsuestia al Salterio', *Atti della Reale Accademia delle Scienze di Torino* 31 (1896): 655–76 (= *Opere minori* I, Studi e testi 76 [Vatican City, 1937]: 318–38).

Scriptures (ἀνιχνεῦσαί τε τὰς τῶν ἑτέρων παρὰ τοὺς ἑβδομήκοντα τὰς ἱερὰς γραφὰς ἑρμηνευκότων ἐκδόσεις). In addition he located a few more, differing from the well-known translations of Aquila, Symmachus and Theodotion (καί τινας ἑτέρας παρὰ τὰς κατημαξευμένας ἑρμηνείας ἐναλλαττούσας, τὴν Ἀκύλου καὶ Συμμάχου καί Θεοδοτίωνος, ἐφευρεῖν). I do not know where he found them, in whatever nook the previous era had hidden them, and brought them to light (ἃς οὐκ οἶδ᾽ ὅθεν ἔκ τινων μυχῶν τὸν πάλαι λανθανούσας χρόνον ἀνιχνεύσας προήγαγεν εἰς φῶς). Since, because they were un-known, he could say nothing about authorship, he reported that he had found one of them in Nikopolis near Actium, and the other in another such place (ἐφ᾽ ὧν διὰ τὴν ἀδηλότητα, τίνος ἀρ᾽ εἶεν, οὐκ εἰδώς, αὐτὸ τοῦτο μόνον ἐπεσημήνατο ὡς ἄρα τὴν μὲν εὕροι ἐν τῇ πρὸς Ἀκτίοις Νικοπόλει, τὴν δὲ ἐν ἑτέρῳ τοιῷδε τόπῳ).

Now, in the Hexapla of the Psalms, where, in addition to the known four editions, he juxtaposed not only a fifth, but also a sixth and a seventh translation, he reports once again that one of them was found in Jericho in a clay jar from the time of Antoninus, the son of Severus (ἔν γε μὴν τοῖς Ἑξαπλοῖς τῶν Ψαλμῶν μετὰ τὰς ἐπισήμους τέσσαρας ἐκδόσεις οὐ μόνον πέμπτην, ἀλλὰ καὶ ἕκτην καί ἑβδόμην παραθεὶς ἑρμηνείαν, ἐπὶ μιᾶς αὖθις σεσημείωται ὡς ἐν Ἱεριχοῖ εὑρημένης ἐν πίθῳ κατὰ τοὺς χρόνους Ἀντωνίνου τοῦ υἱοῦ Σευήρου).

By assembling all the translations and arranging them side by side in columns, together with the Hebrew wording, he left us the manuscript of the so-called Hexapla (ταύτας δὲ ἁπάσας ἐπὶ ταὐτὸν συναγαγὼν διελών τε πρὸς κῶλον καὶ ἀντιπαραθεὶς ἀλλήλαις μετὰ καὶ αὐτῆς τῆς Ἑβραίων σημειώσεως τὰ τῶν λεγομένων Ἑξαπλῶν ἡμῖν ἀντίγραφα καταλέλοιπεν). Apart from that, he arranged the editions of Aquila, Symmachus and Theodotion together with the LXX in the Tetrapla (ἰδίως τὴν Ἀκύλου καὶ Συμμάχου καὶ Θεοδοτίωνος ἔκδοσιν ἅμα τῇ τῶν ἑβδομήκοντα ἐν τοῖς Τετρασσοῖς ἐπισκευάσας) (Eusebius, *Hist Eccl* VI:16).

Eusebius' testimony requires cautious interpretation. From his mentioning of these two manuscripts in his biography of Origen, immediately after the account of his Rome trip of AD 212, it cannot be deduced that those manuscripts were found at that time; this is based not on a chronological but a thematic arrangement.[22] When, at the very end of his report, he relates the production of the Tetrapla in a participial clause in the aorist, in terms of 'and additionally made'—ἐπισκευάζειν—this should not, because of the preposition ἐπί in the verb, be understood as a succession in time[23] nor, because of the aorist, be placed in the past

[22] Cf. E. Schwartz, *GCS* 9/3, 33.
[23] Cf. E. Schwartz, 'Hexapla', 694.

perfect. All that remains certain is the temporal point of the discovery of the Sexta under Caracalla (AD 211–18), which establishes a *terminus post quem* for the completion of the whole work. We need not doubt that the six columns that give the work its name consist of the Hebrew text, the Greek transcription of the Hebrew text, Aquila, Symmachus, the restored LXX, and Theodotion, as Rufinus' Latin translation of Eusebius' report already attests.[24] The Mercati fragments support this arrangement rather than contradicting it. What is important is the evidence of the transcription, while the absence of the Hebrew is not surprising.

The comparison of Eusebius' report with Mercati's Psalter fragments shows that this is an exceptional case, relating, as Eusebius already made explicit, to the transmission of the Psalter. It is of singular significance both for the authenticity of Eusbeius' report and for the theological intention of Origen's textual work, what this manuscript, which is approximately 700 years younger, shows. This later form of the Hexapla tradition takes for granted that which is true of all the biblical books and preserves only the peculiarities.

What all books have in common is the reconstruction of a form of the LXX text according to the criterion of agreement with the Hebrew original by means of the Jewish translations of Aquila, Symmachus and Theodotion. Origen's theological goal was to preserve the ancient tradition, even when it diverges from the original, as canonical Scripture of the Christian church, and to find points of agreement, even if attained only by the new translations of the second Christian century, for possible canonical recognition on the part of Christians and for necessary use in the dispute with contemporary Judaism. In this connection, the adoption of the Tetragrammaton in the LXX column, significantly accompanied in a few passages by the *nomen sacrum* $\overline{\text{κς}}$, also indicates nothing other than the Christian recognition of the Jewish theologumenon of the replacement of the name with אדני.

The peculiarity, true of the Psalter to a remarkable degree, is the focus in Eusebius' report on the tradition of Jewish translation from the second Christian century of unknown origin, discovered at the time of the translations of Aquila, Symmachus and Theodotion: the 'quinta,' the 'sexta' and the 'septima'.

The syntactical difficulty in Eusebius' report is that, after mentioning two translations (one of which was found in Actium near Nikopolis) in addition to the four known (Aquila, Symmachus, the LXX column and Theodotion), nothing is said concerning the discovery of a seventh and an eighth translation. Instead he discusses a sixth and a seventh, one of which, discovered in Jericho from the time of Caracalla. This difficulty is now elucidated by the Mercati fragments; colophons in the Psalter-Catenae confirm this.

---

[24] *Contra* P. Nautin, *Origène* (Paris, 1977), 314–15.

As preserved Hexaplaric notations demonstrate, the final column of the Mercati fragments is not Theodotion (which is not represented) but Quinta. Notations which can be distinguished in a few places in the margin of Quinta (Ps. 49:14 [LXX 48:14] יש־ע: εὐδοκήσουσιν—δραμοῦνται) represent the variants exhibited by the second of those manuscripts Eusebius combined as Quinta over against the first: because they are so similar, they were combined as the Quinta.

The colophons of the Psalter-Catenae confirm this: ε΄ ἔκδοσις, ἣν εὗρον ἐν Νικοπόλει τῇ πρὸς Ἀκτίοις· τὰ δὲ παρακείμενα αὐτῆς ἐστιν ὅσα ἐναλλάσσει παρ᾽ αὐτήν. ς΄ ἔκδοσι, εὑρεθεῖσα μετὰ καὶ ἄλλων Ἑβραϊκῶν καὶ Ἑλληνικῶν ἔν τινι πίθῳ περὶ τὴν Ἱεριχὼ ἐν χρόνοις τῆς βασιλείας Ἀντωνίνου τοῦ υἱοῦ Σευήρου.

The fact that this Hexapla tradition must be genuine Origen known to Eusebius in this form, not a story growing out of Eusebius' report, is apparent especially in that Eusebius retained the statement's halting syntax. The colophon discusses Quinta in the first person: εὗρον 'I (Origen) have found'. Consequently, Eusebius explains ἐπεσημήνατο ὡς ἄρα τὴν μὲν εὕροι ἐν . . . Νικοπόλει, 'He reports that he found one of them in Nicopolis'. The colophon discusses Sexta in the passive voice: ς΄ ἔκδοσις εὑρεθεῖσα. Correspondingly, Eusebius recounts, σεσημείωται ὡς ἐν Ἱεριχοῖ εὑρημένης, 'It was learned that it was found in Jericho'.

The colophon's statement about the Quinta (τὰ δὲ παρακείμενα αὐτῆς ἐστιν ὅσα ἐναλλάσσει παρ᾽ αὐτήν) does not need (contra E. Schwartz) to be completed with a subject, ἑτέρα τις τοιαύτη ἔκδοσις. It is possible to understand ὅσα as the subject. 'On the margin is that which (ὅσα) diverges from it (παρ᾽ αὐτήν): The main column of the "Quinta", in a related manuscript'—I understand ἐναλλάσσει as a rarely used intrasitive mode of the active voice, as found in Eusebius' report: This, too, adopted in this form from the colophon.[25]

The special focus on the Quinta in Origen's Psalter Hexapla, with the related translation noted only when it differs, may derive, indeed, from Origen's second, and theological, intention. According to this goal, the recensional principle of assimilation or approximation to the Hebrew original encounters, and in a few passages even confronts, the LXX when this offers, not a literal translation, but interpretation and when, in this form, independent of the original, it is established as canonical Scripture in the early church. This aspect of Origen's work requires further clarification in relation to the Mercati Psalter fragments. In conclusion, let me refer only to one example once again related to the problem of the divine name.

In Psalm 31(LXX 30):3, the old LXX passes down an interpreting rendering, deeply rooted in the old translation tradition and apparently

---

[25] Cf. also *Hist Eccl* VIII/9:3.

based on the theologumenon of avoiding anthropomorphism; it translates the metaphorical divine epithet צור, 'rock', by the word, 'god', itself (הָיָה לִי־צוּר—γενοῦ μοι εἰς θν), while the Jewish translators preserve the image in various forms (εἰς στερεόν, Aquila and the basis of Quinta; εἰς ἀκρότομον, Symmachus). But the interpreting form of the original LXX, εἰς θεόν, is still preserved in the form of the text noted only as marginalia to the Quinta (ὅσα ἐναλλάσσει). Origen may have taken this as contemporary Jewish confirmation of the accuracy of the old LXX tradition.

The marginalia in the LXX column itself, which reads εἰς θν as εἰς φύλακα, can easily be explained in terms of translation technique: in the older LXX tradition (2 Kgs 22:3,47; 23:3) צור is derived from נצר.[26] Its integration in Origen's textual work may perhaps be explained by the statement in a colophon found before Ezekiel in the LXX Codex Marchalianus: that the Ezekiel text goes back to a manuscript of the Koinobiarch Apolinarius, which, in turn, was based on the Hexaplaric and Tetraplaric edition 'revised and glossed' by Origen himself: αὐτοῦ [i.e. Ὠριγένους] χειρὶ διόρθωτο καὶ ἐσχολιογράφητο.[27] Origen himself glossed his LXX column.

But much has happened here between the origin of the Hexapla and the Tetrapla in the third century AD and the stage of textual history reached in the tenth century with the Mercati fragments in their combination with the catenae tradition. This development in the interim period is evidenced, not only by the Ezekiel Colophon in the Codex Marchalianus, but by colophons preserved for Isaiah LXX in the Syrohexapla and in Codex Marchalianus, and for Esther and 2 Ezra in Codex Sinaiticus. Probably the most important element in the text transformation is the independent tradition of the recension of Origen's LXX column as we find it with his disciples Eusebius and Pamphilus and in its marginal incorporation going back to manuscripts not properly of Origenic origin such as, for the most part, the Codices Sinaiticus and Marchalianus.

With Origen's theological intention, the theologumenon of the exclusive recognition of 'the' LXX translation as Holy Scripture within the Christian church was accepted—the theologumenon which was the intrinsic reason for the exclusive recognition of the Hebrew original within Judaism contemporary with Origen and the rejection of the translation—and thereby of Philo's Hellenistic-Jewish interpreta-

---

[26] Cf. 4 Kgs 17:9; 18:8; Prov 4:13, etc.; Isa 26:3 (φυλάσσειν); Prov 20:28 (φυλακή); Ezekl 19:9 (מצורה, φυλακή for מצודה).

[27] Cf. J. Ziegler, *Ezechiel*, Septuaginta XVI/1 (Göttingen, 1952, 2nd edn 1977), 32–4: 'The glosses may be divided into διορθώσεις and σχόλια: the former were the anonymous marginal readings and the translations of the "three"; the latter were various other marginalia, which did not offer a biblical reading, but exegetical glosses.'

tion of the Aristeas legend as the inspiration of the Seventy. But 'the' translation no longer existed. The goal of Origen's textual work had been the theologically motivated differentiation betwen the ancient tradition as the 'Holy Scripture' of the Christian church and that which had newly been introduced through comparison with the Hebrew original by the Jewish translators of the second Christian century as the object of the dispute with Judaism. Since, however, this differentiation soon lost its significance for the tradents, Origen's textual reconstruction did not, contrary to his original intention, lead to a clear definition and standardization of the translation text in the Christian church. Instead, as Jerome's comment in the preface to his translation of the books of Chronicles attests, it resulted in three *Christian* recensions. Thus there arose within the church itself a confrontation no longer concerned, as had been the debate between Origen and Julius Africanus, with the question of the canonical legitimacy of the Alexandrian canon in contrast to statements and witnesses related to the Palestinian. Instead—given the Christian initiative for a new Latin translation, not of the LXX, but of the Hebrew original—the question concerned the legitimacy of a vernacular translation no longer based on the old tradition of the LXX and other related traditions such as the Old Latin. This is the first decisive break in a periodization of the textual history beyond the 'Urgeschichte'. The Aristeas legend had been understood as a story about the divine inspiration of the Seventy translators, borrowed from Hellenistic Judaism by the church's writers in Origen's time as an argument for the canonical legitimacy of the LXX translation in the apologetic dispute with the Jews. Now it became a weapon in a controversy between Christians. As often happens, it is Augustine (*De civitate Dei* XV:14) who formulates it most clearly—here probably with his opposite, Jerome, in mind:

> Sed ubi non est scriptoris error, aliquid eos [sc. Septuaginta interpretes] divino spiritu, ubi sensus esset consentaneus veritati, et praedicans veritatem, non interpretantium more, sed prophetantium libertate aliter dicere voluisse credendum est. Unde merito, non solum Hebraeis, verum etiam ipsis, cum adhibet testimonia de Scripturis, uti Apostolica invenitur auctoritas.
>
> But, if scribal error is not involved, it must be believed that, where the sense corresponds to the truth and proclaims the truth, they [i.e. the seventy translators], moved by the divine Spirit, wished to deviate [from the Hebrew original], not in the manner of interpreters [translators], but in the freedom of those prophesying. Consequently, the apostles, in *their* authority, when they appealed to the Scriptures, quite rightly utilized not only the Hebrew, but also their own—the witness of the Seventy.

I

A DIFFICULT SUBJECT

The New Testament exegete—perhaps because of the necessity of giving a lecture on the subject—dealing for the first time more thoroughly with the problem of the LXX as a whole, quickly observes how very much he has entered a *terra incognita*, full of surprises. So it was for the author, also, when he was asked to read a paper on 'the Alexandrian canon of the Septuagint' before a theological working group. He suddenly found himself again in a realm in which Old Testament and Patristics scholars are more at home: a realm, however, completely dominated in reality by specialists in LXX research; one of the most exclusive—because it is so complicated—specialities of theology or *philologia sacra*. He is completely aware of the imperfection of his contribution. In essence, it comprises only an extensive outline of the problem[1] (with a few idiosyncratic marginal comments).

The second limitation results from the debatable nature of the subject itself. We cannot prove the existence of a genuine Jewish, pre-Christian collection of canonical value, unambiguously and clearly delimited, distinguishable through its greater scope from the canon of the Hebrew Bible in the realm of the historical books and wisdom writings and written in Greek. Nor, especially, can it be shown that such a 'canon' was already formed in pre-Christian Alexandria. One can only proceed from the fact that the five books of Moses' Torah, the so-called Pentateuch, were translated into Greek under Ptolemy II Philadelphus (282–246), at the latest toward the middle of the third century. The pseudepigraphical *Letter of Aristeas*, written toward the end of the second century, attributed this translation, unique in Antiquity, in legendary fashion to the seventy-two elders from the Palestinian homeland.[2] This is the source of the later designation, οἱ ἑβδομήκοντα, Septuaginta, for the entire Greek Old Testament, a designation first attested in Christian authors (see below, pp. 25–6). It, too, is misleading. The enterprise recounted in the story was, in fact, limited exclusively to the translation of the *Pentateuch* as the Jewish law book. The

---

[1] See references cited in the select bibliography.
[2] A. Pelletier, *Lettre d'Aristée à Philocrate* (SC 89; Paris, 1962); see below, pp. 31–3 and 75–80. N. L. Collins ('281 BCE: The Year of the Translation of the Pentateuch into Greek under Ptolemy', in Brooke and Lindars, 403–503) now seeks to place the translation very early—in my opinion too early.

translation of the historical and prophetic books and of the hagiographa
followed only gradually in a process extending over 300 years down to
the end of the first century CE. In addition, a few writings in the Septuagint
are not translations at all, but were composed in Greek from the outset.

Indeed, upon examining the rest of the independent Judaeo-
Alexandrian writings and the biblical literature employed or attested in
them one is more likely to get the impression that the number of 'Holy
Scriptures' recognized in the Egyptian metropolis was substantially
smaller than in the Pharisaic 'Hebrew canon' developed in Palestine and
(quite certainly) than in the later LXX of the church. Furthermore, it
seems that the Pentateuch stood at the centre even more in the Egyptian
metropolis than in the homeland. Of course one can proceed from the
fact that, beginning with the Pentateuch, not only the majority of the
writings of the Greek Bible but also numerous other works we classify
as apocrypha and pseudepigrapha were translated (and also some
composed) in Alexandria, the great centre of the Jewish Diaspora. But it
remains uncertain—disregarding a core: law, history books, prophets,
Psalms and Proverbs—whether and when the 'scriptures' beyond this
'core' were really recognized there as inspired 'Holy Scriptures', that is
as 'canonical'. Many of them could have even been simply treasured and
utilized, at first, as more or less private religious devotional literature. In
addition, the number of writings translated or composed in Greek in the
homeland itself (or elsewhere outside Egypt, perhaps in Antioch) should
not be underestimated.[3] Diaspora Judaism, scattered over the entire
Roman Empire, had no central court of appeal that could establish a
canon of Holy Scripture. Furthermore, its *religious* centre remained
Jerusalem until the destruction of the temple in 70 CE. Year after year,
a considerable number of Jews from the Greek-speaking Diaspora
assembled for the great feasts, not in Alexandria but in Jerusalem. Before
70 CE Jews in Antioch, Rome, or Ephesus looked for their religious
questions more to the 'holy city' than to the Egyptian metropolis. In
the final analysis, there was no religious court of appeal that could
exercise decisive influence on other centres of 'Hellenistic' Judaism in
the Roman Empire. The assumption of an 'Alexandrian canon' that the
early church adopted without deliberation and to a degree seamlessly is
an eighteenth- and nineteenth-century hypothesis that has proved to be a
wrong turning.[4] One must not forget that the Jewish community in
Alexandria and in Egypt was almost completely annihilated because of
the suicidal rebellion of 115–17 in the territories of the former Ptolemaic

[3] Cf. M. Hengel, *The 'Hellenization' of Judaea in the First Century after Christ*
(London and Philadelphia, 1989), 24–9.

[4] Cf. Sundberg, whose work has refuted the old hypothesis; cf. also Harl, Dorival and
Munnich, 112–19; Beckwith, 382–6; H. von Campenhausen, *Die Entstehung der
christlichen Bibel* (BHTh 39; Tübingen, 1968), 8–9.

kingdom (Egypt, Cyrenaica and Cyprus), similar to the fate of the community in Judaea in 132–5.[5] Furthermore, reports concerning Egyptian Jewry for the next two generations break off almost completely. We do not know what the collection of holy writings in the giant, five-naved synagogue in Alexandria—after the Jerusalem temple the largest religious centre of Judaism[6]—looked like. Like the Jerusalem temple in 70 CE, it too was destroyed in the rebellion of 115. Since, apart from the enigmatic Apollos (Acts 18:25)[7] and the names and doctrines of a few early Gnostics, we possess no dependable reports concerning Egyptian Christianity prior to the second half of the second century, we can also only speculate about a possible early adoption of Jewish writings by the Alexandrian church.[8] Certainly, Clement of Alexandria (*c.* 200) knew a number of biblical and apocryphal writings, but it is impossible to determine whether and when many of them were read in Christian

[5] Cf. M. Hengel, 'Messianische Hoffnung und politischer Radikalismus in der jüdisch-hellenistischen Diaspora', in *Apocalypticisms in the Mediterranean World and the Near East*, D. Hellholm, ed. (Tübingen, 1983, 2nd edn 1989), 655–86; *idem*, 'Hadrians Politik gegenüber Juden und Christen', *JANES* 16/17 (1987), 153–82 (FS E. Bickerman), both republished also in *Judaica et Hellenistica. Kleine Schriften I* (WUNT 90; Tübingen, 1996), 314–43, 358–91. For the situation of the Jews in Egypt in general, cf. A. Kasher, *The Jews in Hellenistic and Roman Egypt* (TSAJ 7; Tübingen, 1985); Harl, Dorival and Munnich, 31–8; E. Starobinski-Safran, 'La communauté juive d'Alexandrie à l'époque de Philon', in ΑΛΕΞΑΝΔΡΙΝΑ, FS C. Mondésert, SJ (Paris, 1987), 45–75. For the Jewish inscriptions, beginning with the late third century BCE, see W. Horbury and D. Noy, *Jewish Inscriptions of Graeco-Roman Egypt* (Cambridge, 1992).

[6] Cf. M. Hengel, 'Proseuche und Synagoge: Jüdische Gemeinde, Gotteshaus und Gottesdienst in der Diaspora und in Palästina', in *Tradition und Glaube*, FS K. G. Kuhn (Göttingen, 1971), 157–84, esp. 177 = *Kleine Schriften I* [I n. 5], 171–95 [188].

[7] Codex D contains the additional information that Apollos was instructed ἐν τῇ πατρίδι in the words of the Lord and thus implies that Christian instruction was already taking place in Alexandria in the year 50 (cf. B. M. Metzger, *A Textual Commentary on the Greek New Testament* [2nd edn; London and New York, 1975], 466). For this problem cf. M. Hengel and A. M. Schwemer, *Paulus zwischen Damaskus und Antiochien* (WUNT 108; Tübingen, 1998), 392–4.

[8] Cf., for example, C. H. Roberts, *Manuscript, Society and Belief in Early Christian Egypt* (Oxford, 1979), as well as Chr. Markschies, *Valentinus Gnosticus? Untersuchungen zur valentinianischen Gnosis mit einem Kommentar zu den Fragmenten Valentins* (WUNT I/65; Tübingen, 1992), 318–23 ('Exkurs IV: Zur Geschichte der christlichen Gemeinde Alexandriens'); B. A. Pearson and J. E. Goehring, eds, *The Roots of Egyptian Christianity* (Philadelphia, 1986), especially the contribution by B. A. Pearson, 'Earliest Christianity in Egypt', 123–56, and the review of it by W. A. Löhr in *ThLZ* 112 (1987), 351–3, concluding with the noteworthy statement: 'Where the sources are silent, the historian's options come to an end'; cf. also now the essays about an alleged Jewish origin of a pre-Christian Gnosticism in Alexandria: B. A. Pearson, *Gnosticism, Judaism, and Egyptian Christianity* (Minneapolis, 1990), esp. 10–12, 165–7, 194–6; see also Harl, Dorival and Munnich, 323, who contend that the division of the transmitted writings into a three-tiered scale of value, as attested in Origen, was a 'classification in use in Alexandrian Judaism' in his time. For the 'canon' of Clement, see J. Ruwet, 'Clement d'Alexandrie: Canon des Écritures et Apocryphes', *Bib* 29 (1948), 77–99, 240–68, 391–408, who wants to draw the boundaries too sharply.

worship. Our knowledge of the spiritual life and literature of the Jewish communities in other centres of the Jewish Diaspora, Antioch, Ephesus, or Rome,[9] is not greater, but much more limited. We have no occasion to speculate that the corpus of sacred writings in use in the synagogues there, stored in the Torah ark and utilized in worship and instruction, was larger than in the homeland.

From the very beginning, Christians—as a Jewish-messianic sect with a strong missionary impulse—utilized and exegeted 'the law and the prophets' under the rubric of eschatological fulfilment. Thus, they also very early employed—I recall only the Hellenists in Jerusalem and the preaching of Stephen in the Greek-speaking synagogues in Jerusalem (Acts 6:1–15)—their Greek translation.[10] This use of the LXX as Holy Scripture is practically as old as the church itself. For New Testament writings, beginning with Paul, it is the rule.[11]

It can easily be deduced from the verbatim citations in the New Testament and the Apostolic Fathers which collection of writings were involved and which books were given preference. A glance in the index of the *loci citati vel allegati* in Nestle/Aland's 26th edition may suffice here. We obviously encounter a fixed core, but a clearly defined, binding canon that can be said to extend beyond the Hebrew Bible cannot be demonstrated. Nor can we assume that the early Christian communities of the first century all had the same books on their bookshelves.[12] Instead, we must assume a considerable range of variation. On the basis of this complicated situation, the question presents itself: how did it come about that the collection of Jewish writings in the Greek language, significantly larger than the scope of the Hebrew Bible, become, under the designation 'the Seventy', the authoritative 'Holy Scriptures' of the Old Testament in the Christian church? For, since the fathers toward the end of the second and the beginning of the third centuries, it becomes more and more clear that this no longer involves a collection employed in the

---

[9] For Rome, see Schürer (rev.) III/1, 73–81; H. J. Leon, *The Jews of Ancient Rome* (Philadelphia, 1960); P. Lampe, *Die stadtrömischen Christen in den ersten beiden Jahrhunderten* (WUNT II/18; 2nd edn; Tübingen, 1989), see the index under 'Juden/ jüdisch'. Many inscriptions have been preserved, to be sure, but they are late; nothing is known of the literary activity of Roman Jewry. See D. Noy, *Jewish Inscriptions of Western Europe, Vol. 2, The City of Rome* (Cambridge, 1995).

[10] Cf. Hengel, '*Hellenization*' (see above, p. 20 n. 3), 14–15, 18, 21, 43–4; *idem*, 'Der vorchristliche Paulus', in *Paulus und das antike Judentum*, M. Hengel and U. Heckel, eds (WUNT I/58; Tübingen, 1991), 177–291, esp. 232–9, 258–60; *idem*, 'Die Schriftauslegung des 4. Evangeliums auf dem Hintergrund der urchristlichen Exegese', *JBTh* 4 (1989), 249–88.

[11] Cf. D.-A. Koch, *Die Schrift als Zeuge des Evangeliums* (BHTh 69; Tübingen, 1986). But the text used by Paul was not uniform. See further below, pp. 108–9.

[12] Cf. M. Hengel, *Die Evangelienüberschriften* (SHAW.PH, 3; Heidelberg, 1984), 37–9. See further below, pp. 111–12 and now *idem*, *The Four Gospels and the One Gospel of Jesus Christ* (London, 2000).

Jewish synagogues, but one utilized in the Christian churches. This observation influences the structure of the investigation. I begin with the 'Christian claim' to the LXX and the consolidation of its canon and then first ask about its Jewish 'prehistory' and the accretion of the writings excluded from the Hebrew canon.

II

THE LXX AS A COLLECTION OF WRITINGS CLAIMED BY CHRISTIANS[1]

1. The Translation Legend in Judaism and the Number of the Translators

First of all, it must be established that—so far as can be demonstrated historically—a *Christian* author first applied the designation 'Septuagint' as a code for the legendary seventy(-two) translators to indicate what was an originally Jewish collection of writings, the scope of which, indeed, had not yet been firmly established. This designation for the Greek translation, whether of the Pentateuch or of the whole Old Testament, does not yet occur in pre-Christian Jewish sources. Consequently, one can only speculate that the Jews already employed it. Notably, the label does not characterize the content, but represents a reference to the story of its origins for which the Jewish translation legend constitutes the starting point. Its oldest witness, the *Letter of (Pseudo-) Aristeas*, relates how, under Ptolemy II Philadelphus (282–246 BC), seventy-two Jewish elders (six from each tribe), brought from Palestine to Alexandria for the task, translated the law of Moses in seventy-two days (see below, pp. 75–80).

Only the dating can be considered the historical kernel of this account. The rest can be explained by the attempt of the *Letter of Aristeas* to legitimize a certain version of the LXX as solely valid (see below, pp. 76–7).

No reference to the number of the translators appears in the writings of the Alexandrian Philo over a hundred years later. Josephus, almost another century later, writes in a report dependent on the *Letter of Aristeas* correctly once again of the seventy-two elders, but then—without harmonizing the contradiction—of the seventy translators.

---

[1] My substantially more extensive essay appeared under this title ('Die Septuaginta als von den Christen beanspruchte Schriftensammlung bei Justin und den Vätern vor Origenes') in the 1991 Durham Symposium volume: *Jews and Christians: The Parting of the Ways*, J. G. D. Dunn, ed. (WUNT I/66; Tübingen, 1992), 39–84 = M. Hengel, *Judaica, Hellenistica et Christiana: Kleine Schriften II* (WUNT 109; Tübingen, 1999), 335–80. Paragraphs 1–4e here are a summary of this larger manuscript. For the sake of easier cross-referencing, the structure of the Durham contribution will be adopted here without alteration (2.1 corresponds to 2a, etc.). Within the current essay, the previous essay will be cited as 'M. Hengel, Durham'.

This may be a first indication of the uniform formula οἱ ἑβδομήκοντα for the entire LXX,[2] although the texts cited always speak only of the translation of 'the law'. Only Philo among Jewish authors empha- sizes the miraculous character of the translation: the 'most eminent Hebrews (*Vit Mos* 2:32) did not each write something different, but, in a prophetic manner and as though under divine motivation (καθάπερ ἐνθουσιῶντες προεφήτευον), all the same terms and words as though one inspiration dictated invisibly in each'. For this reason, those men are 'not to be called translators, but hierophants and prophets, who, because their thoughts were as clear as daylight, could keep pace with the very purest intellect of Moses'.[3]

2. *Justin*

The silence of Jewish as well as New Testament texts, including the Apostolic Fathers, about the LXX and its special character is remarkable, since this theme suddenly attains central status for the educated Christian teacher Justin, a former Platonic peripatetic, in his disputes with Jewish *Dialogue* partners.

a) The Legend in the *Apology* and *Dialogue*

In the *Apology (c.* 152–5 CE), which, judging from its title, is addressed primarily to pagan readers, Justin introduces the translation legend in an otherwise unknown form that contradicts the older Jewish examples at many points. In contrast to the historical tradition, he lays all the weight on the notion that, on the initiative of the Egyptian king Ptolemy, Jews translated into Greek *prophetic writings* written in Hebrew long before Christ. In order to achieve this, Ptolemy is said to have written two suc- cessive letters to the Jewish king Herod (!). In response to the first, Herod sent only the Hebrew Scriptures and, to the second, the translators.[4]

---

[2] *Ant* 12:56. Six men from each tribe, i.e. 12 × 6 translators. Immediately thereafter, in *Ant* 12:57, he speaks of only 'the Seventy'. Josephus also mentions the seventy-two-day period of translation (*Ant* 12:107; cf. A. Pelletier, *Flavius Josèphe adapteur de la Lettre d'Aristée* [EeC 45; Paris, 1962], 125–7, 199; Harl, Dorival and Munnich, 47, 59–61; P.-J. Shutt, 'Notes on the Letter of Aristeas', *BIOSCS* 10 [1977], 22–30). Luke 10:1 (cf. the variant traditions) may also be dependent on this formula. The Seventy(-two) translated the Torah for 'the nations'. Originally, the model of Num. 11:24, 26:70 + 2, may also have played a role. Concerning later rabbinic references, see Bill. III:323 and G. Veltri, *Eine Tora für den König Talmai: Untersuchungen zum Übersetzungs- verständnis des hellenistischen und palästinischen Judentums* (TSAJ 41; Tübingen, 1994). See also the review of Veltri by E. Tov, in *The Greek & Hebrew Bible: Collected Essays on the Septuagint* (VT.S 72; London, 1999), 75–82.

[3] *Vit Mos* 2:37, 40.

[4] We do not yet encounter the two letters in the Jewish sources, but in the peculiar account of Epiphanius (see p. 38 n. 43 below) and in Augustine's *Civ Dei* 18:42 (see below, p. 51 n. 84).

The context discusses neither the Seventy elders nor the fact that under Ptolemy only the Pentateuch was translated. Instead, the entire Old Testament, including the Mosaic law, is understood, in accordance with early Christian interpretation, as prophecy concerning Christ, and all these prophetic writings, he leads the reader to believe, were already translated upon the king's wish at that time. Thus Justin distances himself also from New Testament usage, where ὁ νόμος can still designate the whole Old Testament, although here too we already encounter clear tendencies toward a prophetic understanding of the whole.[5] Nevertheless the five books of the Law remained an exemplary paradigm. The Christian writers of the second century preferred to write works in 'five books', so Papias, Hegesippus, Apollinaris of Laodicea and Irenaeus. The word 'Pentateuch' appears for the first time in the letter of Ptolemy, a contemporary of Justin, to Flora.

The Christian philosopher emphasizes that the translated Scriptures are available to anyone 'even today' in the Alexandrian library and among the Jews, so that anyone can confirm the truth of the scriptural witness with which Justin attempts to convince his pagan addressees.

In contrast, the appeal to the Greek translation made under Ptolemy has an entirely different tendency in Justin's somewhat later *Dialogue* with the Jew Trypho. Here Justin mentions the translation of the Seventy no fewer than six times; this frequency is unique in the early Christian literature of the second and third centuries. It is apparently related to the particular situation of the *Dialogue* with a scholar from Judaea who is nevertheless learned in Greek. Justin twice exhorts his Jewish conversation partner to remain with the acknowledged text of the Seventy elders and not to depart, with the newer translations, from the 'correct' wording.[6] Even in other passages, for the most part, he only appends the (purported) reading of the LXX—apparently authoritative for him—as an afterthought. He first cites another version of the text that could also have been acknowledged by his Jewish *Dialogue* partners, although the text of the LXX in Justin's edition is usually more 'christological'.[7] The Apologist himself is convinced that he has the original work of the

---

[5] Justin, *Apol* I 31:1–5; Moses is described almost stereotypically as a prophet (see Deut. 34:10), once even as 'the first prophet' (32:4; cf. Sir. 46:1). Prophecy itself begins after the Fall (*Dial* 91:4; cf. Gen. 3:14). For the meaning of ὁ νόμος as a reference to the Old Testament in Judaism and Christianity, see Bill. II:542–3; III:159, 462 (on John 10:42; Rom. 3:19; 1 Cor. 14:21). The first signs of a prophetic understanding appear in Rom. 1:2; Heb. 1:1; 1 Peter 1:10, etc. Cf. Campenhausen (see above, p. 20 n. 4), 28–122: 'Seen in this light, the "prophetic", "christological" interpretation of the Old Testament is as old as the church itself' (29). On the 'Pentateuch', see Epiphanius, *Pan.* 33, 4, 1, and M. Hengel, in *Judaica, Hellenistica et Christiana: Kleine Schriften II* (WUNT 109; Tübingen, 1999), p. 20. To write five books against the Gnostics possibly seemed a 'sign of orthodoxy'.

[6] *Dial* 68:7; 71:1.

[7] In these passages, LXX is the subject of ἐξηγεῖσθαι (*Dial* 120:4; 131:1; 137:3 [2×]); the ἐξήγησις of the LXX is mentioned once (124:3).

Seventy in the translation available to him. In reality, this purported LXX text is based in good part on Christian testimonia collections that had been occasionally altered by Christians. In contrast, none of the amplifications and exaggerations in the translation legend encountered in the later Fathers since Irenaeus occur in the *Dialogue*. Nevertheless, Justin's manner of arguing shows clearly that the weight of his arguments against his Jewish opponents could be substantially strengthened by evidence of a divine confirmation of the translation of the Seventy as we find it later. He himself, however, still refrains from such an argument and can in consequence basically appeal only to the credibility of the Seventy.

b) Justin's 'Old Testament Library'

Justin does not explicitly mention in the *Dialogue* which prophetic books were translated under King Ptolemy. He certainly did not think, however, of the five books of Moses only, but, as in the *Apology*, of all prophetically inspired writings, i.e., the Jewish 'canon' forming in his time. This canon, including even the few borderline cases (Qoheleth, Song of Solomon, Esther and—with a negative result—Sirach) concerning which the decision had indeed already been made, already corresponded to the final 'masoretic canon'.[8] Justin cites as Holy Scripture almost all these books except Qoheleth, Esther and the Song of Solomon. Job is employed only twice, Lamentations only once in Christianized form, and the sole citation from 'Ezra' is uncertain.[9] It cannot be determined with certainty whether Justin knew the Old Testament books in their entirety or relied, in part, on testimonia collections, although the latter seems likely in all those cases where strong Christian influence is perceptible in his purported 'text of the LXX'.

Apparently his Scripture collection corresponded to that in use in the Roman church, the last place where he taught. The wide-ranging agreement between biblical books cited by him and by Clement of Rome supports this inference. It is only one or two decades after Justin that the problem of the delimitation of the Holy Scriptures of the Old Testament

---

[8] Cf. *Dial* 30:1–2 which presumes the tripartite division of the canon into the books of Moses, the prophets and the psalms (as in Luke 24:44). The threefold division implies, at the same time, a chronological sequence.

[9] To be sure, Justin mentions the name Ezra twice as the name of a biblical prophet (72:1; 120:5), but the text he cites concerning Passover as a type for Christ is missing in manuscripts of the LXX and probably stems from a Christian testimonia collection (see P. Prigent, 'Justin et l'Ancien Testament', *EtB* [Paris, 1964], 174–5; and O. Skarsaune, *The Proof from Prophecy: A Study in Justin Martyr's Proof-Text Tradition: Text-Type, Provenance, Theological Profile* [NT.S56; Leiden, 1987], 42). Consequently, the question remains open as to the form in which he knew 'Ezra' (1st or 2nd Ezra, Ezra-Apocalypse?); See also M. Hengel, Durham, 46, n. 27.

first becomes clearly apparent in a Christian author, namely Melito of Sardis.[10] Because Christians addressed the problem of the Old Testament 'canon' later than Jews, they were, on this point, never really completely independent of the synagogue. Justin's attitude in the *Dialogue* already demonstrates this: he cites as 'Scripture' none of the texts later excluded from the canon as apocrypha or pseudepigrapha, although he seems to have known the *Book of Enoch* as well as the legends concerning the *Martyrdom of Isaiah*.[11] This may be related to his circumspection in regard to his Jewish *Dialogue* partners, with whom he wants to discuss only 'the passages still recognized among you'.[12]

The various anonymous recensions of the LXX already in circulation at that time, probably by Palestinian Jewish scholars who wished to improve the often inadequate translation of the LXX in light of the Hebrew original, present a problem to this discussion. Even Justin employed such a recensional text in, for example, his citations from the Minor Prophets.[13]

c) The Dispute about the Translation of Isaiah 7:14

The central significance of Isaiah 7:14 for Justin's Christology compelled him to introduce his understanding of the translation of the LXX at this point, for only by means of the Greek text could he adduce scriptural evidence for the virgin birth of the Messiah. Simultaneously, Justin was able to emphasize the divine aspect of Jesus' virgin birth and still hold firmly to the real 'incarnation' of the pre-existent son of God—a matter of supreme importance in the light of his dual intra-church conflict with

---

[10] See below, pp. 60–1. Melito, too, orients himself simply to the Jewish model.

[11] See R. H. Charles, *The Book of Enoch or 1 Enoch* (Oxford, 1912), LXX xi–LXX xii; M. Hengel, Durham, 49 n. 38. Justin may have already known *AscIsa* containing the *Martyrdom*, although his acquaintance with the legends may also stem from oral tradition such as is also apparent in Heb. 11:37. See M. Hengel, Durham, 62, n. 89. Cf. now A. M. Schwemer, *Studien zu den frühjüdischen Prophetenlegenden Vitae Prophetarum* (TSAJ 49; Tübingen, 1995) I, 107–15.

[12] *Dial* 71:2: ἐπὶ τὰς ἐκ τῶν ὁμολογουμένων ἔτι παρ' ὑμῖν τὰς ζητήσεις ποιεῖν ἔρχομαι. See also *Dial* 120:5 and Skarsaune (see above, p. 28 n. 9), 34.

[13] See Skarsaune (see above, p. 28 n. 9), 17–23, 424–6. This dependence on recensional texts becomes clear through a comparison of Justin's citations from the Minor Prophets (esp. Mic. 4:3–7) and the Greek Minor Prophets scroll from Nahal Hever, written at the turn of the era. See D. Barthélemy, *Les devanciers d'Aquila* (VT.S10; Leiden, 1963), 203–12; *idem*, 'Redécouverte d'un chaînon manquant de l'histoire de la Septante', *RB* 60 (1953): 18–29 (now in Barthélemy, 38–50, and *Studies*, 226–38); P. Katz, *Justin's Old Testament Quotations and the Greek Dodekapropheton Scroll* (Studia Patristica I/1; Berlin, 1957), 343–53 (now in *Studies*, 530–40); E. Tov, *The Greek Minor Prophets Scroll from Nahal Hever (8 Hev XII gr)* (DJD 8; Oxford, 1990), esp. 158 concerning Justin's text of the prophets; Tov dates the scroll very early in the middle of the first century BCE. On the problem of recensions, see S. P. Brock, 'To Revise or not Revise', in Brooke and Lindars, 301–38.

the Ebionites on the one hand and with Marcion and his disciples on the other.

The *Dialogue* cites Isaiah 7:14 nine times in the LXX version (ἡ παρθένος); four times Justin contrasts the reading he so vehemently defended with the one he rejected, the one defended by the Jews ('Ἰδοὺ *ἡ νεᾶνις* ἐν γαστρὶ λήψεται).[14] The Ebionite doctrine that Joseph was Jesus' father[15] as well as Tryphon's contention that only a messiah as ἄνθρωπος ἐξ ἀνθρώπου could be the promised son of David[16] force Justin to cling stubbornly to the reading (ἡ παρθένος ...) that he defended. On this point, the apologist cannot yield so much as a finger's breadth. The text is a landmark in his system of prophetic-christological scriptural proofs:

> Now if I demonstrate that this prophecy of Isaiah's was said of our Christ and not, as you contend, of Hezekiah, will I not thereby render you unsure whether you failed to obey your teachers who dared to claim that *the translation of your seventy elders, who were with the Egyptian king Ptolemy, does not correspond in many ways to the truth?* For if scripture passages reproach you for obviously imprudent and selfish thinking, you dare contend that it is not so written.[17]

Justin's argument assumes that, on the whole, his Jewish partners still recognize the authority of the Alexandrian translation of the LXX, even if they fault it for a few errors, presumably because they already know Palestinian recensions that have improved the text. Astonishingly, the fact that the Christian extends the translation legend to all Scriptures, especially to the prophets and Psalms, does not seem to disturb them, since that would have already been a significant objection against Justin's insistence on the authority of the LXX with respect to Isaiah 7:14. At this point, however, there may still have been a certain basic consensus between Christians and Jews concerning the LXX and even the Jewish understanding of the authority of the LXX already included all Greek translations of the writings of the Old Testament. Nor do the Jewish

---

[14] *Dial* 43:3–8 (2×); 66:2–4 and the Jewish response in 67:1; 68:9; 71:3; 77:3; 84:1 (2×), and the Jewish response in 84:3. The *Apologia* cites Isa. 7:14 only once (I 33:1, 4–6). Cf. H. Gese, 'Natus ex virgine', in *Vom Sinai zum Zion* (BevTh 64; München, 1974), 130–46 (145f.): 'The question of whether the Greek translation of *'almā* by παρθένος in Is 7,14 in the midst of the 2nd century BC in Egypt presupposes the idea of a virginal birth of the messiah remains open.' See also A. Kamesar, 'The Virgin of Isaiah 7:14: The Philological Argument from the Second to the Fifth Century', *JThS* NS 49 (1990): 51–75; M. Rösel, 'Die Jungfrauengeburt des endzeitlichen Immanuel: Jesaja 7 in der Übersetzung der Septuaginta', *JBTh* 6 (1991), 135–51.

[15] *Dial* 48:4, cf. Irenaeus, *Adv Haer* 3:21:1.

[16] *Dial* 49:1; 67:2; 68:5.

[17] *Dial* 68:6–8: The definitive passage (68:7) reads: οἵτινες τολμῶσι λέγειν τὴν ἐξήγησιν ἣν ἐξηγήσαντο οἱ ἑβδομήκοντα ὑμῶν πρεσβύτεροι παρὰ Πτολεμαίῳ τῷ τῶν Αἰγυπτίων βασιλεῖ γενόμενοι, μὴ εἶναι ἔν τισιν ἀληθῆ.

opponents appeal to an entirely new and better translation (perhaps that of Aquila), although texts corrected against the original were already in circulation and Justin occasionally utilized such a text. The reading ἡ νεᾶνις, championed by Tryphon and his friends, apparently derives from such a recension.

d) The Appeal to the Seventy and the Charge of Falsifying Scripture

Since the Jewish and Christian versions differ at certain points, despite the still undisputed common reference to the LXX, Justin charged his dialogue partners with falsifying Scripture. In contrast, the idea that his own text could contain Christian expansion does not occur to him. The falsification charge included two elements: translational *alterations*, as for example in Isaiah 7:14, and *omissions* of significant references to Christ.

1. In no way will I allow myself to be convinced by your teachers who will not admit that the Seventy elders of Ptolemy, the king of Egypt, produced a good translation and who, instead, attempt their own translations.

2. I want you to know that they have completely removed from the translation of Ptolemy's elders many passages which clearly demonstrate that the crucified himself is proclaimed as God and Man who will be crucified and die . . .[18]

Dialogue 71:3 makes it clear that the first portion of the citation (71:1) refers once again to the previously mentioned disputed interpretation of Isaiah 7:14; the charge of falsification is once more forcefully repeated in relation to this passage:

You dare, however, to falsify even the translation that your elders prepared under Ptolemy by contending that the scriptures do not read as they translated, but '. . . the young woman . . . will conceive', as though it were a reference to some great event for a woman to bear a child as the result of sexual intercourse—all young women (νεάνιδες), except for the barren, do this.[19]

Isaiah's word to king Ahaz refers to a 'sign' (σημεῖον, 84:2; cf. Isa. 7:10). According to Justin, this can only be true if an extraordinary,

---

[18] 71:1—Ἀλλ᾽ οὐχὶ τοῖς διδασκάλοις ὑμῶν πείθομαι, μὴ συντεθειμένοις καλῶς ἐξηγεῖσθαι τὰ ὑπὸ τῶν παρὰ Πτολεμαίῳ τῷ Αἰγυπτίων γενομένῳ βασιλεῖ ἑβδομήκοντα πρεσβυτέρων, ἀλλ᾽ αὐτοὶ ἐξηγεῖσθαι πειρῶνται. 71:2—Καὶ ὅτι πολλὰς γραφὰς τέλεον περιεῖλον ἀπὸ τῶν ἐξηγήσεων τῶν γεγενημένων ὑπὸ τῶν παρὰ Πτολεμαίῳ γεγενημένων πρεσβυτέρων, ἐξ ὧν διαρρήδην οὗτος αὐτὸς ὁ σταυρωθεὶς ὅτι θεὸς καὶ ἄνθρωπος καὶ σταυρούμενος καὶ ἀποθνῄσκων κεκηρυγμένος ἀποδείκνυται, εἰδέναι ὑμᾶς βούλομαι.

[19] *Dial* 84:3. Cf. M. Hengel, Durham, 60 n. 79.

wondrous event is associated with this birth since giving birth represents nothing extraordinary for young women. Justin justifies the second portion of his charge of falsification (71:2) at his dialogue partner's insistence by giving the following four examples:

First, he mentions 'Ezra's exegesis of the Passover law' which is found neither in the manuscripts of the books of Ezra nor in the apocrypha and which refers to Christ as the paschal lamb (cf. 1 Cor. 5:7). It conceivably originated in a now lost Christian Ezra-apocryphon, or as a Christian addition in a text of 1 or 2 Ezra in the context of the Passover festival.[20]

Disregarding a few variants, the second example (72:2) is identical with the LXX of Jeremiah 11:19 and is found in all manuscripts.[21] Admittedly, Justin adds that this passage can still be found in a few manuscripts from Jewish synagogues since it had only been expunged very recently.[22]

The third example (72:4) concerning the descent of Israel's Lord and God to the dead is also supposed to stem from Jeremiah, but can be found neither in a manuscript of the prophets nor in an apocryphon. Like the Ezra text, it is surely of Christian origin, perhaps from a Jeremiah apocalypse.[23]

The fourth case comes from Psalm 95:10. Justin accuses the Jews of omitting the words ἀπὸ τοῦ ξύλου following the phrase ὁ κύριος ἐβασίλευσεν because they identify the Lord and Creator of the world with the crucified Jesus (*Dial* 73:1–2). But this case, too, concerns a very old Christian addition that appears in only a few witnesses to the LXX.[24] For Justin, the psalm itself is also an important christological text, already cited extensively in his *Apologia*[25] and also quoted in totality in *Dialogue* 73:3–4, although now in the traditional LXX form.

---

[20] 72:1; cf. 1 Ezra 1:1–2; 7:10–12; 2 Ezra 6:19–21. See Skarsaune (see above, p. 28 n. 9), 40, 42.

[21] See Skarsaune (see above, p. 28 n. 9), 40, 42, 187, 301, 452. It is attested in numerous Testimonia lists from the early church period. See Prigent (see above, p. 28 n. 9), 173–5, 178–80, 181, 190–2.

[22] Cf. M. Hengel, Durham, 57 n. 69.

[23] Irenaeus cites the saying six times in slightly varied forms and attributes it once to Isaiah (*Adv Haer* 3:20:4) and twice to Jeremiah (*Adv Haer* 4:22:1; *Epideixis* 78). The remaining references are unattributed (*Adv Haer* 4:33:1; alii—4:33:12; a prophet—5:31:1). See A. Resch, *Agrapha* (2nd edn; Lepzig, 1906 [= Darmstadt, 1967]), 320–2. The text concerns (proto-)Theodotion's version of Dan. 12:1: τῶν καθευδόντων ἐν γῆς χώματι (*Dial* 72:4—τῶν κεκοιμηένων εἰς γῆν χώματος). See also Hengel, Durham, 58 n. 70.

[24] For the evidence see A. Rahlfs, *Psalmi cum Odis*, in, *Septuaginta: Vetus Testamentum Graecum X* (3rd edn; Göttingen, 1979), 31, 247. So already Swete, 423–4; Skarsaune, 35–42. Tertullian (*Adv Marc* 3:19:1; *Adv Jud* 10:11–12; cf. 13:11), Ps-Cyprian (*De Montibus Sina et Sion 9*, CSEL 3/3, G. Hartel, ed. [Vienna, 1871], 113), and *Barn* 8:5 (in a slightly altered form) also mention the reading.

[25] *Apol* I 41:4.

Skarsaune correctly concludes that here Justin utilized a Jewish manuscript of the LXX available to him, but which he regarded as falsified because of the absence of ἀπὸ τοῦ ξύλου.[26]

Trypho cautiously rejects the charge that the Jewish leadership had falsified the text (*Dial* 73:5). For Justin it is a sin more horrendous than the erection of the golden calf. He is prepared, however, to acknowledge the possibility of his own ignorance and, furthermore, with the exception of Isaiah 7:14, to continue the discussion on the basis of the text recognized by both sides.

e) The 'Generous' Treatment of Minor Variants

At three more points in the last quarter of the *Dialogue* Justin takes up three purported differences between the text of the authentic LXX and that purportedly falsified by the Jews. In these cases he does not insist on 'his' reading because the differences concern more peripheral points in his argument. The methodological significance of these treatments may lie in the fact that he wishes to demonstrate to his readers that Christian exegesis is more precise than Jewish exegesis and, consequently, need not fear any objections.

The first variant concerns Jacob's blessing of Judah (Gen. 49:10) cited in *Dialogue* 120:3–4 in two divergent forms. This case, however, involves a pre-Christian divergence in the LXX tradition. Both variants attempt an interpretive translation of the Hebrew text.[27]

The second passage (*Dial* 124:2–3) is Psalm 81:6–7 (MT 82:6–7). The only difference[28] concerns whether ἄνθρωπος in v. 7 stands in the singular or the plural. Because he relates the passage to Adam and Eve, Justin argues for the plural as the authentic LXX reading, a position supported by known manuscripts.[29] The difference is not particularly significant. He is concerned only with demonstrating his superior knowledge of the various recensions of the text. The same is true of the last passage from Isaiah 3:10, which he cites four times in all, twice in the version he finally rejects,[30] once in the form he defends as the LXX reading—in which the weaker 'let us bind the righteous' is replaced by the stronger 'let us do away with the righteous' (Ἄρωμεν τὸν δίκαιον, ὅτι . . . ; *Dial* 136:2)—and finally both readings in succession in *Dial* 137:3, where he explains to his readers the pedagogical rationale for these

[26] Skarsaune (see above, p. 28 n. 9), 38–9.

[27] Cf. Hengel, Durham, 61 and nn. 82–3. Justin rejects the reading of the better attested text.

[28] Disregarding the ὑμεῖς δὲ instead of Ἰδοὺ δή, claimed by Justin as the LXX reading, since it is not pertinent to the discussion. Most LXX manuscripts after Jerome support the text rejected by Justin, however.

[29] Cf. Hengel, Durham, 63 n. 93.

[30] *Dial* 17:2; 133:2: Δήσωμεν τὸν δίκαιον, ὅτι δύσχρηστος ἡμῖν ἐστι.

divergent modes of his citation. He mentioned the 'false' reading twice in order to test them; however, they may well have been inattentive (or thoughtless). But here too, what Justin defends as the LXX reading actually represents a variant probably influenced by passages from the passion narratives of the gospels, while δήσωμεν is original.[31]

f) Justin's Appeal to the Seventy in his Discussion with Jews in Rome

Justin's treatment of the LXX is the result of the experience of over thirty years of Christian instruction and of the discussion with Jewish partners. His knowledge of the LXX and the treasury of citations he assembled in the *Apologia*, as well as in the *Dialogue*, certainly stems, in part, from florilegium collections, but also from his own work with the text of the Greek Old Testament: Justin probably had access to a LXX without recensional influences. The fact that he had at least a dawning awareness of the problems with this translation is evident in his concern for an improved form of the text, as can be discerned in his citations from the Minor Prophets that approximate those in the Naḥal Ḥever scroll.[32] The first slight trace of a scientific interest that will reach its apogee in Origen's Hexapla is evident here. But his astonishingly good knowledge of Judaism is also noteworthy and demonstrates that Justin was in a kind of academic dialogue with the large Jewish community in Rome, which, according to rabbinical reports, had its own school. This discussion would have, however, repeatedly made him aware of the weaknesses of his translation. For this reason, it became essential for him to emphasize the authority of the Seventy elders and of the work they translated. By juxtaposing his text (with its Christian expansions) with the purportedly abbreviated Jewish text, he gave new voice, relatively independently of the older Jewish translation legend (see below, pp. 75–91), to the problem of an *authorized* form of the text. This comparison finally led to the fact that the LXX gradually became the authoritative Christian Old Testament and Aquila's translation after a longer development gave the Jewish community a new authoritative Greek text. In order, however, to lend dignity and authority to the Greek translation appropriated in this manner, the Christian apologist associated it emphatically with the Seventy elders, regardless of the fact that they were the legendary translators only of the Pentateuch. At the same time, however, it should be pointed out that Justin still abstained from all manner of ornamentation and hyperbole, such as the inspiration miracle, in his use of the legend. Justin may have already had a predecessor for this argument concerning the Seventy in the *Dialogue of Jason and Papiscus* from the pen of Ariston of Pella, a

---

[31] Cf. Luke 23:18; Acts 7:52; Wisdom 2:12; John 19:15, and Hengel, Durham, 64 n. 100.

[32] See above, p. 29 n. 13.

contemporary of the Bar-Kochba rebellion. Since this work, perhaps somewhat older than the *Dialogus cum Tryphone*, is now lost, we can only conjecture. Notably, nonetheless, the LXX problem arose in dialogue with the Jews and Isaiah 7:14 played a dominant role.

3. *The Seventy in Later 'Dialogues'*

Two later Christian-Jewish Dialogues from the fifth and sixth centuries respectively emphasize, much as did Justin, the significance of the translation of the Seventy for the church and for its differentiation from and discussion with the synagogue. In contrast, in the other Dialogues oriented literarily toward Justin's model, and also in the Adversus-Judaeos literature,[33] interest in the question of the LXX and its text receded significantly. This diminished interest indicates once again that Justin's statements are bound up with his own experiences and do not represent mere literary convention.

In the fifth or sixth century *Dialogue of a Christian and a Jew*,[34] between the Christian Timotheus and the Jew with the significant name Aquila, the latter objects that Christians adduce texts that do not exist in Hebrew and thus falsify the Scriptures. The Christian responds with an extensive report of the translation by the seventy-two elders, who were inspired by the Holy Spirit, while the Jews, for their part, are said to possess a falsified text in the Aquila translation. Here, in contrast to Justin's situation, the LXX has become an unequivocally Christian book, while Aquila's translation had achieved sole supremacy in the syna-gogues. This is even clearer in the somewhat later disputation between Bishop Gregentius of Tafra in Yemen and the Jew Herban[35] who confesses at the outset: 'Our fathers wrongly and capriciously translated the (holy) books of Israel into Greek so that you could take possession of the same and silence us.' The Jews' final repudiation of the LXX made it henceforth exclusively the church's book.

A Passover homily falsely attributed to Chrysostom raises the objec-tion that the Jews permitted themselves to be deceived 'by a certain proselyte' (Aquila) into rejecting the translation of their best and wisest men, although 'all Hebrews' were once threatened with curses if they altered it (Arist 311). Consequently, Christians are Moses' true followers

---

[33] Cf. H. Schreckenberg, *Die christlichen Adversus-Judaeos-Texte und ihr literarisches und historisches Umfeld (1.–11. Jh.)* (Frankfurt am Main und Bern, 1982). On the charge of falsification, see 186, 197.

[34] F. C. Conybeare, ed., *The Dialogues of Athanasius and Zacchaeus and of Timothy and Aquila* (Anecdota Oxoniensia, Classical Series 8; Oxford, 1898), 66–104. See also Jellicoe, 78. The form of the legend is dependent on Epiphanius, see below, p. 37 n. 42.

[35] *PG* 86/1, 622–783. The disputation is supposed to have taken place in 535. The legendary report stems from a life of Gregentius and is substantially later. See also Schreckenberg (see above, n. 33), 397–400, 632. For the rabbinic parallels, cf. Hengel, Durham, 69 n. 118.

since they accepted their translation 'not just because of two (Deut. 10:15), but on the basis of seventy-two witnesses'.[36] The peculiar transformation in *Ps-Clem Hom* 3:47–49 probably goes back to a Judaeo-Christian legend and a conflict about the validity of the whole Law: Moses transmitted the Torah to the seventy elders on Sinai *only* in oral form (contrast *mAv* 1:1). Later, someone wrote them down—from memory. For this reason, truth and lies are intermixed in the Torah. This diametrically contradicted all Jewish concepts of the Torah.

4. *The Translation Legend in the Early Fathers after Justin*

a) Persistent Problems

Teachers of the church after Justin faced a number of open problems fundamentally beyond solution: the claim of the authority of the Seventy for the whole Christian Old Testament, whose contents still varied; the fact that the Greek collection of books itself contained portions of texts and whole books that do not appear in the Jewish canon and thus were not covered by the translation legend at all, while other works appear to be abbreviated in comparison to the Hebrew original (see below pp. 83–96); and, finally, the existence of competing Greek text traditions whose contradictions could only be masked, but not removed, by the charge of falsification.

Consequently, Origen created the Hexapla[37] to obtain an overview of the confusing chaos. But he too defended the LXX text as approved by the church since it represented the translation that had come into existence by God's providence and was binding in the churches. Nevertheless, he never mentions the translation or even the inspiration legend. For him, the Hebrew original gained a certain importance once again. Indeed, the first two columns of his magnum opus were devoted to it. Thereby the church was continually reminded that the LXX is only a *translation* that can never exceed the Hebrew original in dignity, but must, rather, always succeed it. This was also true—*cum grano salis*—for the question of the true scope of the Holy Scriptures. At least a few Christian intellectuals were somewhat sensitive to this issue.[38]

[36] For the quotations from the disputations, see *PG* 86/1, 624. For Pseudo-Chrysostom, see *PG* 59, 747 and P. Wendland (see below, p. 37 n. 39), 165–6.

[37] C. P. Bammel, 'Die Hexapla des Origenes: Die Hebraica Veritas im Streit der Meinungen', *Augustinianum* 28 (1988): 125–49. See also the collection of essays in A. Salvesen (ed.), *Origen's Hexapla and Fragments: Papers presented at the Rich Seminar on the Hexapla. Oxford Centre for Hebrew and Jewish Studies 25th July–3rd August 1994* (TSAJ 58; Tübingen, 1998), with a comprehensive bibliography, pp. 453–74.

[38] Cf. the letter of Julius Africanus to Origen (N. de Lange, ed., in *SC* 301 [Paris, 1983], 514–21) and P. Nautin, *Origène: Sa vie et son oeuvre* (Paris, 1977), 303–61; see below, pp. 47–9. Later this was true especially of Jerome, see below, pp. 49–50. Even Augustine could not entirely avoid the critical arguments, see below, pp. 50–4. Another example is

b) Pseudo-Justin's *Cohortatio ad Graecos*

Nevertheless, the majority of Christians sought a way around this difficulty by appealing to the translation legend, now—by far surpassing Justin—highly enriched with inspiration miracle motifs borrowed from Philo, coloured ever more fantastically.[39]

These reached their peak in the *Cohortatio ad Graecos*, falsely attributed to Justin, which probably originated in the second half of the third century.[40] For the first time, this work expressly maintains that the Seventy elders, isolated in separate quarters, independently translated 'the story of Moses *and the other prophets*'. According to him, the foundations of the cells are supposedly still visible on the island of Pharos. According to this report, each of the Seventy prepared his own translation and when King Ptolemy compared them they were in exact verbal agreement.[41] The joint work of the translators, who discussed their text with one another, as presumed in the *Letter of Aristeas* (302; and still in Irenaeus, see below, pp. 38–40), has fallen prey to the miracle. This transformation into a miracle probably reflects the influence of Philo's report which, although much more cautious, can be interpreted in accord with the *Cohortatio*. Possession of the LXX made it possible for Christians, so the author claims, to produce the proof of their religion for Jews and pagans without appeal to their own genuine texts (the New Testament) since the LXX could be found in the synagogue even in his day.

The legend receives further novelistic flavour only from Epiphanius,[42] while his contemporary Jerome rejected the whole account as a lie, on the basis of his thorough familiarity with the sources:

Lucian of Antioch, martyr in the time of Maximinius Daza, 312 (Eusebius, *Hist Eccl* 8:13:2, cf. 9:6:3). According to Philostorgius, *Kirchengeschichte*, J. Bidez and F. Winkelmann, eds. (GCS; Berlin, 1981³), 187, he corrected the corrupt LXX text according to 'the Hebrew language, which he mastered perfectly'; cf. G. Zuntz, 'Lukian von Antiochien und der Text der Evangelien', AHAW.PH (1995), 2, 9–17.

[39] P. Wendland, ed., *Aristeae ad Philocratem epistula cum ceteris de origine versionis LXX interpretum testimoniis* (Leipzig, 1900), 87–166, 228–9, counts over seventy references by Christian authors appealing to the legend. A complete bibliography on the legend 'which probably represents the most widely distributed account in antiquity concerning the translation of a sacred text' (1) in Jewish, Christian, Islamic, Samaritan and Karaitic sources can be found in Veltri (see above, p. 26 n. 2), 1–2 n. 2. See also 'Legende der LXX'.

[40] Pseudo-Iustinus, 'Cohortatio ad Graecos', M. Marcovich, ed., *PTS* 32 (Berlin and New York, 1990), 1–78. See pp. 4–6 for the dating and characterization of the unknown author. The thirteenth chapter deals with the LXX. See also Jellicoe, 44.

[41] 13:3 (Marcovich, ed., 40–1): Ἐπεὶ δὲ ἔγνω τοὺς ἑβδομήκοντα ἄνδρας μὴ μόνον τῇ αὐτῇ διανοίᾳ, ἀλλὰ καὶ ταῖς αὐταῖς λέξεσι χρησαμένους, καὶ μηδὲ ἄχρι μιᾶς λέξεως τῆς πρὸς ἀλλήλους συμφωνίας διημαρτηκότας . . .

[42] *De Mensuris et Ponderibus*, chaps 5 and 6; cf. M. Hengel, Durham, 74 n. 143 and Jellicoe, 45–7.

Nor do I know who was the first author to erect the seventy cells through his lies, since Aristeas, the bodyguard of the same Ptolemy, and much later Josephus, reported nothing of the kind. Instead, they wrote that those assembled in the hall had compared among themselves and not prophesied. It is one thing to be a prophet, and something else to be a translator (*sed in una basilica congregatos contulisse scribant, non prophetasse. Aliud est enim vatem, aliud esse interpretem*) . . . I do not condemn the Seventy, I raise no objection against them, but, with complete respect, I prefer the Apostles to them all.[43]

c) Irenaeus

For the history of interpretation, the most significant interpretation of the legend of the origin of the LXX, however, is that of Irenaeus (barely a century before the *Cohortatio*), who influenced Clement of Alexandria and the whole church tradition after him.

Here, too, it is the problem of Jesus' incarnation and the prophecy of the Virgin Birth in Isaiah 7:14 which occasions the discussion of the LXX problem. Irenaeus emphasizes the antiquity of both the Hebrew prophecy and the Greek translation in order to forestall any charge of Christian falsification. His version of the translation legend follows in its entirety:

Before the Romans established their dominion and the Macedonians still ruled Asia, Ptolemy, the son of Lagus, . . . eager to supply the library in Alexandria he had built with the most important writings of all humanity, communicated to the Jerusalemites his wish to possess their writings in the Greek language. They . . . sent Ptolemy seventy elders, especially learned among them in scriptural exegesis and in both languages, so that they might fulfil his wish.[44] Since Ptolemy, fearing that they could obscure the true content of the writings by agreement, wanted to test each one, however, he separated them from one another and commanded that all should translate the same work; he did this for all the books.[45] But when they assembled before Ptolemy and compared their translations to one another, glory be to

---

[43] 'Prologus in Pentateucho', cited in *Biblia Sacra iuxta Vulgatam versionem*, B. Fischer OSB and others, ed. (3rd edn; Stuttgart, 1983), 3–4; so also in the *Apologia adv Rufinum* 2:25 (CChr.SL 79: Hieronymus III/2, P. Lardet, ed. [Turnhout, 1982], 62–3).

[44] In his citation from Irenaeus, Eusebius (*Hist Eccl* 5:8:12) has ποιήσαντος τοῦ θεοῦ ὅπερ ἠβούλετο for *facturos hoc quod ipse voluisset*. At issue is a significant, secondary theological interpretation. This may be an example of the influence of Clement of Alexandria (*Strom* 1:149:2): θεοῦ γὰρ ἦν βούλημα upon Eusebius.

[45] Here, too, Eusebius (5:8:13) has an interpretive change: instead of *iussit omnes eandem interpretari Scripturam*, he reads ἐκέλευσε τοὺς πάντας τὴν αὐτὴν ἑρμηνείαν γράφειν. The demand for the same basis for the translation becomes a demand for an identical written translation.

God, the writings were proven to be truly divine. For all had rendered the same texts with the same words and the same meanings . . . so that even the pagans present acknowledged that the books had been translated by divine inspiration (κατ' ἐπιπνοίαν τοῦ θεοῦ = *per aspirationem Dei*).[46]

The complete isolation of the translators is adduced here for the first time as evidence of the inspiration of this translation. In a certain sense, it can thus even be regarded as superior to the Hebrew text since any variations or instances of greater precision in relation to the original that may appear in the Greek version can be regarded as divinely legitimized through the agreement of the Seventy. As evidence of the credibility of the miraculous inspiration, Irenaeus refers to a second similar miracle involving Ezra, whom God enabled by inspiration to record anew the Hebrew Scriptures of pre-exilic times which had previously been lost.[47] This means that even the preservation of the Hebrew text following the first destruction of Jerusalem by Nebuchadnezzar depends on a special miraculous inspiration, and the translation of the Seventy only continues in heightened fashion what had already taken place. Thus, the extreme antiquity and the divine confirmation of the LXX are, for Irenaeus, the definitive basis of his appeal to the LXX version of Isaiah 7:14:

The faith of the Christians is 'not fabricated, but alone is true', because he has his 'obvious evidence in those scriptures that were translated in the manner narrated above; even so the preaching of the church is free of falsification (*sine interpolatione*)'. The apostles, who are older than the new translators Theodotion and Aquila, and also their followers, 'preached the words of the prophets just as they are contained in the translation of the elders (*quemadmodum seniorum interpretatio continet*)'. Thus, it is the same Spirit of God who spoke through the prophets of the coming of the Lord, 'who properly translated through the elders what was really prophesied (*in senioribus autem interpretatus est bene quae bene prophetata fuerant*), and who preached the fulfilment of the promise through the apostles.[48]

Thus, the inspired LXX constitutes the bridge between the 'prophets' and the apostles. At the same time, the seventy translators and the apostles who depend upon them appear as the true tradents and guarantors of the divine word, being inspired, like the prophets themselves, in contrast to the new 'translations' of Theodotion and Aquila which were apparently at least somewhat preferred by the Jews in

---

[46] *Adv Haer* 3:21:2 = Eusebius, *Hist Eccl* 5:8:11–14. Irenaeus attributes the translation to Ptolemy I in contrast to the other sources. This chronology may be related to the fact that the Demetrius of Phaleron who plays a decisive role in the *Letter of Aristeas* was counsellor to Ptolemy I and not Ptolemy II. See also above, p. 20 n. 3.

[47] Irenaeus, *Adv Haer* 3:21:3 = Eusebius, *Hist Eccl* 5:8:15. The basis is the Jewish Ezra legend present also in 4 Ezra 14:37–46. On this see below, pp. 54 and 72–3.

[48] *Adv Haer* 3:21:2–3. For Augustine see below, pp. 50–3.

Irenaeus' day; the novelty of these translations simultaneously expresses their inferiority. In Irenaeus, toward the end of the second century, Christians seem to have already largely appropriated the LXX for themselves.

d) Clement and Tertullian

A little later Irenaeus' version of the translation legend was also adapted in slightly altered form by Clement of Alexandria, although he knew the reports of both Philo and Josephus; i.e. Irenaeus' version must have very much impressed this most learned Christian author of his time. He, too, emphasizes the inspired agreement as a unique characteristic which he understands as a divinely produced 'prophecy in the Greek language' (ὁιονεὶ ʽΕλληνικὴν προφητείαν).[49]

In Carthage Tertullian, who had read both Justin and Irenaeus, was, in contrast to them, the first Christian author to appeal to the *Letter of Aristeas*[50] when, in the *Apologeticum*, he informs his pagan and Christian readers concerning the documents of his own faith. He especially emphasizes the role of Ptolemy in the translation enterprise, which he extended with equal care to the prophetic literature, by speaking not of the law, but by maintaining that 'the prophets had always spoken' to the Jews. Tertullian's emphasis on the philosopher Menedemus, a member of the Ptolemaic court, mentioned once in the *Letter of Aristeas* as a defender of divine providence, is so arranged that an allusion to the total agreement of the individual translators can also be heard in it.[51] The characteristically more cautious use of the translation legend here, tantamount almost to neglect, is symptomatic of developments in the West where the dispute with Jews and Jewish Christians was apparently less urgent or at least less bound to the canon than in the East, which was influenced by Alexandria. This circumstance may also be the basis for the fact that the West could permit greater freedom in relation to the Scriptures present in neither the Hebrew nor the LXX canons. For Tertullian this was true in particular of the *Book of Enoch* (see below, pp. 54–6). From the beginning of the third century the Western fathers also increasingly used the Old Latin translation based only upon the Greek Septuagint. The distance from the Hebrew original became therefore still larger.

e) Summary

The witnesses assembled here make it clear that the legend of the seventy translators, extended to the whole Old Testament understood in its

---

[49] *Strom* 1:149:3.

[50] *Apologeticum* 19:5–9 contends that the original books can still be seen in Alexandria.

[51] See C. Becker, ed., *Tertullian Apologeticum: Lateinisch und deutsch* (Munich, 1961), 303, and M. Hengel, Durham, 80–1 nn. 164–5.

entirety as a collection of prophetic literature, fulfilled a hermeneutical function intended to justify the exclusive use of the Greek translation. The more logical recourse to the Hebrew canon or even to the original text was not possible—yet; Origen and Jerome remain the few, but significant, exceptions. At the same time, the fact must be emphasized that only the Christianized LXX permitted the church to adhere to the Old Testament. The alternative would have been its total rejection, as Marcion and some Gnostics had done. Finally, the hermeneutical function of the Christianized translation legend is also evident in the fact that almost all the twenty-plus *Aristeas* manuscripts introduce a catena to the Octoteuch (Genesis–Ruth).[52]

One could say that it served as a justification for the use of the Greek translation of the Old Testament in the church.

5. *The Form of the Christian LXX*

The thorough Christian appropriation of the LXX also manifests itself in the external form of the documents. Long before there was a 'New Testament', the Christian LXX was distinguished by the use of the *codex* rather than the Jewish *scroll*. Further, the tetragrammaton, as a rule continued in use in Greek scrolls of Jewish provenance, but in the Christian codices it was replaced by κύριος, which was now written, like χριστός and other *nomina sacra*, for emphasis with only the initial and final letters and a line above ($\overline{\text{ΚΣ}}$, $\overline{\text{ΧΣ}}$, etc.).[53] This distinction must reach back into the first century and thus makes it possible to distinguish between Jewish and Christian manuscripts practically from the very beginning. It also points externally to a new beginning intended to distinguish between the use of Scriptures in 'ekklesia' and 'synagogue'. We possess only nine fragments of Jewish biblical scrolls in the Greek language dating to between the second century BCE and the first century CE from Egypt, despite its sizeable Jewish population, Qumran, and the Judaean wilderness.[54] Yet in Egypt at least fourteen Christian codex fragments of

---

[52] Wendland (see above, p. 37 n. 39), vii–viii; Pelletier (see above, p. 19 n. 2), 9–10.

[53] Cf. Kenyon and Adams, 17; K. Aland, 'Repertorium der griechischen christlichen Papyri I: Byblische Papyri', *PTS* 18 (Berlin and New York, 1976), 3: '. . . presence in a codex signifies from the outset a certain indication of Christian origin'. Conversely, it is not true that all LXX scrolls are of Jewish origin; compare, for example, P Oxy 1166 (AT 9 in Aland, no. 944 in Rahlfs). An index of the *nomina sacra* can also be found in Aland, 420–8. About this problem see also M. Hengel, *The Four Gospels and the One Gospel of Jesus Christ* (London, 2000).

[54] PRyl 458; 4QLXXLev^a+b; 4QLXXNum; 7Q1LXXEx; 7Q2EpistJer; PFouad inv. 266; 8Hev XIIgr; cf. J. Van Haelst, *Catalogue des Papyrus Littéraires Juifs et Chrétiens* (Paris, 1976), 409. To this may now be added 4QLXXDeut; cf. E. Ulrich, 'The Greek Manuscripts of the Pentateuch from Qumrân, including Newly-Identified Fragments of Deuteronomy (4QLXXDeut)', in A. Pietersma and C. Cox, eds, *De Septuaginta*, FS J. W. Wevers (Missisauga, Ontario, 1984), 71–82; cf. also *idem*, 'A Greek Paraphrase of

the Old Testament and one scroll fragment from Psalm 77 dating to between the end of the first and the beginning of the third centuries have been preserved. Included are five verse-Psalm manuscripts (i.e. the Psalms were sung as Christian hymns), five different Torah fragments, one each of 2 Chronicles and Jeremiah, an additional copy each of Ezekiel, Daniel and Esther in *one* codex and in the Alexandrian sequence.[55] This frequency of Psalter manuscripts is no accident. In terms of frequency in citations in the early Christian literature up to Justin, the Psalms rival and even exceed Isaiah. With a view to use in worship, the Psalter as a 'Christian hymnbook' was probably the most important 'prophetic' document.

This distribution of the Christian LXX in Egpyt contradicts the popular theory that—otherwise unknown—early Egyptian Christianity was thoroughly Gnostic. Three of these papyrus codices (Num. and Deut.; Jer.; Ezek.-Esther) came from the great library of the Chester Beatty find which also contained a large fragment of *Enoch* from the third/fourth century, as well as valuable New Testament texts.[56] In the period mentioned, only about eleven New Testament fragments accompany the thirteen Christian LXX fragments. The Christian codex, in contrast to the scroll, made it possible to assemble various larger documents in a fixed sequence. The Daniel text of the Chester Beatty Papyrus (no. 967) contains all the expansions, but the text does *not* correspond to the recension of '(Proto-)Theodotion' that dominates

---

Exodus on Papyrus from Qumran Cave 4', in D. Fraenkel, U. Quast and J. W. Wevers, eds, *Studien zur Septuaginta: Robert Hanhart zu Ehren* (MSU 20; Göttingen, 1990), 287–98. As far as can be determined given their very fragmentary condition, the eighty fragments of 4Q127 represent a free Greek rendition of Exodus. The LXX fragments from Qumran have now been collected in P. W. Shekan, E. Ulrich and J. E. Sanderson, *Qumran Cave IV: Palaeo-Hebrew and Greek Biblical Manuscripts* (DJD 9; Oxford, 1992), 161–92, 217–42. A list of the Jewish witnesses to the LXX can be found in P.-M. Bogaert, 'Les études sur la Septante: Bilan et perspectives', *RTL* 16 (1985), 174–200 (198–200); see also Eissfeldt, 959f., and the summary by E. C. Ulrich, 'The Septuagint Manuscripts from Qumran: A Reappraisal', in Brooke and Lindars, 49–80; and E. Tov, 'The Contribution of the Qumran Scrolls to the Understanding of the LXX', in Brooke and Lindars = *idem, The Greek and the Hebrew Bible* (VT.S 72; Leiden, etc. 1999), 285–300. The earliest Greek fragment of Esther E 16–9.3 (later first or early second century) upon a scroll probably indicating Jewish provenance, has been published by K. Luchner, P Oxy 65 (1998), 4–8 no. 4443, 11–47.

[55] Cf. Van Haelst (see above, p. 41 n. 54), Index, pp. 409–10. For the codex mentioned last, cf. n. 118 = p. 627; Aland (see above, p. 41 n. 53), 30–3 (no. 101, Rahlfs no. 967). See also Exodus 20:10–11, 18–22, ed. D. Coloma, P Oxy 65 (1998), 1–4 no. 4442 early third century upon a codex. On the Psalm scroll see Haelst n. 174; Aland AT 77. It is Christian (nomina sacra) but has recto payment orders.

[56] Cf. the catalogue in Aland, 459 and P Oxy 64 (1997), 5–11 no. 4403–5.

[57] See above, n. 55. The text is available in W. Hamm, *Der Septuagintatext des Buches Daniel Kap. 1–2 nach dem Kölner Teil des Papyrus 967* (PTA 21; Bonn, 1969); *idem, Der Septuagintatext des Buches Daniel Kap. 3–4 nach dem Kölner Teil des Papyrus*

the transmission of Daniel, but to the original 'LXX' version[57] that sometimes more resembles a relatively free paraphrase than an exact translation. This phenomenon explains the prompt new translation and the suppression of this version in favour of '(Proto-)Theodotion'.

6. The Jewish Reaction

The consistent appropriation of the Greek Bible—one could also speak of its 'Christianization'—did not take place, to be sure, without resistance. Already in the pre-Christian period efforts were apparent in Palestine to gain currency for forms of the text prominent there also among the Greek-speaking Diaspora. This may be related to the growth of Pharisaic influence in the first century BCE, a growth also evident in numerous other phenomena. Such an interest led to revisions of the text intended to correct the older, freer, translations of the prophetic books, for example, as well as to new translations, a tendency that intensified after 70 CE and, especially in the second century, now with a certain anti-Christian character.[58] The enigmatic, almost legendary, and controversial Jewish recensionists or translators Theodotion and Aquila, and the Jewish-Christian Symmachus,[59] as well as other unknown editors,[60] were active during the second century. The protest of the Jew Trypho against

---

967 (PTA 21, Bonn, 1977). A. Geissen, *Der Septuagintatext des Buches Daniel Kap. 5–12, zusammen mit Susanna, Bel et Draco, sowie Esther Kap. 1,1a–2,15 nach dem Kölner Teil des Papyrus 967* (Bonn, 1968); a new edition of the LXX-text was edited by O. Munnich and J. Ziegler, *Septuaginta gottingensis XVI,2*, Susanna Daniel Mel et Draco, ²1999; cf. also R. Albertz, *Der Gott des Daniel: Untersuchungen zu Daniel 4–6 in der Septuagintafassung sowie zu Komposition und Theologie des aramäischen Danielbuches* (SBS 131; Stuttgart, 1988). In contrast, Justin's Daniel text probably follows '(Proto-)Theodotion'. See Skarsaune, 88–90, as well as the citation of Daniel which already appears in the Shepherd of Hermas (see below, p. 113 n. 27).

[58] Harl, Dorival and Munnich, 119–25. Concerning the Pharisaic influence beginning in the middle of the first century BCE, see R. Deines, *Jüdische Steingefässe und pharisäische Frömmigkeit* (WUNT II/52; Tübingen, 1993), esp. 15–17, cf. *idem*, *Die Pharisäer* (WUNT 101; Tübingen, 1997), 534–55.

[59] Cf. Irenaeus, *Adv Haer* 3:21:1 (= Eusebius, *Hist Eccl* 5:8:10); Eusebius, *Hist Eccl* 6:14–15; Epiphanius, *De Mensuris et Ponderibus*, 14–15; Swete, 29–58; Kenyon and Adams, 27–9; Jellicoe, 74–99; Schürer (rev.) III/1, 493 = 503; Harl, Dorival and Munnich, 142–61. On Aquila, cf. also K. Hyrvärinen, *Die Übersetzung von Aquila* (Uppsala, 1977). The chronicle of Jerachmeel b. Solomon from the twelfth century adopts the Christian reports concerning the LXX recensionist Theodotion (Thodos, perhaps identical with the legendary Theudas in Rome, see Bill. III:23), Aquila, identified with Onkelos and Symmachus (סומכוס) in the time of Hadrian, see R. Medina-Lechtenberg and P.-R. Breger, 'Eine späte Theodotion-Tradition vom Danielbuch?' in: *Begegnungen zwischen Christen und Juden in Antike und Mittelalter* (FS H. Schreckenberg), D. A. Koch and H. Lichtenberger, eds (Göttingen, 1993), 303–11 (–309). The seventy are dated here to the time of Antiochus IV.

[60] Such as Ben La'ana and Ben Tilga. Cf. S. Krauss, 'Two Hitherto Unknown Bible Versions in Greek', *BJRL* 27 (1942–3), 97–105, now in *Studies*, 261–9.

Justin's capricious use of the LXX seems moderate in comparison to the much later rabbinic tradition that the day the seventy elders translated the Torah into Greek for king Ptolemy 'was as bad for Israel as the day they made the golden calf'.[61] Justin contended, on the other hand, that the Jewish removal of offensive passages in the text is worse than that apostasy.[62] A very late addition to the *Fast Scroll* maintains that after 'the Torah was written in Greek in the days of king Talmai, darkness covered the world for three days'.[63] The day of its translation must therefore be a fast. In addition, we also find in the legend of the miracle in the older Philonic version,[64] admittedly with the—surely anti-Christian—addition of R. Yehuda (c. 150), that permission to write the Holy Scriptures in Greek is limited to the Torah, i.e. the Pentateuch alone.[65] In other words, the Christian claim concerning the translation of *all* the prophetic literature contradicts the truth; it is fundamentally impious. Indeed, we do not know how long the LXX was in use in Jewish synagogues in the Diaspora. The *Cohortatio ad Graecos* (after 260) presupposes such use to a degree (see above p. 37). In contrast, only fragments of Aquila were found in the Cairo Geniza. The suppression will have taken the form of a gradual development, probably paralleling the growing influence of rabbinical scholars from Palestine on the worship of the Diaspora synagogues.

Even the final closing of the Hebrew canon by the Pharisaic teachers, constituting themselves as rabbinate toward the end of the first century— a process that lasted into the middle of the second century with respect to individual books and that presupposes a long period of preparation reaching back into pre-Christian times—must be categorized in the final analysis as 'anti-heretical', indeed anti-Christian. Expanding upon the rabbinical discussion in Mishnah *Yadayim* (3:5; cf. 4:6) concerning the 'pollution of the hands', the *Tosefta* (2:13) emphasizes that 'the Gospels (*hag-gilyônîm*, literally "the book margins", in my opinion probably a phonetic allusion to εὐαγγέλιον) and the books of the heretics (*mînîm*)

---

[61] *Sefer Torah* 1:6; *Tractate Soferim* 1:7 (= *Sof*). Cf. Veltri, 114–28. The rationale is that the Torah cannot be adequately translated.

[62] See above, pp. 33–4 and Justin, *Dial* 73:6.

[63] MegTaan 13 (text in B. Z. Lurie, *Megillath Taanit* [Jerusalem, 1964], 200–1; as cited in Bill. IV:414); cf. Veltri, 2, 16–17; *idem*, 'Der Fasttag zur Erinnerung an die Entstehung der Septuaginta und die Megillat Ta'anit Batra', *Frankfurter judaistische Beiträge* 19 (1991), 63–71.

[64] *BMeg* 9a-b (as cited in Bill. IV:414); cf. Veltri, 157–62, who also examines the parallels to the pseudo-Justinian *Cohortatio*.

[65] Cf. Sof 1:8.

[66] Cf. D. Barthélemy, 'L'état de la bible juive depuis le début de notre ère jusqu'à la deuxième révolte contre Rome (131–135)', in Kaestli and Wermelinger, 9–45 (30–4); H.-P. Rüger, 'Das Werden des christlichen Alten Testaments', *JBTh* 3 (1988), 175–89 (181–2); but contrast G. Stemberger ('Jabne und der Kanon', *JBTh* 3 [1988], 163–74), who cites K. G. Kuhn ('Giljonim und sifre minim', in W. Eltester, ed., *Judentum—*

do not pollute the hands. The books of Ben Sirach and all books written *from that point onward* do not pollute the hands'.[66] In other words, this statement also introduces a chronological boundary. Ezra, Nehemiah, Haggai, Zechariah and Malachi were considered the last prophetically inspired writers.[67] With these writers, the Scriptures inspired by God's Spirit came to an end. Tosefta *Shabbat* 13:5 adds that 'one does not keep the *Gilyonim* and the books of the heretics, but has them and the divine name contained in them burned on the spot'. R. Nahum adds (*bGit* 45b): 'We had been taught that a Torah book written by a heretic should be burned. . . .' All biblical manuscripts of the 'heretics' fell under this verdict. Judging from the context, Jewish Christians especially were in view. Ben Sirach, known to have been read by Christians, and the 'books written after him', also bring into view the so-called Apocrypha, also

---

Urchristentum–Kirche [FS J. Jeremias; BZNW 26; Berlin, 1964], 24–61) and contests both the identification of the Gilyonim with the Gospels and also the association of the *minim* with Jewish-Christian writings. In his opinion, *tYad* 2:13 deals 'with irregular Torah exemplars and those written by *minim* or in their possession, but not with heretical, non-biblical literature, which simply cannot "pollute the hands". *Minim* here, as elsewhere in rabbinical literature, are not simply Jewish Christians or any Christians, but all Jews who diverge from the main line of Jewish life' (168). So also Sundberg, 121–4. But this passage must deal with books stored in the (meeting) houses of the *minim* and the question is how this unusual euphemism for 'irregular Torah exemplars' comes to be. The discussion in *bShab* 116a/b, which refers to Jewish Christians not only through '*awän-gilyôn* = Evangelium, but probably also through the loaded reference to the 'houses' of the 'Ebionites' and of the 'Noṣrîm', demonstrates that at least the Amoraim established a relationship between *gilyônim* and the Gospel of the Jewish-Christians. The Jewish Christians (including Gnostic groups) were the most significant component of the *minim*. *Gilyonim* and 'books of the heretics' belong together in substance and are not entirely different matters.

[67] Cf. Josephus, *Ap* 1:40–1; 4 Ezra 14:18–20; Sirach 49:13–15 (the conclusion of the Praise of the Fathers), see below pp. 99–103 and *bBB* 14b (citation in Bill. IV:424–5). The oldest prior reference is 1 Macc. 9:27 (cf. 4:46; 14:41). Cf. now especially passages referring to the common 'canon' of recognized Scriptures in the halakic letter from the Teacher of Righteousness to the high priests in Jerusalem (4QMMT C 10–11): 'so that you may understand the book of Moses [and the words of the pro]phets and of Davi[d together with the words of the days] of that generation', i.e. the books of Chronicles (probably including Ezra/Nehemiah) at the end; see A. M. Schwemer, *Studien zu den frühjüdischen Prophetenlegenden: Vitae Prophetarum II* (TSAJ 50; 1996), 188 n. 58 about the introduction formulas. This concept found its conclusion, however, only in the second post-Christian century; cf. P. Schäfer, *Die Vorstellung vom Heiligen Geist in der rabbinischen Literatur* (StANT 28; Munich, 1982), 94–6, cf. also 98–9: 'the cessation of the Holy Spirit since the beginning of Greek dominion'. On the other hand, some texts associate the cessation of the Holy Spirit with the destruction of the first temple, cf. Schäfer, 100–1 and 143–6; Beckwith, 369–76; Barthélemy, 22–5. On the closing of the prophetic canon from an Old Testament perspective, compare now, H. Steck, *Der Abschluss der Prophetie im Alten Testament: Ein Versuch zur Frage der Vorgeschichte des Kanons* (BThSt 17; Neukirchen, 1991), whose dating of the closing around *c.* 200 BCE is somewhat too late, however. See M. Hengel, 'Schriftauslegung und Schriftwerdung in der Zeit des 2. Tempels', in *Schriftauslegung im antiken Judentum und Urchristentum*, M. Hengel and H. Löhr, eds (WUNT 73; 1994), 27, n. 94 = *Kleine Schriften II*, 27 n. 94.

widespread among Christians. R. Aqiba includes among those who
'possess no portion in the coming world' those 'who read in the excluded
(בספרים החיצונים) books' (*mSanh* 10:1).[68] Strict prohibitions mislead,
however. Aqiba's rigorous dictum did not prevent such 'apocryphal'
books from being read and treasured in Judaism, nonetheless. On the
contrary, Origen and Jerome attest a Hebrew book of Maccabees,[69] and
Jerome, *contra* Origen, Aramaic versions of Tobit and Judith.[70] The
Babylonian Talmud (*bSan* 100b) cites Sirach extensively. Five Hebrew
manuscripts were found in the Cairo Geniza and fragments of Tobit (one
in Hebrew and four in Aramaic) and Sirach roughly 1000 years older
were found at Qumran and Masada respectively.[71] The Jews, too—
despite their rigorous attitude—had a continuing 'apocrypha problem'.
Some Christian 'apocrypha' were also re-translated or freely paraphrased
in abbreviated form in Aramaic or Hebrew, as was the case with the
Aramaic Tobit and Judith, or the originally Aramaic *Megillat Antiochus*
later translated into Hebrew.[72]

In addition, the Hebrew canon involved the problem that the
individual documents found highly diverse usage in temple or synagogue
worship and that many books held no firm place whatsoever in the
liturgy. Only the Torah and the prophets were regularly read, the latter in
no fixed order, however, although Isaiah and the minor prophets seem to
have been preferred. One of the five Megilloth (Ruth, Lamentations,
Esther, Canticles, Qoheleth) were read on the various festivals, but, with

[68] Contrast Stemberger (see above, p. 44 n. 66), 172f. But even if one does not identify
in this statement any 'specifically anti-Christian point', one cannot overlook the fact that
it forbids literature that found particular interest among the Christians from the second to
the fifth century (including Christian-Gnostic groups) and that was preserved at least
partially for us only by these groups. Even Stemberger admits that it involves excluded
'religious scriptures' (in contrast to pagan writings). It is of little help, too, to problematize
the concept of canon with respect to the Hebrew Bible; this can be done with greater
justification for the early church. The matter was unequivocal: a corpus of Holy Scriptures,
clearly defined since at least the second century. The Christians in the second and third
centuries had not yet done this in such a firmly established manner. The term 'canon' for
an officially acknowledged collection of books appears only in the fourth century.

[69] Schürer (rev.), III/1, 182.

[70] Cf. Origen, *Epistola ad Africanum* (see above, p. 36 n. 38), 13; Jerome, *Prologus
Tobiae*, 676; *Prologus Iudith*, 691 (n. 43 above).

[71] A collection of all fragments and editions of the text appears in A. S. van der Woude,
'Fünfzehn Jahre Qumranforschung', *ThR* 55 (1990), 303. For Sirach, cf. also Eissfeldt,
811–12; Schürer (rev.) III/1, 202–4; and now E. Tov, 'The Unpublished Qumran Texts
from Cave 4 and 11', in *BA* 55/2 (1992), 94–103 (esp. 97).

[72] For the *Megillat Antiochus*, cf. H. L. Strack and G. Stemberger, *Einleitung in Talmud
und Midrasch* (7th edn; Munich, 1982), 302–3 = *Introduction to the Talmud and Midrash*
(Edinburgh, 1992), 364–6; Texts in A. Jellinek, *Bet ha-Midrasch I* (originally in six parts,
1853–77; 4th edn, Jerusalem, 1982), 142–6 (Hebr.), compare the introduction, xxv;
concerning the original Aramaic version see VI, 4–8 (and the introduction, vii-ix). For
Tobit, see Schürer (rev.) III/1, 224, 230 and for Judith, 219–20 and Jellinek I, 130–1 (cf.
the introduction, xxii–xxiii).

the exception of Esther, this practice is attested only very late. The neglect of certain texts in worship also indicates a certain 'secondariness' confirmed by the Targums, much overlooked, to the Hagiographa known to us only in very late versions. On the other hand, an abbreviated Aramaic translation of Job was discovered in Cave 11 at Qumran and Rabbi Gamaliel I, Paul's teacher, is supposed to have already removed a Job Targum from circulation. Special interest in this connection attaches to the Psalms, some of which at least played an outstanding role in the temple cult, although, apart from the Hallel, they had no fixed place in synagogue worship. Something approaching a devaluation took place. Is this related to the fact that in the early Christian communities the Psalms played an essential role as inspired songs and were the most important biblical texts above all?[73]

7. *The Question of the Hebrew 'Originals'*

As I have already said, the Christians' appeal to the inspired and thus infallible translation of all sacred Hebrew Scriptures by the Seventy resulted, nonetheless, in several enduring complications. The transmission of the LXX text was thoroughly confused under the influence of the Jewish revisions and Christian testimonia collections, as may already be seen in Justin. Not only this, but since in disputed questions it was necessary to check doubtful cases against the original text, the dependence of the Christian LXX on the older Hebrew prototypes was also essentially confirmed in case after case. What was one to do if the Hebrew and the various Greek texts differed substantially or if the Jews maintained that for certain additional texts and documents utilized by Christians there was no original? Could one always simply accuse them of abbreviating or falsifying as Justin had already done, or, subsequently, Hippolytus in his treatment of the story of Susanna and the Elders in his commentary on Daniel,[74] and with him many other Fathers? And what if one were to acknowledge, as did the highly educated Julius Africanus, the librarian of the Emperor Severus Alexander, that the style and content of the Susanna story marks it as a 'counterfeit' and not a translation from the Hebrew, casting doubt on whether it belongs to the Old Testament? His

---

[73] Cf. Strack and Stemberger, 228–30. For the Job Targum, see *bShab* 115a; J. P. M. van der Ploeg and A. S. van der Woude, eds, *Le Targum de Job de la Grotte XI de Qumran* (Leiden, 1971). For the singing of psalms in the temple and the development of early Christian hymns, see M. Hengel, 'The Song about Christ in Earliest Worship', in *idem, Studies in Early Christology* (Edinburgh, 1995), 227–92.

[74] In the exegesis of Dan. 1:14 (in the Ps.-Theodotion version, Susanna constitutes the first chapter of Daniel); on the text, see Hippolytus, *Commentaire sur Daniel*, SC 14, M. Lefèvre and G. Bardy, eds (Paris, 1947), 40 and *GCS Hippolytus* I, G. Bonwetsch and H. Achelis, eds (Leipzig, 1897), 1–340, esp. 23; see also Schürer (rev.) III/2, 725–7.

critical letter to Origen is formulated with astonishing acerbity. In his
response to the scholar, Origen was able to counter these doubts only
with great difficulty and very unconvincingly by emphasizing early
church practice.[75]

Thus the greatest philologist and theologian of the early church found
it difficult to maintain the balance here between philologico-historical
truth and church tradition. He basically attempted to take a wise middle
way which, however, often encountered misunderstanding, since there
were many uncritical adherents to the anti-Jewish counterfeit theory, who
gave no consideration to the dubious state of the transmission of the
Septuagint, and they were unwilling to confront the uncomfortable
truth. Origen's Hexapla, the endeavour to regain the 'pure' text through
comparing the Hebrew original and the various versions of the Greek
translation, is a remarkable attempt to resolve the difficulties and to place
on a scientific basis the dialogue with the Jews about the correct text.
Jerome pursued an even more consistent path with his appeal to give
preference to the assured Hebrew tradition. While Origen simply passed
over the legend of the translation by the Seventy in silence, Jerome
energetically rejected as a lie the Christian legend, lovingly depicted by
his friend and contemporary Epiphanius, who spoke about 2×36
translators in their cells.[76]

Consequently, according to Jerome, the additions of the translators of
the Hebrew text to the books of Chronicles could have resulted 'vel ob
decoris gratiam, vel ob Spiritus Sancti auctoritatem' (from consider-
ations of style or through the counsel of the Holy Spirit): they must not

---

[75] Julius Africanus was the only early church father to dispute the canonicity of the
additions to Daniel; compare his *Epistola ad Origenem* (see above, p. 36 n. 38) and
Origen's response *Epistola ad Africanum*. Julius Africanus designated Susanna
σύνγραμμα νεωτερικὸν καὶ πεπλασμένον. Cf. H. Engel, *Die Susanna-Erzählung:
Einleitung, Übersetzung und Kommentar zum Septuaginta-Text und zur Theodotion-
Bearbeitung* (OBO 61; Freiburg, Switzerland and Göttingen, 1985), 68–70; Nautin, 176–
82. To be sure, the question of a Hebrew or Aramaic original of the additions must remain
open, cf. Schürer (rev.) III/2, 724: 'It cannot be stated as certain whether any or none of
the additions were originally composed in either Hebrew or Aramaic before being translated into Greek' (in the new Schürer this passage appears in paragraph 33 B: 'Jewish
Literature of which the original language is uncertain'), but I prefer to assume with
Africanus that the Greek is the original, which does not preclude the possibility that
individual portions were also in circulation as Aramaic stories; cf. M. Hengel, 'Der
alte und der neue "Schürer"', *JSS* 35 (1990): 19–64, esp. 61 (= *Kleine Schriften II*,
127–99 [190]). J. T. Milik's attempt to identify the Susanna story at Qumran ('Daniel
et Susanne à Qumrán?' in M. Carrez, J. Doré and P. Grelot, eds, *De la Tôrah au Messie*
[FS H. Cazelles; Paris, 1981], 337–59) is plucked from thin air; cf. van der Woude,
303–4.

[76] See above, pp. 37–8. Cf. O. Wermelinger, 'Le Canon des Latins au Temps de Jèrôme
et d'Augustin', in Kaestli and Wermelinger, 153–96, esp. 187–93. For Origen see
B. Neuschäfer, *Origenes als Philologe (Schweizer Beiträge zur Altertumswissenschaft)*
18/1 u. 2 (Basel, 1987). For Jerome, cf. O. Wermelinger and the contribution of
Chr. Markschies, *Hieronymus* (see below, p. 51 n. 83).

necessarily have been 'inspired', although he still refers positively here to the translators 'who translated filled with the Holy Spirit, for that they certainly were'.[77] Later he is much more reserved on this point. As far as I can tell, Jerome is also the only author in the early church who repeatedly emphasizes that the Seventy did not translate all the Hebrew Scriptures of the prophets, but only the five books of Moses.[78] His one-time friend and later opponent, Rufinus, energetically opposed him on this point, appealing to Origen's more cautious opinion and to the translation miracle of the Seventy. The Apostles of the church transmitted the LXX which was inspired by the Holy Spirit. Had it been erroneous, they would have corrected it.[79] In the East the (traditional) position of Rufinus prevailed in essence, even when Origen's Hexapla was utilized appreciatively, although less for correction than for comparison. The fact that Pope Damasus officially accepted Jerome's translation may be characterized as a minor miracle. Augustine still defended the LXX against Jerome's *Hebraitas*. Jerome himself, who was not only a great and combative scholar but also a smooth diplomat, largely abandoned

---

[77] '. . . qui Spiritu Sancto pleni, ea quae vera fuerant, transtulerunt', *Praefatio in Librum Paralipomenon juxta LXX interpretes* PL 29, 424, 426. In later prefaces to translations of portions of the Bible, however, Jerome completely abandoned the thesis of an inspired LXX; cf. Wermelinger (see above, p. 48 n. 76), 187–9, and M. E. Schild, 'Abendländische Bibelvorreden bis zur Lutherbibel' (*QFRG* 39; Gütersloh, 1970), 19–23: 'The "hexaplaric" preface to the books of Chronicles is the only one that speaks so positively of the LXX' (23).

[78] Thus in the introduction of *Hebraica Quaestiones in Libro Geneseos: Hieronymus* I/1, CChr. SL 72, P. de Lagarde, G. Morin and M. Adriaen, eds (Turnhout, 1959), 2: '. . . Iosephus, qui LXX interpretum proponit historiam, quinque tantum ab eis libros Moysi translatos refert . . .'; *Commentatorium in Hiezechielem, Buch 2 zu Hes 5, 12: Hieronymus* I/4, CChr.SL 75, F. Glorie, ed. (Turnhout, 1965), 60: '. . . sed per multa saecula scriptorum atque lectorum uitio deprauatum, quamquam et Aristaeus et Josephus et omnis schola Iudaeorum quinque tantum libros Moysi Septuaginta translatos asserant'; *Commentariorum in Michaeam Prophetam, Buch 1, zu Mi 2,9f.: Hieronymus* I/6, CChr.SL 76, M. Adriaen, ed. (Turnhout, 1970), 446–7: 'Interpretatio Septuaginta—si tamen Septuaginta est: Iosephus enim scribit, et Hebraei tradunt, quinque tantum libros legis Moysi translatos ab eis, et Ptolemaeo regi traditos—. . .', see Wendland (see above, p. 37 n. 39), 164; Pelletier (see above, p. 19 n. 2), 90. On the critique of the translation legend, see also Schild, 36–7.

[79] *Apologia contra Hieronymum*, Rufin, CChr. SL 20, M. Simmonetti, ed. (Turnhout, 1961), 111–16; see Bammel (see above, p. 36 n. 37), 137. On Rufinus, cf. Wermelinger, 160–6. One of Jerome's most important arguments against Rufinus and others was precisely his observation that many Old Testament quotations in the New Testament authors did not correspond to the LXX text sanctioned by the church, but represent a Greek translation improved through comparison with the Hebrew text, for which reason the reclamation of the *hebraica veritas* carried apostolic sanction; at the same time, he emphasized that the Hebrew text even had a christological advantage over the LXX, cf. Wermelinger, 192; Schild (see above, n. 77), 33–5. It is remarkable that Rufinus, the translator and disciple of Origen, understood so little of the philological concerns of Jerome, who became a critic of Origen due to theological reasons although he followed in his footsteps as a biblical theologian.

any effort to defend the Hebrew original in the Apocrypha question. In the prologue to Tobit he writes: 'Sed melius esse iudicans Pharisaeorum displicere iudicio et episcoporum iussionibus deservire.'[80] For the most part, the development continued despite the protests of the scholars. A final example: in the Emperor Justinian's notorious Novella 146 *De Hebraeis*, cap. 1 (published 8 February 553), in which he prohibited the reading of the Hebrew Bible in the synagogues, he recommended the LXX to the Jews since the Seventy, although divided into pairs (this follows Epiphanius' account), 'all produced *one* version' (μίαν ἅπαντες ἐκεδώκασι σύνθεσιν). The Seventy are to be admired because, long before the appearance of Christ, 'like those (fore-)seeing the future, they undertook the transmission of the Holy Scriptures as though prophetic grace streamed around them'.[81] In the end, then, the *vates* and his *prophetare* triumphed over the *interpres* and the mere *conferre* of Jerome (see above, pp. 37–8). So that the Jews need not break entirely with their trusted tradition, Justinian permitted them to read Aquila's version despite its misleading variants. The Christian emperor magnanimously refrained, therefore, from imposing the true, inspired, Holy Scriptures that 'almost all use (ταύτῃ μὲν χρήσονται μάλιστα πάντες)' on the unbelieving Jews. The usurpation of the LXX by the now ruling Christians thus itself entered into the law of the state; the Greek Bible appeared to have displaced the Hebrew. But even this imperial use of force was only a late episode in an extraordinarily complicated and complex development[82] and was by no means the last word on the matter.

---

[80] *Biblia zacra* . . . (see above, p. 38 n. 43), 676. It should be noted that Jerome was the first to employ the term 'apocrypha' for the deuterocanonical writings (in the *Prologus in libro regum*, 365). He indicated 'those writings' in the older canon lists and book catalogues 'unattested, unmentioned by the Fathers . . . but in usage among the heretics . . .' 'Jerome's innovation consists in the application of the expression "apocrypha" to the marginal books, non-canonized (Athanasius' term), contested (Cyril's), or ecclesiastical (Rufinus'), but recommended for reading and use in catechism', so Wermelinger (see above, p. 48 n. 76), 190. Wisdom, Sirach, Judith, Tobit and the additions to Daniel are sanctioned by long use in the church; he attributes to them a *chaldaica veritas*, i.e. a kind of secondary 'Aramaic' truth; cf. Schild (see above, p. 49 n. 77), 29–30; on his defence of the *hebraica veritas*, see 31–41. The history of the impact of Jerome's prologues is related to the fact that every Vulgate manuscript and also, from 1455, many printed editions, included them, so that the Latin church always remained aware of the question of the Hebrew original as well as the problem of the Apocrypha, even though it had decided the canon question more unequivocally than the Greek church; cf. M. E. Schild (see above, p. 49 n. 77), 29f., and see below, pp. 56 and 70–4. Cf. also D. Barthélemy, 'La place de la Septante dans l'Eglise', in *idem*, 111–26 (originally in *Recherches Bibliques* 8 [Paris, 1967], 13–28). See also below, p. 66 n. 22. Jerome was a constant stimulus to the humanists of the fifteenth and sixteenth centuries.

[81] Cf. already Irenaeus, *Adv Haer* 3:21:2 (see above, pp. 38–40). See also Veltri (see above, p. 26 n. 2).

[82] Text in, *Corpus Iuris Civilis* III, R. Schoell and W. Kroll, eds (Berlin, 1954), 715. See also Schreckenberg (see above, p. 35 n. 33), 413–14.

8. *Augustine's Attempt at Compromise*

In his *City of God* Augustine deals extensively with the LXX and the new situation created by Jerome. He demonstrates both his conservative attitude and his awareness of the problem so that, in the end, he can suggest a compromise. First, however, he wants fundamentally to affirm the authority of the church's traditional text despite every difficulty. For him too, the starting point and unshakeable basis is the translation legend of the *Letter of Aristeas* in the more developed Christian version, as attested since Irenaeus, concerning the prophetic inspiration of the Seventy and the resulting miraculous agreement of the translators who translated the entire Hebrew Scriptures: 'Their translation was so similar as to have been produced by *one*: indeed, *one* translator was active in all of them.'[83] Precisely by this means their work attains a level of 'authority' that pertains not to human, but only to 'divine writings'.[84] The work of the Seventy differs in this way from that of all other translators of the Hebrew original such as Aquila, Symmachus, Theodotion, or the unknown translator of the Quinta. With good reason the church has adopted their translation as, so to speak, 'unique',[85] so that Greek-speaking Christians use it only, and as a rule do not even know that there are other translations. This text of the Seventy was also translated into Latin and utilized by the churches of the West. Now, however, 'the extraordinarily learned, trilingual presbyter Jerome has recently translated, not from the Greek, but from the Hebrew into Latin. But, as philologically sound as his contribution may be, and even though the Jews recognize it as reliable, while they maintain that the seventy translators erred in many cases, the churches of Christ are convinced, nonetheless, that, with respect to authority, no one is to be preferred to the many men chosen by the high priest Eleazar.'[86] This applied even in the event that the translations—as the *Letter of Aristeas* reports—harmonized the text comparatively; in reality their agreement still came

---

[83] *Civ Dei* 18:42 (*Augustinus* XIV/2, CChr.SL 48, B. Dombart and A. Kalb, eds [Turnhout, 1955], 638). Regarding Augustine, see C. Markschies, 'Hieronymus und die "Hebraica Veritas"', in *Die Septuaginta zwischen Judentum und Christentum*, M. Hengel and A. M. Schwemer, eds (Tübingen, 1994), 163–9.

[84] Loc. cit: '... ut illarum scripturarum non tamquam humanarum, sed, sicut erant, tamquam diuinarum etiam isto modo commendaretur auctoritas'.

[85] 18:43: '... hanc tamen, quam Septuaginta est, tamquam sola esset, sic recipit ecclesia'.

[86] Loc. cit. 693:10–18: '... quamvis non defuerit temporibus nostris presbyter Hieronymus, homo doctissimus et omnium trium linguarum peritus, qui non ex Graeco, sed ex Hebraeo in Latinum eloquium easdem scripturas converterit. Sed eius tam litteratum laborem quamvis Iudaei fateantur esse veracem, septuaginta vero interpretes in multis errasse contendant: tamen ecclesiae Christi tot hominum auctoritati ab Eleazaro tunc pontifice ad hoc tantum opus electorum neminem iudicant praeferendum.' Cf. Markschies (see above, n. 83), 168–9.

about through the miraculous work of the Spirit. In other words, from
the outset the Seventy have greater weight than a single translator like
Jerome. Augustine thereby rejects Jerome's critique of the Seventy and
would prefer to deny his new translation recognition by the church by
appealing to the seventy witnesses (see above, p. 36). But he is unable to
escape the argument that significant differences exist between the work
of the Seventy and the Hebrew text. He resolves the difficult point
(*aporia*) by postulating a dual prophetic revelation: 'Since, however,
such a magnificent divine miracle took place through them, every other
reliable translator from the Hebrew, regardless of the language into
which he translates, "must either agree with the seventy translators or,
if he differs, believe that a deeper prophetic sense is present in them
(*altitudo ibi prophetica esse credenda est*)"'. For the very same Spirit
was at work in the Seventy as in the prophets. Various possibilities result
from this contention:

1. The Spirit could, with divine authority, say something new through the
   Seventy, just as he could speak twice in succession through the same
   prophet and thus reveal different messages—in this case the LXX attains
   the quality of additional revelation;
2. It could be that, even where variant wordings occur in the prophets and in
   the Seventy, the same meaning is nonetheless present if only the text is
   correctly interpreted;
3. The Spirit could—in contrast to human copyists and translators (see
   below, pp. 76–7)—also add or subtract, thus demonstrating that, in the
   translation of the Seventy, 'the intellect of the translator was filled and
   guided' not by 'human, slavish literality, but by divine might'.

The Bishop of Hippo paid little attention to the historical objections
of the scholar from Bethlehem, i.e. that the Seventy translated only the
Pentateuch and not all the Scriptures, or that they were only translators
and not inspired prophets. For him, both the prophets and the seventy
translators were equally important, spirit-filled mediators of divine
revelation. The Greek text wondrously produced by the latter group
remained authoritative for church and worship.

And yet the greatest theologian of the Latin church must seek a
compromise, for Origen's Hexapla had led to revisions of the text in the
attempt 'to improve the Greek text in light of the Hebrew manuscripts'
and even many Latin Bible manuscripts had been influenced by these
efforts. To be sure, the revisers did not remove LXX passages unrepre-
sented in the Hebrew text, but only indicated them with a 'horizontal'
mark (*iacentis virgules*)—the obelos. They expanded the LXX text with
what they considered additions in the Hebrew text and marked these
expansions with an asterisk.

The difficult problem of the revealed text can be resolved by making
God's Spirit alone responsible for all these differences, whether

marked additions and omissions or variants in wording established through comparison: 'That which appears in the Hebrew codices but not in the seventy translators, God did not want to say through the Seventy but through the prophets themselves'; conversely, 'In this manner he demonstrated that *both* were prophets.'[87] Basically, the only difference between prophets and translators consists in the fact that the former prophesied earlier: 'for just as the one Spirit of peace was in the true and consistent witness of the former, so the same Spirit was evidently active in the latter who did not converse with one another and nonetheless translated everything in agreement'. The problem that had concerned Origen, and, in a different way, Jerome, seemed to have been resolved in the most elegant and harmonious manner: both the Hebrew original and the Greek translation of the Seventy are correct; both texts are similarly inspired and to be taken seriously in the church.

And yet Augustine's suggested compromise implicitly contains the impetus for individual thinkers to concern themselves ultimately with the Hebrew original and not to be satisfied with the prophetic gifts of the Seventy. On the basis of Origen's comparative work and the manuscripts influenced by it, he must admit the existence of substantial variations from the Hebrew text which are not the result of intentional falsification and, thus, the justification and necessity of textual comparison. Therefore, one or another scholar could be emboldened to investigate the original, himself. This concept, together with Jerome's sharp 'historical-philological critique' must gradually awaken scholarly curiosity. The thorn was not removed; instead it continued to work. Pre-Reformation humanism, as exemplified in, say, Reuchlin, already picked up on this indication. At the same time, it becomes clear how fortunate it was that Jerome's new Latin translation found acceptance in the church despite Augustine's protest.

Augustine himself offers an example of such textual comparison in the following paragraph (18:44). In Jonah 3:4, Nineveh's period of contrition prior to the threatened divine judgement lasted three days according to the LXX and forty according to the Hebrew text and the later recensions of Aquila, Symmachus and Theodotion. Despite his previous 'protestations', Augustine prefers as the original prophetic text the 'historically' more plausible forty days of the Hebrew text and the later Jewish revisions. Yet the three days in the translation of the Seventy also refer to the same matter and the same meaning, although through a different image.[88] The reader is warned in this manner 'not to disregard either of the two authorities, but instead, beginning with the historical

---

[87] Loc. cit. 640:57: '. . . sic ostendens utrosque fuisse prophetas'.
[88] *Civ Dei* 18:44 (loc. cit., 640:10–12): '. . . tamen ad rem pertineret et in unum eundemque sensum, quamvis sub altera significatione'.

report, to rise above it and to investigate what it and its copy actually mean'. In fact, these real details have a deep christological significance, which becomes apparent in Jonah's three days in the belly of the fish (2:10), interpreted as referring to Christ's three days in the grave (Matt. 12:40). Nevertheless, the forty days also support this deeper christological interpretation on the basis of Acts 1:3.

'The seventy translators, who are also prophets, desire . . . nothing other than to rouse from sleep the reader who wants to attend only to the historical details, to seek the deeper sense of the prophecy.' This harmonizing allegorical interpretation can effortlessly resolve all difficulties. Augustine can appeal to the apostles since even they already 'cited prophetic witnesses from both texts, from the Hebrew and from the Seventy'. The church was satisfied with his truly 'Solomonic' solution for a long time—too long.

9. *The Problem of the* Book of Enoch

The direction taken by Tertullian, working almost 200 years earlier, was entirely different from Jerome's defining efforts. Like many of his contemporaries, he considered *1 Enoch* a biblical, inspired text.[89] He knew of Christians, to be sure, who did not accept it 'because it was not permitted entry into the Jewish Torah shrine (*non recipi a quibusdam, quia nec in armarium Iudaicum admittitur)*'. In addition, there was the historical argument that it could not have survived the Flood. Tertullian countered with the explanation that Noah either received the Enoch tradition orally or—as did Ezra later—reconstructed it in the Spirit. The determinative argument, however, is: 'Since Enoch *too* spoke *from the Lord* that which pertains to us may in no way be rejected.' I believe that Tertullian refers to the figure of the Son of Man in the book of Similitudes, implying that he knew *Enoch* already in the form transmitted to us in the Ethiopic text. In *Enoch* too, Holy Scripture is that which 'urges Christ' (Martin Luther, WA.DB 7, 384: 'ob sie Christum treibet').

In addition, according to Tertullian, the epistle of Jude cites *1 Enoch*. The Jews, by contrast, later rejected the work precisely because it deals with Christ. 'It is no wonder that they did not accept a few documents that speak of him since they did not recognize him himself, when he spoke to them in person.'[90] Naturally, the decisive weakness in Tertullian's argument is that he cites no evidence that *Enoch* was ever part of a Jewish 'canon' from which it could have been removed.

[89] *De Idololatria* 4:2; 15:6. See J. H. Waszink and J. C. M. van Winden, *Tertullianus De Idololatria: Critical Text, Translation and Commentary* (VigChr Suppl. 1; Leiden, 1987), 113f., and J. T. Milik, *The Books of Enoch: Aramaic Fragments of Qumran Cave 4* (Oxford, 1976), 78–80; M. Hengel, Durham, 81–3.

[90] *De Cultu Feminarum* 3:1–3. The texts are assembled in Schürer (rev.) III/1, 262, together with the other statements of the fathers concerning *Enoch* (261–4). Cf. also Th. Zahn, *Geschichte des neutestamentlichen Kanons* 1 (Erlangen, 1888), 120–2.

Admittedly, the Aramaic *Enoch* manuscripts (apart from the similitudes of *1 En.* 37–71 which have not yet been found there) play a significant role at Qumran, but the existence there of a fixed, closed 'canon' of sectarian documents cannot yet be demonstrated.[91] On the other hand, its citation as a prophetic work in Jude, about 100 years before Tertullian, shows that the work was already regarded by many Christians at the time as 'Holy Scripture' and was favoured reading because of its special 'protological' and christological revelations.[92]

But the only two Greek papyrus fragments of *Enoch* from the fourth century do not come from codices containing Old Testament Scriptures. In addition to *Enoch* 97:6–107:3, the Chester-Beatty Papyrus XII includes the Passover homily of Melito of Sardis and minute portions of an Ezekiel apocryphon,[93] while the five fragments of P Oxy 2069 contain only a portion of *Enoch* 75–87.[94] In addition, the so-called Gizeh fragment (Codex Panopolitanus, or Akhmimic fragments), a parchment codex from the fifth or sixth century, containing, along with *Enoch* 1:1–32:6; 19:3–21:9, portions of the *Gospel of Peter* and the *Apocalypse of Peter*.[95] The uncertainty with respect to the delineation of the 'Scriptures of the Old Covenant' (Melito, see below, pp. 60–1) which is perceptible throughout the second century may be related to the fact that Christian theologians (including the Gnostics) in this period attempted for the first time to work carefully through the rich Jewish literature which was originally Greek or had been translated into Greek and to investigate its usefulness for church doctrine and practice and theological speculation. The simultaneous increase in literary education and related interests—one could even speak of curiosity—led not only to a growing adoption of Greek philosophical—especially Platonic—perspectives, but

[91] Tov ('Unpublished Qumran Texts', 97) catalogues twelve manuscripts of the various portions of the *Enoch* literature which do not yet constitute a unit. Included is the 'Book of Giants' which does not appear in *1 Enoch* but plays a role among the Manicheans. See also Milik, above, p. 54 n. 89), *The Books of Enoch*, and now L. T. Stuckenbruck, *The Book of Giants from Qumran* (TSAJ 63; Tübingen, 1997), who demonstrates against Milik that the 'Book of Giants' was independent of the *Enoch* collection.

[92] Cf. Jude 14 with *Eth En* 1:9; see also Jude 6 = *En.* 10:6; 12:4; Jude 13 = *En.* 18:5; etc. See also below, pp. 66–9. Notably, 2 Peter omits the *Enoch* citation.

[93] We also find four manuscript fragments of Ezekiel apocrypha at Qumran. See Tov, 'Unpublished Qumran Texts', 100. According to Josephus, *Ant* 10:79, Ezekiel is supposed to have left two books.

[94] Cf. Aland (see above, p. 41 n. 53), 57–60, 366 (no. 0204), 390 (no. Ap 29); van Haelst (see above, p. 41 n. 54), 202–4 (no. 576–7 = Aland no. Ap 29), 204 (no. 578 = Aland no. 0204). On P Oxy 2069, compare also J. T. Milik, 'Fragments grecs du livre d'Hénoch (P Oxy XVII 2069)', *Chronique d' Égypte* 46 (1971), 321–43. Even in his *Verzeichnis der griechischen Handschriften des Alten Testaments*, prepared for the Septuagint project (*MSU* 2; Berlin, 1914), A. Rahlfs omitted *Enoch* since it does not occur 'in an actual Bible manuscript' (xi).

[95] Van Haelst (see above, p. 41 n. 54, 201–4 (no. 575–7). He notes attempts at dating that range from the fourth century to the twelfth. Introduction and text in M. Black, ed., *Apokalypsis Henochi Graece* (PVTG 3; Leiden, 1970), 7–9, 19–37.

also to an intensive reception of Jewish writings in the Greek language. This includes the great Gnostic-Christian teachers of the second century. The best majority church example is Clement of Alexandria. Reactions to this from the third century onward involve on the one hand the LXX legend and on the other a return to the Hebrew canon, in the attempt to establish the collection of Scriptures broadened by this interest in the churches. Here, a few leading churches such as Rome (first) and (later also) Alexandria may have played determinative roles. The preference of a few heretics for apocryphal scriptures[96] supported this tendency. In addition, during this time individual documents still existed as single codices or scrolls. Thus, Tertullian might well have believed that *Enoch* belonged among the books translated for Ptolemy.

These examples, which could be multiplied, demonstrate the problem and associated struggles resulting from the church's claim to the LXX as a significantly expanded (in comparison to the Hebrew Bible) *Christian* Scripture collection, a collection admittedly not yet strictly defined nor universally accepted at the beginning of the third century. In the dispute both with Jewish opponents and with the new recensions of the Greek Bible, as well as in withstanding the unrestricted production of new documents by 'biblical' authors and unlimited interpretations by the Gnostic and other 'heretics', a certain clearer, permanent delimitation was unavoidable.

[96] The meaning of 'apocryphal' or 'Apocrypha' has varied widely. As a designation for the deutero-canonical Scriptures, i.e. Scriptures contained in the Christian Old Testament not present in the Hebrew canon, the term was used first by Jerome (see above, p. 50 n. 80) and thence passed into common usage. For Athanasius, in his thirty-ninth Festal Letter, in contrast, 'Apocrypha' designates a third group after the canonical books and those suitable for public reading (= deutero-canonical Scriptures): '. . . Beloved, although those are canonized and these are suitable for public reading, no mention of the Apocrypha can be found (οὐδαμοῦ τῶν ἀποκρύφων μνήμη). These are, rather, a matter for the heretics who wrote them when they chose and dated them as they wished in order to be able to pass them off as old and so have a pretence for deceiving the simple with them' (trans. following H.-P. Rüger, 'Apokryphen I', in *TRE* III [1978], 289–316 [esp. 292], see below, p. 64 n. 17). They are the 'excluded' books and should not be read in church. They include books designated pseudepigrapha today. The origin of this term in patriarchal literature is quite unconnected with the debate about the canon, but arises from disputes with false teachers who appealed to their secret documents; cf. Irenaeus, *Adv Haer* 1:20:1, who refers to the apocryphal books of Zoroaster on which the Gnostic Prodikos relied (cf. also Clement of Alexandria, *Strom* 3:4:29). For a brief period, then, the church itself attempted to respond to this phenomenon through appeal to its own secret documents, but very soon abandoned this effort. Nevertheless, a parallel usage persisted, associated especially with the exegesis of those 'scripture citations' that cannot be located in the Old Testament and that, therefore, must derive from 'hidden', but completely legitimate texts. Here, the usage approaches that of the rabbis (see below, p. 91 n. 46). Cf. A. Oepke, 'Βίβλοι ἀπόκρυφοι im Christentum', in the addendum 'Kanonisch und apokryph', to the article 'κρύπτω κτλ', *ThWNT* III (Stuttgart, 1938), 979–99 (987–9, esp. 996–8) = *TDNT* III.987–1000; G. W. H. Lampe, *A Patristic Greek Lexicon* (Oxford, 1961), 198–9, s.v. ἀπόκρυφος. The term 'pseudepigraphal' we find first in the polemic of Serapion of Antioch against the gospel of Peter in Eusebius Hist. Eccl. 6, 12, 3.

III

THE LATER CONSOLIDATION OF THE CHRISTIAN 'SEPTUAGINT CANON'

1. *The First Codices: The Writings Contained in Them and Their Order*

In the West, at the Synod of Carthage in 397, a relatively but by no means definitively closed Scripture collection was *gradually* nearing more definite delimitation, culminating in the final decision taken at the fourth session of the Council of Trent in 1546.[1] At this point we encounter the Greek Old Testament in the three great codices of the fourth and fifth centuries: Vaticanus, Sinaiticus and Alexandrinus. But even there the data exhibit such significant differences that one can not yet speak of a truly fixed canon even in this period.[2] All exceeded the scope of the Hebrew Bible by including Judith, Tobit, Sirach and Wisdom, as well as the expanded books of Daniel, Esther and Psalm 151. In Vaticanus, however, all four of the books of Maccabees are missing and in Sinaiticus, 2 and 3 Maccabees, as well as 1 Ezra, Baruch and *Letter of Jeremiah*—presumably only the result of lacunae in the text. Codex

---

[1] The text of the biblical canon at the Synod of Carthage appears in E. Preuschen, 'Zur Kanonsgeschichte', *Analecta* (SQS 8/2; 2nd edn; Tübingen, 1910 = repr. Frankfurt, 1968), 72–3. It names the following Old Testament canonical Scriptures (*canonicae scripturae*) that may be read as Holy Scripture in the church: the Pentateuch, Joshua, Judges, Ruth, 1–2 Samuel, 1–2 Kings, 1–2 Chronicles, Job, Psalms, five books of Solomon (including Sirach), twelve Minor Prophets, Isaiah, Jeremiah, Ezekiel, Daniel, Tobit, Judith, Esther, two books of Ezra, and two books of Maccabees. For Trent, see G. Bedouelle, 'Le Canon de l'Ancien Testament dans la Perspective du Concile de Trente', in Kaestli and Wermelinger, 253–74 and an appendix of the most important textual sources, 275–82. The following were canonized (variations from the previous list are italicized): the Pentateuch, Joshua, Judges, Ruth, 1–2 Samuel, 1–2 Kings, 1–2 Chronicles, *1 Ezra and Nehemiah*, Tobit, Judith, Esther, Job, Psalms, *Proverbs, Qoheleth, Song, Wisdom, Sirach*, Isaiah, Jeremiah *with Baruch*, Ezekiel, Daniel, twelve Minor Prophets, and two books of Maccabees, *the first and the second*.

[2] The order of the books in the three codices appears in Kaestli and Wermelinger, 151. Compare Swete, 201–14, who also assembles the other book lists from the patristic literature in addition to the codices. But also compare E. E. Ellis, *The Old Testament in Early Christianity* (WUNT I/54; Tübingen, 1991), 34–5, who warns against drawing conclusions about the canon from the content of the codices: 'No two Septuagint codices contain the same apocrypha, and no uniform Septuagint "Bible" was ever the subject of discussion in the patristic church. In view of these facts the Septuagint codices appear to have been originally intended more as service books than as a defined and normative canon of scripture.'

Alexandrinus, approximately one century younger, is, in contrast, much more extensive; it includes the LXX as we know it in Rahlfs' edition, with all four books of Maccabees and the fourteen *Odes* appended to Psalms. The Odes also include the *Prayer of Manasseh*, previously attested only in the Syriac *Didaskalia* and the *Apostolic Constitutions*. This form, usually without *4 Maccabees*, then became the rule in the East. A peculiarity of Codex Alexandrinus is that its table of contents mentions the *Psalms of Solomon* after the books of the Old and New Testaments in a sort of appendix (which also includes the two letters of Clement) and further separated from the 'canonical' books by a number of blank lines.[3] Moreover, their text is not to be found in the codex as it has been preserved for us. They may have been lost together with a portion of *2 Clement*, a document that immediately preceded them in the list. J. Rendel Harris suspects that in Codex Sinaiticus, where six leaves are missing, they were to be found between *Barnabas* and *Hermas*. This remains, however, completely uncertain. In addition, they were listed in later canon catalogues among the ἀντιλεγόμενα, or disputed books. Thus, for example, in the stichometry of Nicephorus between Sirach and Esther, and in the *Synopsis scripturarum sacrarum* of Ps-Athanasius between the books of Maccabees and Susanna. The text itself is preserved in private manuscripts from the tenth to sixteenth centuries.[4]

---

[3] S. Holm-Nielsen (*Die Psalmen Salomos* [JSHRZ IV/2; Gütersloh, 1977], 52) writing about the order in Codex Alexandrinus: 'It seems, then, that the PsSal did not, in fact, belong to the canon, but was nevertheless closely associated with it.' In my opinion, this statement goes too far. The *Psalms of Solomon* did not belong—as indicated by the order of their appearance—to the corpus of acknowledged Holy Scriptures. One may not even speak of a 'canon' in the strict sense. It is a document at the extreme boundaries of the LXX. Essentially, *PsSol* does not belong in the LXX.

[4] Cf. Swete, 293, see also 202, 206–8; Schürer (rev.) III/1, 195–6 (read Alexandrinus instead of Vaticanus!); A. Rahlfs, *Septuaginta: Editio minor* (Stuttgart, 1935 = 1979) II, 471 (introduction to *PsSal*); R. R. Hann, 'The Manuscript History of the Psalms of Solomon', *Septuagint and Cognate Studies* 13 (Chico, California, 1982), 3–6. In all, eleven Greek and four Syriac manuscripts are extant, the older Greek from the tenth/ eleventh century (Rahlfs no. 260; the manuscript was already copied exactly in the eleventh century = no. 253). It contains a catena of Job and Proverbs, marginal glosses to Qoheleth and Song, and Wisdom and Sirach; in a manuscript from the eleventh century. (Rahlfs no. 149; cf. *idem, Verzeichnis*, 249), which contains Job, Proverbs, Qoheleth, Song, Wisdom, *PsSol* and Sirach in immediate succession; the last three books are described in the prologue to Wisdom as ἀδιάθετα ('extra-testamental'). The same books appear in the identical sequence in Rahlfs no. 336 from Athos (fourteenth century), where the biblical texts are followed by scholia to Qoheleth, Song and Proverbs. Else- where, too, the *PsSol* can be found between catena and scholia to the canonical wisdom books, without, however, ever being commented on itself: no. 471 (thirteenth-fourteenth century): catenae on Job and Proverbs, marginalia on Qoheleth and Song, followed by Wisdom, *PsSol* and Sirach (cf. nos 253 and 260); no. 629 (thirteenth century): after a catena on the *Psalms* and *Odes*, followed by a later Gospel commentary; no. 769 (four- teenth century?): *PsSol* follows a Psalm commentary and the *Odes*, and is followed by a Song commentary. Finally, Rahlfs no. 606 (from the year 1419) contains Wisdom, *PsSol* and Sirach. Nos. 655 and 659 are two manuscripts from the sixteenth century, written by

It should be considered, further, that the *Odes* (sometimes varied in number), attested from the fifth century in all Greek Psalm manuscripts, contain three New Testament 'psalms': the Magnificat, the Benedictus, the Nunc Dimittis from Luke's birth narrative, and the conclusion of the hymn that begins with the 'Gloria in Excelsis'. This underlines the fact that the LXX, although, itself consisting of a collection of Jewish documents, wishes to be *a Christian* book.[5] The relative openness of the Old Testament portion of these oldest codices also corresponds to that of its 'New Testament': Sinaiticus contains *Barnabas* and *Hermas*, Alexandrinus *1* and *2 Clement*.

In contrast to the relatively fixed order of the Hebrew Bible, the sequence of the documents in these early codices also differs widely at points. It was truly clear only for the 'historical books' which up to and including Chronicles follow a temporal sequence. Alexandrinus follows them with the prophets, beginning with the Minor Prophets and ending with Daniel, then the 'lesser historical works' of Esther to *4 Maccabees*. Finally come the poetico-wisdom documents from the 'Psalterion' to Sirach (compare the reference to the *Psalms of Solomon* in the table of contents). In Vaticanus the historical books conclude with 1 and 2 Ezra, followed by the Psalms and the wisdom books through Sirach, then Esther, Judith and Tobit. Last—as in the Rahlfs edition—stand the prophets with Daniel as the last book in the Old Testament. Sinaiticus has the prophets after *4 Maccabees*, beginning, like the Masoretic Text, with Isaiah and concluding with the Twelve. The wisdom books, beginning with the 151 Psalms of David and concluding with Job, stand at the end of the codex. Even in the late, eighth/ninth century double codex, Basiliano-Venetus, containing the LXX only, the historical books are separated. The main group at the beginning concludes with 2 Ezra and Esther (the Hebrew canon may have exerted influence here), followed by the poetic and prophetic writings, and ends with Tobit, Judith and 1–4 Maccabees. A peculiarity is a second entirely unique form of the text of the Canticle of Habakkuk (Hab. 3) in some manuscripts (V. 62.86.147.407), containing a translation of unknown origins. It had already caught the attention of the scribe of codex 86 (Rome, ninth/tenth century) who commented that it did not agree with either the LXX,

---

one copyist, and no. 3004 is only a fragmentarily preserved codex (twelfth/sixteenth century) where *PsSol* follows a Song commentary. Notably, in a relatively limited number of manuscripts the triplet Wisdom, *PsSol* and Sirach as a nearly fixed component follow the other 'canonical' texts as an appendix, but were never supplied with scholia, catenae or marginalia.

[5] See Rahlfs, *Psalmi cum Odis*, 78–80. 'Of the Greek MSS., B and S, from the fourth century, do not yet have this appendix. But from the fifth century onward, all Greek manuscripts have it' (78). See also Harl, Dorival and Munnich, 301–2, 325; H. Schneider, 'Die biblischen Odem in christlichen Altertum', *Bib* 20 (1949), 28, 65.

Aquila, Theodotion or Symmachus.[6] In the early New Testament codices the order of the books is as a rule much more uniform.

In reference to the highly variable order, one can speak, generally, of four blocks: 'major' and 'minor' historical books (the latter often at the end), prophets and poetico-wisdom documents. But even within these blocks no fixed scheme dominates, with the exception of the first group, which follows the historical order of the Hebrew Bible. Everything is still in flux. This is also partly true even of the late Byzantine manuscripts. Notably, in contrast to the Hebrew canon, Daniel essentially belongs to the prophetic books, as a rule following Ezekiel, and the Minor Prophets are generally placed (except in Sinaiticus), before Isaiah. This order seems to be very old.

It is important to add that as long as the individual books were written in scrolls and stored in a scroll cabinet it was relatively difficult to maintain a fixed order. This was especially true for the Jewish preliminary of the LXX, where the sequence of the scrolls in the ark of the Torah became definitive. Only the codex with several scriptures facilitated a fixed order. But a comparison of the sequence of the books in early church LXX codices shows that a totally fixed sequence was basically never truly attained. In fact, significant variations can be found. There was an astonishing multiplicity, especially at the margin of the canon. In the first centuries of the Church only few large and rich communities possessed the whole Bible.

2. *The Earliest Canon Lists*[7]

If we examine the earliest canon lists we find a substantially different picture from what appears in the codices. The number of unequivocally acknowledged books is much smaller. To a certain extent, a second group of lesser importance, also permitted for church use, joins the books which are 'canonical' in the full sense.

Melito of Sardis (*c.* 170) sent a fellow Christian, Onesimus, 'excerpts from the law and the prophets' currently popular among Christians and, since Onesimus wanted to know 'the exact number and order of the ancient Scriptures', a list of the 'books of the Old Covenant' (τὰ τῆς παλαιᾶς διαθήκης βιβλία): here the term 'Old Testament' appears for the first time. Melito had probably learned this from Jewish Christians or

---

[6] For Basiliano-Venetus, see Kenyon and Adams, 46. For Hab 3, see J. Ziegler, *Duodecim Prophetae*, Septuaginta: Vetus Testamentum Graecum XIII (2nd edn; Göttingen, 1967), 137–8, 273–5. For the order of the Gospels see M. Hengel, *The Four Gospels and the One Gospel of Jesus Christ* (London, 2000).

[7] Texts in Preuschen, 27–9; cf. also Sundberg, 58–9; E. Junod, 'La formation et la composition de l'Ancien Testament dans l'église grecque des quatre premiers siècles', in Kaestli and Wermelinger, 105–34 (esp. 107–8). All of the total of twelve lists are printed in the appendix (pp. 135–51).

Jews during a journey to the Holy Land.[8] A consequence of the second-century church's total appropriation of the LXX, contemporaneous with the dispute with Marcion, was that it distinguished for the first time between its new Scriptures and the traditional Scriptures of 'the Old Covenant'. Both were read and interpreted alike in worship. According to Justin's *Apologia* I:67:3, 'the reminiscences of the apostles (ἀπομνημονεύματα τῶν ἀποστόλων) or the scriptures of the prophets were read, followed by the sermon, before the Eucharist'.[9] Melito's term 'Old Covenant' for the Holy Scriptures of the Jews suggests the hypothesis that the growing body of Christian Scriptures regarded as 'apostolic' were already sometimes designated as the 'New Covenant'. We meet this still somewhat unclear terminology—not yet found in Irenaeus, a generation after Melito—in Clement of Alexandria and Tertullian.[10] In addition, Melito is the first Christian pilgrim to Palestine known to us. A particular biblical interest surely stood behind this journey. The catalogue he sent admittedly names only the books of the Hebrew canon, with the exception of the book of Esther, itself still somewhat controversial in second-century Jewish circles. As transmitted to us, the list contains twenty-one titles; with Esther, or with a division of the four books of Kings into two documents as in the Hebrew canon, it would have been twenty-two books, similar to Josephus' list in *Ap* 1:38–41 (see below, pp. 99–100).[11]

Since the Hebrew alphabet has twenty-two letters, twenty-two later became almost a 'holy number' among Christians, especially for Origen and Jerome, as determining the number of canonical books, even though

---

[8] Eusebius, *Hist Eccl* 4:26:13–14. Here Daniel appears after Jeremiah and before Ezekiel, so also in Origen (see Eusebius, *Hist Eccl* 6:52:2).

[9] See J. Salzmann, *Der frühchristliche Wortgottesdienst bis Origenes* (WUNT II/59; Tübingen, 1994). This order follows that of the synagogue. M. Hengel, *The Four Gospels and the One Gospel of Jesus Christ* (London, 2000), 37f., 116, 162f. It is important that here the Gospels are mentioned before the prophets.

[10] Cf. already the antimontanist author Eusebius, *Hist Eccl* 5:6:3: ὁ τῆς τοῦ εὐαγγελίου καινῆς διαθήκης λόγος; further, *Strom* 1:28:1 (GCS 52:17:37); 5:3:3 (327:26); 5:58:1 (382:17); see also the more extensive citations in Zahn, 104–6. Tertullian, however, more often employs *instrumentum* rather than *testamentum*, since the legal term possessed the special meaning of 'evidence' or 'the document to be produced before the court' (Zahn, 106).

[11] The order in Melito is as follows: Pentateuch (with Num. before Lev.!), Joshua, Judges, Ruth, 1–2 Samuel, 1–2 Kings, 1–2 Chronicles, Psalms, Proverbs of Solomon *or Wisdom* (Σαλομῶνος Παροιμίαι ἢ καὶ Σοφία, i.e. Melito preferred the title Sapientia for the Proverbs, cf. Eusebius, *Hist Eccl* 4:22:9), Qoheleth, Song, Job, Isaiah, Jeremiah, twelve Minor Prophets, Daniel, Ezekiel, Ezra. Significantly, Melito's friend asked for 'excerpts from the *law and the prophets*, insofar as they pertain to our Redeemer and our whole faith', and he wanted to know 'precisely the *number* and *sequence* of the Old Testament books'. Melito responded with the list above and concluded: 'From these scriptures I give excerpts from six books', that is, he understood 'law and prophets' as in the New Testament (see below, p. 105 n. 1) self-evidently as a designation for the *entire* Old Testament, including the 'Hagiographa'.

attempts to do so encountered great difficulty with the Scriptures actually used in worship. Notably, however, beginning with *4 Ezra* 14:45, all Jewish sources, except for Josephus, universally speak of twenty-four books. The rabbinic sources mention the number, however, only from the beginning of the third century.[12] An early Jewish controversy over the extent of the Hebrew canon may be concealed behind the two competing numbers twenty-two and twenty-four, since Canticles and Qoheleth were debated in that period. More likely, however, is a difference among the Jews concerning how the books should be counted. As Jerome reports, some counted Ruth and Lamentations among the Hagiographa and thus arrived at twenty-four books.[13] In any case, Christian uncertainty about claiming support from the Greek LXX in

[12] Citations in Bill. IV:419–20. Cf. also Schürer (rev.) II:314–21. Notably, nonetheless, neither Origen nor Jerome maintains that the analogy (twenty-two Hebrew letters corresponding to the twenty-two biblical books) was of Jewish origin. (The citation of Origen in Eusebius, *Hist Eccl* 6:25:1 ['It should be noted that according to the tradition of the Hebrews there are twenty-two biblical books, corresponding to the number of Hebrew letters'] does not contradict this, since the 'tradition of the Hebrews' refers primarily only to the first part of the sentence. Presumably, Josephus' reference to twenty-two books inspired the Christian theologian, who generally preferred numerological symbolism to this comparison; compare Origen's exegesis of John 2:6 and see A. Smitmans, 'Das Weinwunder von Kana', *BGBE* 6 [Tübingen, 1966], 65–6, 130–1; cf. p. 46 n. 68). Josephus himself nowhere mentions in his report that texts in the Hebrew language are involved; the analogy was apparently not significant to him. Beckwith, 235ff., sees the oldest source for the twenty-two books corresponding to the Hebrew alphabet already in *Jub.* 2:22–3, where, according to R. H. Charles, a lacuna occurs after 2:22 that he supplies with the help of later citations. Admittedly, the extant text speaks only of the twenty-two founding fathers from Adam to Jacob and of the twenty-two works created on the seventh day; see K. Berger (*Das Buch der Jubiläen* [JSHRZ II/3; Gütersloh, 1981], 330) who refers to additional parallels in Origen, among others.

[13] Cf. Beckwith, 235–73: 'It is thus clear that the two rival counts do not imply different canons. The two books on which the difference depends are not among the five disputed books. The numeration of twenty-two arose not from a smaller canon but from the number of letters in the Hebrew alphabet' (256). Jerome then compares the twenty-four old books with the twenty-four elders in the Apocalypse of John: the latter represent the former (cf. *Prologus in Libro Regum* [= *Prologus Galeatus*] (see above, p. 38 n. 43), 364–6, citation, p. 365). This comparison is, however, attested prior to Jerome. The oldest evidence for it may come from the *Gospel of Thomas*, dating back to the second century CE (saying, 52: 'Twenty-four prophets spoke in Israel, and they have all spoken of you', *NTApo* I [5th edn], 107); the other citations are in Victorinus of Pettau (d. 304, *Commentarii in Apocalypsin* 4:3, 5 [text in CSEL 49, J. Haussleiter, ed. (Vienna, 1916), 50, 56]) who mentions the lost Epitome of Theodorus as his source; Ps-Tertullian, *Carmen Adv Marcionem* 4:198–210 (fourth century, text in *Tertullian 2*, CChr. SL 2, R. Willems, ed. [Turnhout, 1954], 1417–54): 'Alarum numerus antiqua volumina signat, / Esse satis certa viginta quattuor ista . . .' (198–9); Hilary of Poitiers (d. 367) mentions the twenty-two books in accordance with the Hebrew alphabet and then adds Judith and Tobit because the Greek alphabet has twenty-four letters; compare his preface to his commentary on the Psalms, *Instructio Psalmorum* 15 (text in CSEL 22, A. Zingerle, ed. [Vienna, 1891], 13) and the Mommsenian list (text in Preuschen, 36–40); cf. also Beckwith, 271 n. 70 and 273 n. 86.

contrast to the neglected—indeed completely ignored—original text is apparent in Melito's list. The ongoing dialogue with Jewish opponents and their reference to the (as had to be acknowledged, more original) Hebrew canon kept this uncertainty alive and, in the third and fourth centuries, intensified it once again. It was necessary constantly to submit willy-nilly to criticism from that perspective.

Even the lists of books assembled by Origen 'in the exegesis of the first Psalm'[14] are limited to twenty-two 'biblical books as transmitted by the Hebrews, corresponding to the number of their letters'. Remarkably, the Minor Prophets are missing, although Esther is mentioned. It is clear that this must simply be an accidental omission since, without the Twelve, the list contains only twenty-one books. So in Rufinus' translation the Twelve are inserted after Canticles, as also in the list of Hilary of Poitiers, who otherwise agrees entirely with the sequence of the Alexandrian scholar.[15] Origen mentions the Greek and Hebrew titles together and appends 'outside the series' (ἔξω δὲ τούτων) the Maccabean histories (τὰ Μακκαβαϊκά) under the designation— still extremely enigmatic—of 'Sarbethsabanaiel'.[16] To be sure, this learned list is not meant simply to reproduce the Old Testament books used in the church; Origen was much too aware of tradition for this. But Eusebius, who knew the work of this honoured scholar and confessor like no other, follows the list immediately with Origen's statements concerning the Gospels and the New Testament Epistles. In the introduction, he calls the list a 'list of the Holy Scriptures of the Old Covenant' (τοῦ τῶν ἱερῶν γραφῶν τῆς παλαιᾶς διαθήκης καταλόγου). Origen defended the authenticity of Susanna (one of the additions to Daniel) in dialogue with Julius Africanus by appealing, for example, to the Jewish (proto-)Theodotion version which he, and after him almost all the other Fathers, utilized exclusively; yet he—unlike Jerome—sought not to devalue LXX texts which had no Hebrew equivalent. At the same time, as the greatest biblical philologist of the early church, he was unwilling to disregard the consequences of the text-comparative work documented in his monumental Hexapla. For one who took such pains with the 'original' and the improvement of the chaotic text tradition, the Hebrew Bible must indeed have attained substantial importance. Even Augustine was forced, although unwillingly, to take into account the results of the philological textual comparison inaugurated by Origen (see above, pp. 50–3).

The famous thirty-ninth Easter Letter of Athanasius in 367 CE made it evident that lists such as Origen's later assumed a certain prescrip-

---

[14] Eusebius, *Hist Eccl* 6:25–6; Swete, 203.

[15] Cf. Beckwith, 185–6.

[16] Σαρβηθσαβαναελ, 'Prince of the house of the Son of God' (?). Cf. above R. Hanhart p. 11.

tive function and that the Hebrew canon continued to maintain its 'normative' (or—perhaps better—disruptive?) role. He, too, appeals to the 'magical' number 22 attained by following the Hebrew canon, for the most part, although he considers 1 and 2 Kings (= 1 and 2 Samuel), 3(1) and 4(2) Kings, 1 and 2 Chronicles, 1 and 2 Ezra, as well as—in accordance with older tradition (see below, pp. 113–14)—Jeremiah, Baruch, Lamentations, and the Epistle of Jeremiah as one book each. In this manner, Baruch and the Epistle of Jeremiah, as well as 1 Ezra and the additions to Daniel found shelter in the canon lists and could be integrated into the number 22 (see below, pp. 101–2). On the other hand, Athanasius wished no more than did Jerome later to abandon completely the 'other books' distributed in the churches, books 'which are to be distinguished from these and are not canonical, but which the fathers have determined should be read to new converts to be instructed in the word of wisdom'. Such books were Wisdom, Sirach, Esther (despite the Hebrew canon, still not yet fully recognized in the Greek church), Judith and Tobit. As in Vaticanus, the books of Maccabees are omitted entirely from the Easter Letter. This omission may have been in accordance with contemporary Alexandrian tradition. Of those works now known as the 'Apostolic Fathers', however, the *Didache* and the *Shepherd* of Hermas are included in the New Testament. By contrast the 'hidden' (apocryphal) books of Moses, Isaiah and Enoch— highly regarded well into the third century—are rejected with sharp polemic.[17]

Here we find for the first time a clear differentiation between three categories: certain books have been *canonized* (κανονιζόμενα) by the fathers; others are only *read publicly* (ἀναγιγνωσκόμενα); others, the 'Apocrypha', they would have preferred not to mention at all (οὐδαμοῦ τῶν ἀποκρύφων μνήμη, ἀλλὰ αἱρετικῶν ἐστιν ἐπίνοια)—they are to be *rejected* because they have been counterfeited by the heretics. The distinction, whose development can be perceived here, prepared by church practice and based on the dispute with the Jews over the true scope of the Holy Scriptures as well as on the containment of heretical influences, has its beginnings as far back as the second century. Significantly, during the process an 'intermediate group' was formed, somewhere between the strictly 'canonical' books and those that were to be rejected, an intermediate group that Jerome first designated with the once-again neutral term 'apocrypha' (see above p. 49 n. 80 and p. 56 n. 96) and that was used primarily for the ethical instruction of catechumens.

---

[17] ἕτερα βιβλία τούτων ἔξωθεν, οὐ κανονιζόμενα μέν, τετυπωμένα δὲ παρὰ τῶν πατέρων ἀναγιγνώσκεσθαι τοῖς ἄρτι προσερχομένοις καὶ βουλομένοις κατηχεῖσθαι τὸν τῆς εὐσεβείας λόγον (text in Preuschen, 42–5, the Coptic fragments, 45–52; cf. also Junod, 124–30. On *Enoch*, see above, pp. 54–6).

The (provincial) Synod of Laodicea (*c.* 360)[18] acted even more rigorously in its Canon 60 (admittedly of disputed authenticity). This first prohibits the recitation of private (i.e. non-biblical) psalms, Christian hymns, and the reading of 'non-canonical books' in the church and then lists the twenty-two books permitted for reading;[19] the list, in contrast to that of Athanasius, also includes Esther. To achieve the number 22, Ruth is appended to Judges. Furthermore, only the 150 psalms of the Hebrew Bible, but not Psalm 151 of the LXX, are admitted. In other words, this synod adhered even more closely to the 'Hebrew canon' and limited hymn-singing in worship to the biblical Psalter.

This clear distinction—that will naturally reflect the actual use of Scripture during the first three centuries of the church in only a very limited way—corresponds to a large number of catalogues from the Greek church from roughly the same period—for example, the contemporaries of Epiphanius, Amphilochus of Iconium, Gregory of Nazianzus and Cyril of Jerusalem (d. 386). In his fourth catechesis, after first relating the Aristeas legend in the Christian form, already traditional, that emphasizes the inspiration of the separated translators, Cyril lists the twenty-two Holy Scriptures: twelve 'historical books' from Genesis to Esther, five 'poetical' books written in stichoi, and, finally, five 'prophetic' books. There is no intermediate group; he expressly rejects the apocrypha.[20] The dependence on the Hebrew canon is also noteworthy here. In Palestine, the constant dispute with Jewish inhabitants, who were very self-confident and influential in the fourth century, may have played a role. Even the patriarch Nicephoros of Constantinople (*c.* 750–828) clearly distinguished the intermediate group from the twenty-two books of the Old Testament; he allocated nine titles to the intermediate group: three books of Maccabees, Wisdom, Sirach, the Psalms and *Odes* (!) *of Solomon*, Esther, Judith, Susanna and Tobit. These were followed by fourteen 'apocrypha' to be rejected, with *Enoch* at the head.[21]

---

[18] The precise date of this assembly of bishops is uncertain. Cf. B. M. Metzger (*The Canon of the New Testament* [Oxford 1987], 292), who accepts the date 363. In contrast C. Nardi, Art. 'Laodicea (concili)', in A. Di Berardino, ed., *Dizionario patristico e di Antichità Christiane* II (Casale Monferratto, 1983), 1889–99 (French edn, p. 1407) speaks only of the time of Theodosius (347–95), but regards as possible an even later date during the time of Theodoret of Cyrus (393–458). For canon law see Zahn II/1, 193–202; the text is in P. P. Joannou, *Discipline générale antique* I/2 (Grottaferrata, 1963), 1027–55. I am grateful to Dr Chr. Markschies for these references.

[19] ὅτι οὐ δεῖ ἰδιωτικοὺς ψαλμοὺς λέγεσθαι ἐν τῇ ἐκκλησίᾳ, οὐδὲ ἀκανόνιστα βιβλία, ἀλλὰ μόνα τὰ κανονικὰ τῆς καινῆς καὶ παλαιᾶς διαθήκης (text in Preuschen [see above, p. 57 n. 1], 72–3). On the prohibition against reciting private psalms, see M. Hengel, 'Das Christuslied im frühesten Gottesdienst', in *Weisheit Gottes-Weisheit der Welt* I (FS J. Card. Ratzinger), W. Baier and V. Pfnür, eds (St Ottilien, 1987), 357–404, esp. 366–8 = idem, *Studies in Early Christology*, Edinburgh, 1995, 227–91 (275f.).

[20] *Catechesis* IV, 33–6. Text in Preuschen, 79–82; cf. also Junod (see above, p. 60 n. 7), 129–30.

[21] Text: Preuschen, 62–4; German translation in *NTApo* I (5th edn), 33–4.

It is against this background that we may understand Jerome's battle for the priority of the *hebraica veritas* and the Western counter-reaction in the undiscerning inclusion by the Synod of Carthage (397 CE) of the books from the intermediate group not represented in the Hebrew Bible but in church use. The conflict over the scope of the Old Testament in the Reformation proceeds from the problems already evident quite soon in the early church and the unresolved dispute, broken off at that time, continues in a new form.[22]

3. *The 'Second Class' Character of the Writings Not Contained in the Hebrew Canon*

The fact that one may speak of the relatively 'second class' character of the 'intermediate group' not contained in the Hebrew canon is also evident from a certain reluctance to cite them or use them as readings in worship. Despite its inclusion in the Hebrew Bible, Esther continues to be numbered among these only half-heartedly recognized writings. The Apostolic Fathers—except for Clement of Rome (see below, pp. 121–2)—and the Apologists, from Justin to Theophilus of Antioch, ignored these documents almost entirely. The same is essentially true, although to a somewhat lesser degree, even from Irenaeus to Tertullian, with the exception of Clement of Alexandria's use of Tobit, Wisdom and Sirach (see below, pp. 115–17); he utilized the latter work especially in the *Paidagogos*, addressed to educated catechumens and Christians. Here the educational motive mentioned by Athanasius becomes apparent. At the same time, he also frequently employed pseudepigrapha, even

---

[22] For the situation in North Africa, cf. Wermelinger (see above, p. 48 n. 76), 170–4. The text of the biblical canon of the Synod of Carthage is in Preuschen, 72–3: 'Item placuit, ut praeter scripturas canonicas nihil in ecclesia legatur sub nomine divinarum scripturarum, sunt autem canonicae scripturae hae: . . .' In addition to the usual canonical books, the following are mentioned: five books of Solomon (Prov., Qoh., Cant., Wisd., Sir.!), Tobit, Judith, Esther, 1 and 2 Maccabees. For the Reformation controversy, see H. Bornkamm, *Luther und das Alte Testament* (Tübingen, 1948), 158–9 and 234. Luther preached on only two passages from Sirach, otherwise there are no commentaries or sermons on the Apocrypha; H. Volz, 'Luthers Stellung zu den Apokryphen des Alten Testaments', *LuJ* 26 (1959): 93–108; K. D. Fricke, 'Der Apokryphenteil der Lutherbibel', in *Die Apokryphenfrage im ökumenischen Horizont*, S. Meurer, ed. (Stuttgart, 1989), 51–82; W. Neuser, 'Calvins Stellung zu den Apokryphen des Alten Testaments', in, *Text-Wort-Glaube* (FS K. Aland), M. Brecht, ed. (AKG 50; Berlin and New York, 1980), 298–323; *idem*, 'Die Reformierten und die Apokryphen des Alten Testaments', in Meurer, ed., 83–103; J. Quack, *Evangelische Bibelvorreden von der Reformation bis zur Aufklärung* (QFRG 43; Gütersloh, 1975), 15, 40–6, 48, 67–8, 80, 115, etc.; Rüger (see p. 61 n. 10), 294–6; B. Lohse, 'Die Entscheidung der lutherischen Reformation über den Umfang des alttestamentlichen Kanons', in *idem*, *Evangelium in der Geschichte. Studien zu Luther und der Reformation* (Göttingen, 1988), 211–36, also in *Verbindliches Zeugnis* I, 169–94.

works by heretical and pagan authors. He, the most truly educated early Christian author before Origen, loved to display his comprehensive learning and is consequently rather atypical. In view of the grand scope of the totality of his work, even Origen made rather limited use of writings such as Esther, Tobit, Judith, and the books of Maccabees. This also applies to the later fathers.[23] It seems to me that in this early period works such as *1 Enoch* (or related works attributed to Enoch) were cited as often if not more. Besides the letter of Jude (v. 14), the *Letter of Barnabas* refers to it twice as γραφή;[24] furthermore, Tatian[25] and Athenagoras[26] mention (or know) it; Justin, too, who does not cite it, apparently knew it.[27] Irenaeus[28] refers to it frequently, as does Tertullian, who valued it especially and defended it against rejection by the Jews (see above pp. 54–5). Others who knew it include Minucius Felix, Clement of Alexandria, Julius Africanus, Hippolytus, Commodian, Cyprian, etc.[29] Even Origen knew that it was not universally recognized in the church and was rejected by the Jews. He vacillated, therefore, in his judgement, but nonetheless refers to it

---

[23] Compare the indices in *Biblia Patristica, I: Des Origines à Clément d'Alèxandrie et Tertullien* (Paris, 1975): of 172 pages dealing with the Old Testament, only a mere 7 refer to the books of Tobit, Judith, 1 and 2 Maccabees, Wisdom, Sirach and Baruch; *II: Le troisième siècle (Origène excepté)* (Paris, 1977): 168 pp. Old Testament, of which 9 pages Tobit-Baruch; *III: Origène* (Paris, 1980): 187 pp. Old Testament, only 5 pages Tobit-Baruch; *IV: Eusèbe de Césarée, Cyrille de Jérusalem, Épiphanie de Salamine* (Paris, 1987): of 174 Old Testament pages, only 4 for Tobit-Baruch.

[24] 4:3 says: τὸ τέλειον σκάνδαλον ἤγγικεν, περὶ οὗ γέγραπται ὡς ᾽Ενὼχ λέγει. About this, K. Wengst remarks: 'The Enoch literature known to date offers no reference to this; the remaining references to Eth En 89:16–64 and 90:17–18 are lapses. This may be an error on the author's part' (*Schriften des Urchristentums* II [Darmstadt, 1984], 145 n. 36). In addition, Codex L (Corbiensis) reads Δανιήλ instead of Enoch and thus interprets the 'complete scandal' in the sense of the βδέλυγμα ἐρημώσεως of Daniel 9:27; 11:31; 12:11 (cf. Wisd. 14:11 where βδέλυγμα and σκάνδαλα stand in parallel [see K. Wengst, loc. cit., 197 n. 35]). The substitution of Daniel is apparently an 'orthodox' correction citing a canonical book in the place of a 'heretical' one. In any case, one may assume that *Barnabas* knew 'Enoch literature'. The second instance in 16:5 does not mention the source of the citation. It is merely introduced with γέγραπται γάρ and then follows a free, abbreviated rendition of *Eth En* 91:13. Even more than the *Dialogue* of Justin, the *Letter of Barnabas* is also a scholastic document created almost entirely from testimonia collections (cf. K. Wengst, 123–5).

[25] *Oratio ad Graecos* 8:1 (an allusion to *En.* 8:3) and 20:4 (cf. *En.* 6:6; 15:8). Text in *Corpus Apologeticum Christianorum* VI, J. C. Th. Otto, ed. (Jena, 1851), 34, 88.

[26] *Legatio Pro Christianis* 24:1 (ll. 4–5), M. Marcovich, ed. (PTS 31; Berlin and New York, 1990), 82. The same appears as *Libellus pro Christianis* (E. Schwarz [TU 14; Leipzig 1891]), and *Supplicatio* (E. J. Goodspeed, *Die ältesten Apologeten* [Göttingen, 1914 = 1984], 315–17). The variants result from differing translations of Πρεσβεία.

[27] See M. Hengel, Durham, 49 n. 38.

[28] *Adv Haer* 1:10:1 = *1 En.* 10:13–14; 5:4; etc.; *Adv Haer* 1:15:6 = *1 En.* 8:1; etc.; *Adv Haer* 4:36:4 = *1 En.* 9:8; 10:2; *Adv Haer* 5:28:2 = *1 En.* 19:1; 99:7.

[29] A collection of the citations in Charles (above n. 11, p. lxxxi–xcv; cf. also Milik, see above, p. 54 n. 89), 70–2, 79–81, and above, pp. 54–6.

relatively often and favourably. In the dispute with Celsus, who adduced a citation from *Enoch* in order to demonstrate Christian inconsistency, however, Origen accuses him not only of being unfamiliar with the book, but also of 'not seeming to know that the literature attributed to Enoch is not even regarded as divine in the churches'.[30]

The manuscript evidence for the books of this 'intermediate group' and their use in the lectionaries is also substantially more modest than that for the other writings.[31] It is especially noteworthy that they were not commented on or interpreted in a homily either in the East, or even in the West where a few of them attained apparent equal status through the Synod of Carthage (397).[32] In the West, Rhabanus Maurus (780–856) wrote the first commentary on Wisdom, Sirach, Judith and Esther. Only Tobit was excepted. Since he was considered a prophet, already in the fourth century Ambrose and later Bede commented on the book.[33]

In contrast, the first commentaries on the Song of Songs and Qoheleth—whose 'religious content', on the surface, seems indeed hardly greater than that of Sirach or Wisdom—were already appearing in the third and fourth centuries (Hippolytus, Origen, Gregory Thaumaturgus, Dionysius of Alexandria, Didymus the Blind, etc.). This early preference for the Song is remarkable. The impulse toward allegorical interpretation already perceptible earlier in Judaism will have prompted the writing

---

[30] *Contra Celsum* 5:54; ἐν ταῖς ἐκκλησίαις οὐ πάνυ φέρεται ὡς θεῖα τὰ ἐπιγεγραμμένα τοῦ Ἐνὼχ βιβλία; see Harl, Dorival and Munnich, 323. For the *Enoch* citations, see also Schürer (rev. III/1, 261–4). Beckwith (391–2, 397–405) emphasizes that the canonicity of Jude became a problem because of this citation and that 2 Peter already corrected this point. In his opinion, Jude did not employ *Enoch* as inspired Scripture but as 'narrative haggadah—edifying, but not necessarily historical' (430); compare also Ellis (see above, p. 57 n. 2), 5: '. . . while canonical Scripture was regarded as prophetic, prophetic writing did not necessarily become canonical'. It should be noted that, at the time when Jude was written, there was still no fixed 'Christian canon' and even the Jewish canon was still problematical. Beckwith's reasoning on this point is anachronistic.

[31] A. Rahlfs, *Die alttestamentlichen Lektionen der griechischen Kirche* (MSU I/5; Berlin, 1915), 226–30: Judith, Tobit and 1 Maccabees are totally absent. See also G. Zuntz, *Prophetologium Monumenta Musicae Byzantinae Lectionaria* I (Copenhagen, 1970), 603–5, index locorum. Of the 'Apocrypha', only two Wisdom and two Baruch texts are utilized (567–70, 42–3, 556).

[32] Junod (see above, p. 60 n. 7), 118.

[33] For Tobit as a prophet, see already the Ophitic prophet list in Irenaeus, *Adv Haer* 1:30:11. The book is often cited in the Apostolic Fathers, Clement and Origen (cf. the citations in Schürer [rev.] III/1, 227). Ambrose, too, in his commentary *De Tobia* (CSEL 32/2, C. Schenkl, ed. [Vienna, 1897], 517–73) treats the work as a prophetic book. The commentary begins with the words: 'Lecto prophetico libro, qui inscribitur Tobis, quamvis plene virtutes sancti prophetae scriptura insinuaverint, tamen conpendiario mihi sermone de eius meritis recensendis et operibus apud vos utendum arbitror, ut ea quae scriptura historico more digessit latius nos strictius comprehendamus virtutem eius genera velut quodam breviario colligentes.' For Bede and the other commentators, see J. Gamberoni, *Die Auslegung des Buches Tobias in der griechisch—lateinisch Kirche der Antike und der Christenheit des Westens bis 1600* (StANT 21; Munich, 1969).

of commentaries,[34] for without such an interpretive strategy it was incomprehensible as Holy Scripture. Byzantine commentaries on Wisdom (by Matthaeus Cantacuzenus and Malachias Monachos) appear only late in the fourteenth century; the latter is supposed to have also commented on Sirach. There are no commentaries whatsoever on Esther, Judith, Tobit and the books of Maccabees from the Greek church.[35]

Remarkably, *4 Maccabees*, which was not received in the West, appears substantially more often in Byzantine manuscripts than the other books; this is related to its particular martyriological character. The work stands at the boundary between (deutero–)canonical Scripture and hagiographical-liturgical narrative.[36]

This 'second class' character is certainly to be understood in the first instance in terms of the absence of a prototype in the Hebrew Bible, but cannot, however, be explained solely in these terms since this 'second class' character is also substantially true for Esther. Quite unlike Esther by contrast, since the third century, the fathers highly treasured and allegorically interpreted the books of Canticles and Qoheleth, whose 'canonization' was also highly debated by the rabbis.

Educated users observed already long before Jerome, that Wisdom— in itself quite significant for Christology—was originally written in Greek and could not have originated with Solomon.[37] In the prologue to his commentary on Canticles, Origen mentions only three books attributable to Solomon (Proverbs, Canticles and Qoheleth), although he usually cites Wisdom as Solomonic. The passage in *De Principiis* IV

---

[34] The Song of Songs was presumably already interpreted allegorically at Qumran where we find three manuscript fragments (two of Qoheleth): Tov, *Unpublished Qumran Texts*, 96. In my opinion, 2 John already alludes to the Song through ἐλεκτῇ κυρίᾳ and ἀδελφή. See M. Hengel, *Die johanneische Frage* (WUNT I/67; Tübingen, 1993), 136 and idem, Die auserwählte Herrin, die Brant & die Gottesstadt, in *La Cité de Dieu/Die Stadt Gottes*, eds. M. Hengel, S. Mittmann and A. M. Schwemer (WUNT 129: Tübingen 2000), 245–85. In the second century, the Valentinians with their bridal mysticism may have interpreted it allegorically. See below, pp. 91–3.

[35] Compare the bibliographies on the history of exegesis compiled by W. Werbeck at the end of the relevant articles in RGG (3rd ed.) and Rahlfs, 385, 420–2 (for commentaries on Wisdom and Sirach); an anonymous commentary on Wisdom from a sixteenth-century manuscript should also be mentioned (p. 424).

[36] Rahlfs (see above, p. 55 n. 94), 387–90; Eusebius and Jerome count the book among the writings of Josephus (*Hist Eccl* 3:10:6; *De Viris Illustribus* 13; *Contra Pelagianos* 2:6); in the canon lists, it never appears among the canonical books, but it is contained in codices Sinaiticus, Alexandrinus and Venetus (eighth/ninth century), as well as in Josephus manuscripts. No catenae or commentaries exist for any of the four books of Maccabees. Only Rhabanus Maurus wrote a commentary in the West in the ninth century (MPL 109). It found a successor, however, only in the fifteenth century.

[37] Cf. *Prologus in libris Salomonis* (957): 'Secundus apud Hebraeos nusquam est, quin et ipse stilus graecam eloquentiam redolet; et nonnulli scriptorum veterum hunc Iudaei Filonis adfirmant. Sicut ergo Iudith et Tobi et Macchabeorum libros legit quidem Ecclesia, sed inter canonicas scripturas non recipit, sic et haec duo volumina legat ad aedificationem plebis, non ad auctoritatem ecclesiasticorum dogmatum confirmandam.'

4:6,[38] where he refers to the document as 'Sapientia *quae dicitur Salomonis*' and then points out that 'this book is not recognized by all', demonstrates that he follows convention more than conviction in this respect. Jerome says that, 'some of the old authors attribute it to the Jew Philo'. The Muratorian Canon even lists it among the New Testament writings. Apparently the comment in the Muratorian Canon Muratori 69–71, 'Sapientia ab amicis Salomonis in honorem ipsius scripta', reflects a possible mistranslation of ὑπὸ Φίλωνος.[39]

Already (*Hist Eccl* 2:16–17), Eusebius refers to the older report that, on the occasion of his mission to Caligula, Philo had contact with Peter and in *De vita contemplativa* described the life of the Therapeutae as that of early Christian ascetics; Jerome (*De Viris Illustribus* 11) even makes him out to be a Christian author. Consequently, it would be quite understandable if Roman Christians toward the end of the second or beginning of the third century—the scholar Hippolytus comes to mind here—had included Wisdom in the New Testament canon as Philo's work. It may have also been an attempt to incorporate the popular book into the New Testament, at least after its absence from the Hebrew Bible became apparent.

'Disqualifying' grounds, then, in addition to absence from the Hebrew canon, were late origins (Sirach and the books of Maccabees, as well as Wisdom), but, for some also, questionable content (Esther, Judith and, as the protest in Julius Africanus shows, the Susanna story). A certain misogyny may also be involved here. The latter three works are typical novelistic products of the Hellenistic period, including even the erotic elements. In the predominantly 'pacifist' Christianity of the second and third centuries, the nationalistic, bellicose accounts of 1 and 2 Maccabees or Judith may also have excited objections.

4. *The Rejection of Authentic 'Apocrypha'*

It remains yet to ask why, beginning with the third century, 'Apocryphal books' (as they were later called) such as Esther, Judith, Tobit, Baruch,

---

[38] At issue is an instance of ὕλη in Wisd. 11:17 in a meaning otherwise unattested *in scripturis canonicis*. The whole passage reads: 'First, one must know that, to date, we have not found the word "material" (*hyle*) used anywhere in the canonical scriptures for the substance underlying the body [Isa. 10:17 LXX follows along with an exposition]. And, in the event that the word "material" should appear in another passage of scripture (*in alio loco scriptum*), one will still not find it, in my opinion, in the meaning with which we are concerned here, except in the so-called "Wisdom of Solomon"; but this book is not recognized by all (*qui utique liber non ab omnibus in auctoritate habentur*)' (Text and German translation by H. Görgemanns and H. Karpp, 'Origenes: Vier Bücher von den Prinzipien', *TzF* 24 (1976), 801). Cf. also Junod (see above, p. 60 n. 7), 118.

[39] Cf. Schürer (rev.) III/1, 54. This also explains its appearance among the New Testament books; cf. already Swete, 268. In his prologue to Wisdom, Luther, too, considers Philonic authorship a possibility; cf. B. Lohse (see above, p. 66 n. 22), 188.

Wisdom, Sirach and the books of Maccabees were accepted at all—even though rather grudgingly—while other somewhat theologically interesting documents were finally completely rejected. These documents include, especially, the much-cited book of *Enoch*, but also the *Assumption of Moses* already presupposed in the letter of Jude, the *Martyrdom of Isaiah* as a portion of the early Christian apocalypse, the *Ascension of Isaiah*,[40] alluded to in Hebrews 11:37, the book of the *Repentance of Jannes and Jambres*,[41] underlying 2 Timothy 3:8, the book of *Eldad and Modad*, based on Numbers 11:26–7,[42] the only document formally cited in Hermas 2:3:4 (7:4), not to mention the *Testament of the Twelve Patriarchs*, which is so closely related to New Testament ethics and which was already subjected to Christian revision in the second century, or the *Prayer of Joseph*, favoured by Origen.[43]

---

[40] See Schürer (rev.) III/1, 335–41. The legend of the dismemberment of Isaiah occurs in Justin, *Dial* 120:5 (cf. M. Hengel, Durham, 49); Tertullian, *De Patientia* 14:1; *Scorpiace* 8:3. Origen also knows the document, cf. *Epistola ad Africanum* 9: 'The traditions (αἱ παραδόσεις) say that the prophet Isaiah was dismembered, and this appears in an apocryphon (ἔν τινι ἀποκρύφῳ τοῦτο φέρεται); this was, however, intentionally corrupted by the Jews for they have inserted a few unsuitable words so that the entire document becomes unreliable.' The same is true, according to Origen, of the Susanna story because it also depicts the Jewish elders in a very bad light. It should be emphasized that Origen employs the word 'apocryphal' here in a literal sense, corresponding to the Hebrew גנז (see below, p. 91 n. 46): the book is not forbidden, but 'hidden', that is excluded from public reading. It did not yet have any derogatory connotation for the Alexandrian, but neither did it yet indicate, as it did after Jerome in the fifth century, the 'intermediate group'.

[41] This is a midrash of sorts on Exodus 7:8–11, already presupposed in CD 5:18. The story of the two Egyptian magicians, who lost a magicians' contest with Moses, is known both in the rabbinic literature and in Pliny the Elder and Apuleius. Early Christian literature also makes frequent reference to it, but never as Holy Scripture, instead always as a story in relation to Moses. Origen even cites it as evidence that the New Testament often refers to 'hidden books': '. . . sicut Iamnes et Mambres restiterunt Moysi' non invenitur in publicis libris, sed in libro secreto qui suprascribitur liber Iamnes et Mambres' (Matthew commentary on Matt. 27:9 [*Commentariorum series* 117], GCS Origenes 11, E. Klostermann, ed. [Leipzig, 1933], 250; cf. also on Matthew 23:37–9 [*Comm. Ser.* 28], loc. cit., 50–1). All citations from Schürer (rev.) III/2, 781–3. The actual book is only preserved in a few papyrus fragments; see A. Pietersma and R. T. Lutz, 'Jannes and Jambres', in *The Old Testament Pseudepigrapha* II, J. H. Charlesworth, ed. (London, 1985), 427–42, and the edition of the Greek text by A. Pietersma, *The Apocryphon of Jannes and Jambres the Magicians* (RGRW 119; Leiden, 1994).

[42] ἐγγὺς Κύριος τοῖς ἐπιστρεφομένοις ὡς γέγραπται ἐν τῷ Ελδὰδ καὶ Μωδάδ, τοῖς προφητεύσασιν ἐν τῷ ἐρήμῳ τῷ λαῷ. Otherwise, it is only mentioned in the stichometry of Nicephorus among the Old Testament Apocrypha; cf. Schürer (rev.) III/2, 783; Preuschen (see above, p. 57 n. 1), 64. Only the verse cited has been preserved; cf. also E. G. Martin, 'Eldad and Modad', in Charlesworth II (see above, n. 41), 463–5.

[43] According to the stichometry of Nicephorus, the prayer had 1100 stichoi and, according to Origen, was still in use among the Jews of his time. Only nine christologically very interesting verses are preserved as citations in Origen; cf. Schürer (rev.) III/2, 798–9, and J. Z. Smith, 'Prayer of Joseph', in Charlesworth II (see above, n. 41), 699–714. Cf. M. Hengel, *The Son of God* (London, 1976), 47–8.

One could continue here at length and list all those books rejected in the later catalogues such as the Gelasian Decree, regarded as heretical forgeries and mostly lost, if not preserved in translations, on the fringes of the church, such as the theologically important apocalypse, *4 Ezra* in its Latin, Syriac and Ethiopic versions, or the related apocalypse, the *Apocalypse of Baruch*, surviving only in Syriac. Also significant are the *Book of Enoch*, canonical in the Ethiopic church, the *Book of Jubilees* in the same language, and, finally, *2 Enoch* and the *Abraham Apocalypse* in the Old Slavonic.[44]

Another look at the Hebrew canon will assist in answering the question of the origin of this distinction. The canon contains only documents between Moses and Ezra. Consequently, according to a baraita in *bBB* 14,[45] even the book of Job—which according to Jewish tradition stemmed from a descendant of Esau in the patriarchal period— was *written* by Moses. Thus, judgement was pronounced upon all writings claiming to stem from an author before Moses. Christians, too, could not permanently avoid the Jewish model. This tendency was strengthened because the Gnostics not only appealed to previously 'hidden' (ἀπόκρυφοι) traditions and documents,[46] but also themselves produced documents attributed to patriarchs. Indeed, they had a certain preference for such 'primeval writings'. The Gnostic library at Nag Hammadi contained twelve pseudepigraphical 'apostolic writings', but also an Adam Apocalypse, two texts that appealed to the ancient revelations of Seth, Adam's third son, who became the eponymous hero of so-called Sethian gnosis, and one document each from Shem, Melchizedek and Norea, purportedly a daughter of Adam or Noah.[47] Such excessive production could best be counteracted by an appeal to the basic

---

[44] For the canon of the Ethiopic church, which exhibits a number of peculiarities related to the isolation of this church, cf. Beckwith, 478–505. In addition to *Enoch, 4 Ezra* and *Jubilees*, it also includes, for example, *Josippon*, the early medieval Hebrew revision and expansion of Josephus by Joseph ben Gorion; cf. also H.–P. Rüger, 'Der Umfang des alttestamentlichen Kanons in den verschiedenen kirchlichen Traditionen', in Meurer (p. 66 n. 22), 137–45. Cf. also below, p. 73 n. 49. On the *Slavonic Enoch*, see now Ch. Böttrich, *Weltweisheit, Menschheitsethik, Urkult* (WUNT II/50; Tübingen, 1992); on the *Abraham Apocalypse*, see R. Rubinkiewicz in Charlesworth I, 681–705.

[45] Citation in Bill. IV:434; cf. also Beckwith, 122; Barthélemy, 'L'état de la Bible juive', 14; Ellis (see above, p. 57 n. 2), 13: 'It is significant that the baraita is concerned not with the *identity* of the canonical books but with their *order*. That is, it suggests no controversy about the *limits* of the canon, but it may reflect a situation in which there were uncertainties or divergent traditions among the Jews about the sequence and divisions of the canon, for example, which books belonged among the Prophets and which among the Writings' (ital. in original). A comprehensive bibliography of all Old Testament Apocrypha and Pseud-epigrapha is available in A. Lehnardt, *Bibliographie zu den jüdischen Schriften aus hellenistisch-römischer Zeit* (JSHRZ VI, 2; Gütersloh, 1999).

[46] Cf. Irenaeus, *Adv Haer* I:20:1; Hippolytus, *Refutatio Omnium Haeresium* 7:20:1.

[47] Regarding Seth, Norea, Cain and Melchizedek among the Gnostics, see the various essays by Pearson (see above, p. 21 n. 8), 52–123.

principle whereby one followed the old biblical-Jewish tradition that the first books of the Holy Scriptures were written by Moses and none other. The conclusions of *4 Ezra* (14:44–46), stemming from a Jewish 'apocalypticist' closely related to Pharisaism around 100 CE, attempts to resolve the dilemma between the known writings of the canon and the 'hidden' books by having the inspired seer dictate ninety-four books in forty days. Of these, on God's command, he published the first twenty-four, i.e. the books of the Hebrew canon—'for the worthy and the unworthy (*priora quae scripsisti in palam pone, et legant digni et indigni*)', but 'preserved'[48] the other seventy. Such a compromise, however, ultimately found adherence neither in the rabbinic synagogue nor the church.

Since Tobias supposedly belonged in the Assyrian period and Judith and Baruch in the time of Nebuchadnezzar, Esther and Ezra fell in the period of Artaxerxes I, while Wisdom and Sirach (the prologue to minuscule 248 from the thirteenth century calls Sirach a 'companion of Solomon') were included in the Corpus Salomonis, there remained only the books of Maccabees. As a consequence, Codex Vaticanus and Athanasius excluded them. Their final inclusion in the recognized collection of church writings may be related to the fact that they formed the historical bridge to the present, the time of fulfilment. Furthermore, the motif of the wondrous deliverance of God's people and their martyr theology was a model for the early church for the roughly two and a half centuries' period from 64 to 311 CE because they encouraged communities suffering from uncertain legal status and sporadic persecution. Here, one could further point to the church's high regard since Origen and Eusebius for Josephus, whose *Jewish Wars* was considered evidence of the fulfilment of Jesus' prophecy about the destruction of Jerusalem and the temple, thus confirming Christian truth over against Judaism; Book 6 of the *Wars* in a Syriac translation was even included in manuscripts of the Peshitta.[49]

The question remains open as to how, from the Hebrew Bible, so significantly divergent a Christian collection of Scriptures as the LXX came to be in the first place. On the one hand, despite the usurpation of

---

[48] *Conservatis*, Aram. נטר; cf. 12:37; 14:6; *SyrBar* 20:3. On this text, compare J.–D. Kaestli, 'La Récit de IV Esdras 14 et sa Valeur pour l'Histoire du Canon de l'Ancien Testament', in Kaestli and Wermelinger, 71–102. On the one hand, Ezra's dictum mirrors for the first time the fixed Hebrew canon of twenty-four books. On the other, the emphasis on the seventy hidden books is to be evaluated as an attempt to legitimize the apocalyptic literature against the decisions of the rabbis in Jabneh; that is, the statement is to be classified as canonocentric. Regarding the miracle of inspiration in *4 Ezra*, see pp. 39 and 99.

[49] H. Schreckenberg, *Die Flavius–Josephus–Tradition in Antike und Mittelalter* (ALGHL 5; Leiden, 1972), 61–2: 'Book Six of the *Wars* appears as "5 Maccabees" in the Syriac Vulgate' that was translated from the Greek in the fourth/fifth century.

the LXX as the corpus of 'prophetic' Scriptures translated by the Seventy through divine inspiration, it was indeed never possible to be entirely free of the authority of the Hebrew Bible, precisely because of the appeal to the inspired, miraculous translation at the time of Ptolemy II Philadelphus in the third century BCE. Consequently, documents written later, some transmitted only in Greek, could never be regarded as fully equal, but essentially always only as 'second class'. On the other hand, one did not wish—as, to a degree, did some of the later Reformers—simply to disregard these extra books in comparison to the Jewish 'canon' because of their acculturation and practical value in the church. Even Luther, in his forewords to individual documents, emphasized their value for piety and right living (Jud., Tob., Wisd., Sir. and 1 Macc.), while he sharply criticized others (2 Macc., Additions to Dan. and Esth.).[50] In order to answer the question of how the expanded 'collection of books' came to be, we must turn in Part IV to the pre-Christian development of the LXX writings. We concentrate, first, on its peculiar differences from the Hebrew Bible and, related to this, the history of its influence in the earliest Christian communities.

---

[50] WA DB 12 on the individual documents and B. Lohse (see above, p. 66 n. 22), 188–91.

IV

THE ORIGIN OF THE JEWISH LXX

1. *The Translation of the Torah and Its Enduring Significance*

The legend of the translation of the five books of the Torah into Greek by the seventy-two Palestinian elders is certainly not a historically reliable report, although it goes back to a historical event.

Thus, already by about 170 BCE, the first known Jewish philosopher of religion, Aristobulus, attests that the Torah was translated under Ptolemy II Philadelphus (284–246).[1] The great Jewish Diaspora in Egypt and Alexandria hellenized very rapidly in the first decades of the third century. Consequently, an urgent liturgical need for such a translation of Moses' Torah into the Greek lingua franca arose rather quickly. It is not unlikely that the king legitimized the translation in some form since he, the first truly 'absolutist' ruler in antiquity, would not have been uninterested in the laws followed by a large ethno-religious minority in his realm. Judaea, too, was under Ptolemaic dominion through the third century. Presumably the Samaritans were not slow to prepare a competing revision of the Pentateuch for their Diaspora, the so-called 'Samareitikon', only fragments of which are preserved. We meet the first evidence of this Diaspora as early as *c.* 100 BCE on Delos; in the fourth century CE we find a Samaritan synagogue in Thessalonica from which comes a bilingual inscription with an unusual Greek version of the priestly blessing.[2] Already under the son of the second Ptolemy, Ptolemy

---

[1] Fragment 4 (= Eusebius, *PraepEv* 13:12:1–2; German text in, N. Walter, *Fragmente jüdisch–hellenistischer Exegeten: Aristobulos, Demetrios, Aristeas* (JSHRZ III/2; 2nd edn; Gütersloh, 1980), 257–96; the passage in question, 273–4; English translation by A. Y. Collins, in OTP II, 831–42 [839]). At the same time, he maintains that older partial translations had already been read by Pythagoras and Plato; cf. Swete, 1–2. Anatolius, the later bishop of Caesarea and former peripatetic and mathematician from Alexandria (second half of the third century) counts Aristobulus himself among the seventy translators of Ptolemy's time; cf. the introduction to Fragment 1 (= Eusebius, *Hist Eccl* 7:32:16); Fragment 3 contradicts this position, however. 2 Macc. 1:10 suggests that Aristobulus was the teacher of young Ptolemy VI Philometor (180–145 BCE); cf. in general N. Walter, *Der Thoraausleger Aristobulos* (TU 86; Berlin, 1964); M. Hengel, *Judentum und Hellenismus* (WUNT I/10; 3rd edn; Tübingen, 1988), 295–307 = *idem, Judaism and Hellenism* (London, 1974), 163–9; Schürer (rev.) III/1, 579–87.

[2] *CIJ* I 2nd edn. B. Lifshitz, 1975 I/2, no. 693a; additional literature in Schürer (rev.) III/1, 66–7; Delos: P. Bruneau, BCH 106 (1982), 565–7. On the 'Samareitikon' see S. Noja, 'The Samareitikon', in A. D. Crown, ed., *The Samaritans* (Tübingen, 1989),

III Euergetes (248–222) and his spouse Berenice, we also possess the first Graeco-Jewish synagogue inscriptions. (CIJ II, 1440.1532a = Horbury/Noy 22.117). We find the earliest literary use of the new translation in the Jewish historian Demetrius under Ptolemy IV Philopator (222–205).[3] Two Jewish inscriptions from the island of Rheneia near Delos from *c.* 100 BCE[4] imply the use of the LXX outside Egypt also. The Alexandrian translation of the Pentateuch marched victoriously throughout the whole Greek-speaking Jewish Diaspora.

The various remains of the learned Jewish-Hellenistic literature, originating predominantly in Alexandria, concentrate notably, almost exclusively indeed, on the Pentateuch, especially on Moses and his giving of the law; the later historical and prophetic tradition diminishes strikingly in significance in relation to its importance in the Palestinian motherland. This is true also of the reports from pagan authors con-cerning the Jews. Only the Torah appears in the *Letter of Aristeas* itself; not a single word concerns the prophets (quite in contrast to later Christian interpretation since Justin; see above pp. 26–8). The Jewish motherland appears to be relatively foreign to the pseudepigrapher; his report about it is remote from reality and points politically to a later period of independence between *c.* 130 and 63 BCE. He is primarily concerned with defending the translation, already revered in his time, against competing translations or revisions. It was apparently publicly recognized by the Jewish community of Alexandria; any 'revision' was forbidden. By means of the threat, adopted from Deuteronomy, that any alteration would invoke God's curse, it was declared sacrosanct:

> (310) As the scrolls were read, the priests, the oldest of the translators, representatives of the [Jewish] population and the heads of the entire community met together and said: 'Since the translation is good, pious, and complete, it is right that it be preserved as it is and that no revision take place.' (311) Now since everyone agreed to these words, they placed under a

---

407–12; *A Companion to Samaritan Studies*, ed. A. D. Crown et al. (Tübingen, 1993), 209–10; E. Tov, *The Greek and Hebrew Bible* (VT.S 72; Leiden, 1999), 459–75 (459 n. 1) and 513–17. The Samareitikon also used *nomina sacra* like x͞ς, see above p. 41 n. 53.

[3] The surviving work of Demetrius shows no relationship to the Hebrew text; the chronology and the Greek spelling of the biblical proper names are identical with the LXX. The fragments occur in excerpts from Alexander Polyhistor (ca. 100 BC) cited by Eusebius and Clement of Alexandria; cf. N. Walter, in JSHRZ III/2, 280–92; see also Hengel, *Judentum und Hellenismus*, 128 = *Judaism and Hellenism*, Vol. 1, p. 69 and n. 96; Schürer (rev.) III/1, 513–17.

[4] CIJ I 725; cf. Schürer (rev.) III/1, 70. For a German translation and an extensive discussion of the LXX parallels, see A. Deissmann, *Licht vom Osten* (4th edn; Tübingen, 1928), 351–62.

curse, as is the practice among them, those who would revise [the translation] through additions, rearrangements or omissions. They did this rightly, so that it should remain perpetually unchanged for all time.[5]

Indeed, we find a similar formula at the end of the only thoroughly 'prophetically inspired' document in the New Testament, Revelation 22:18, 26. Josephus, who incorporates the *Letter of Aristeas* in his major history (*Ant* 12:12–118), takes the edge off this dangerous passage and, indeed, reverses it, even though he emphasizes the intention that the extant translation remain unchanged, by replacing the concluding curse with the instruction:

> If, however, someone discovers something in the law that is superfluous, or missing, he should be concerned with making it publicly known and correcting it (12:109).

Here speaks the learned priest and Pharisee, originally from Palestine, writing in Rome toward the end of the first century CE, aware that the Alexandrian translation of the Torah required improvement, and thus justifying the efforts at correction originating in Palestine, probably in Pharisaic circles. Additionally, Josephus' knowledge of the supple-

---

[5] German translation, N. Meisner: ἵνα διαμείνῃ ταῦθ' οὕτως ἔχοντα, καὶ μὴ γένηται μηδεμία διασκευή ... ἐκέλευσαν διαράσασθαι, καθὼς ἔθος αὐτοῖς ἐστιν, εἴ τις διασκευάσει προστίθεις ἢ μεταφέρων τι τὸ σύνολον τῶν γεγραμμένων ἢ ποιούμενος ἀφαίρεσιν ... Cf. Deuteronomy 4:2; 12:32; 29:19, 26 and Josephus, *Ant* 4:196; see also W. C. van Unnik, 'De la règle Μήτε προσθεῖναι, μήτε ἀφελεῖν dans l'histoire du canon', *VigChr* 3 (1949), 1–36 (= *idem, Sparsa Collecta* II [NT.S 30; Leiden, 1980], 123–56). For the intention of the *Letter of Aristeas*, cf. V. Tcherikover, 'The Ideology of the Letter of Aristeas', *HThR* 51 (1958), 59–85 (= *Studies*, 181–207), who sees in it an apology for the Greek language and an opening to the Greek world: 'From now on the Jews would not need the Hebrew language any more, even in their religious service; Greek, the language of the kings and the state, would serve for all their spiritual needs, and there would be no language barrier between the Jews and Greeks' (198; cf. also pp. 205–7); D. W. Gooding, 'Aristeas and Septuagint Origins: A Review of Recent Studies', *VT* 13 (1963), 357–79 (= *Studies*, 158–80); Jellicoe, 47–52, 59–61; D. Barthélemy, 'Pourquoi la Torah a-t-elle été traduite en Grec', in *idem*, 321–40 (originally in *On Language, Culture and Religion*, FS E. A. Nida [La Haye, 1974], 23–41) and Brock, 63: 'The tendency hidden behind Aristeas' portrayal must be understood as a defense of the original LXX Pentateuchal text in the face of contemporary efforts to revise it on the basis of the Hebrew text. In the second and first century BCE, two diametrically opposed options regarding the LXX seem to have surfaced: one [presumably Palestinian, M. Hengel, see above p. 29 n. 13] school thought that the LXX did not render the Hebrew precisely enough and thus required correction. The other [Alexandrian, M. Hengel] maintained that the translations themselves were inspired and thus no revision was necessary.' The *Letter of Aristeas*, however, does not yet speak of inspiration. The beginnings of this notion first occur in Philo. The Jerusalemite priest Josephus knows of no theory of the inspiration of the Seventy, but represents a more pragmatic standpoint; see above, p. 268). Cf. also Brock (see above, p. 29 n. 13), 308–9.

mentary and corrective oral Torah must be presumed (*Ant* 13:297–8, 408; 18:15). The experience of the Jewish historian some time around the year 90 CE, involving disputes with Christians in Rome who appealed to the LXX in response to their Jewish dialogue partners (much like Justin in responding to Trypho), may already stand behind this conscious reversal of the exemplar.

Two generations earlier Philo unfolds the Aristeas story quite differently in his *Vita Mosis* 2:33–44: whereas in the *Letter of Aristeas* the seventy-two translators bring the text into agreement through reciprocal comparison and majority decision (32:302), in Philo, who does not mention the numbers, this occurs through divine inspiration.[6] According to Philo, the anniversary of the translation was regularly celebrated on the island of Pharos as a Jewish folk festival. The translation had worldwide significance, for Philo was certain that when the fate of the now unfortunate people of Israel was reversed—i.e. in the Messianic era—all peoples would accept the law as divine instruction.[7] The testimony of the Jew Philo holds inestimable significance for Christian estimation of the LXX as inspired Scripture. Christians consistently followed the path he pointed out.

The later Christian interpretation already mentioned expanded the translation to include all acknowledged Old Testament Scriptures that were, for them, inspired 'prophetic' writings (see above pp. 26–8), although the scope of the corpus of inspired Scriptures was not firmly established at the outset. In addition, the wondrous process was magnified by the legend of the completely isolated work of the translators in single or double cells where, led by the Holy Spirit, they produced an identical text. Thus the miracle of inspiration acquired the function of assuring the equality of the Greek translation with the Hebrew original (see above, pp. 37–40). That is, the same Holy Spirit was at work in the prophets and in the translators. In the event of a difference between the Hebrew and the Greek text, both texts (should no later error be present) conformed to the divine Spirit and were consequently—thus Augustine—to be taken equally seriously. In contrast, Philo's interests were still limited strictly to the Torah; this is what he has in mind, as a rule even when he speaks of 'Holy Scriptures'. According to Leisegang's index, Philo cites roughly 1100 passages from the Pentateuch (roughly a third from Genesis, followed by Exodus, while the three remaining books play a relatively minor role), but only forty-seven texts from other books (seventeen from the Psalms, twelve from Kings, eleven from the prophetic books, Proverbs four times, and one each from Joshua, Judges

---

[6] The quotation already occurs above, see p. 26; regarding Philo's testimony; cf. also Harl, Dorival and Munnich, 46–7.

[7] See his *De praemiis et poenis* and U. Fischer, *Eschatologie und Jenseitserwartung im hellenistischen Diasporajudentum* (BZNW 44; Berlin and New York, 1978), 184–213; (1984), 476–86.

and Job). The so-called 'apocrypha' do not appear at all.[8] He seems to have either not known, or, more likely, to have ignored or rejected them. This is all the more remarkable since he extensively cites Greek authors from Homer to Hesiod, the pre-Socratics, Plato, Aristotle, and all the way to the Stoics. Indeed, even tragedians and poets such as Pindar are not omitted. Here we encounter the 'aristocratic' attitude of the comprehensive scholar who was atypical in comparison with the rest of Diaspora Judaism. Jewish Sibylline texts and forged classical poetry were also—consciously—avoided.

Thus Philo's work is consistent with the fact that the Pentateuch also held central importance in the other 'Judaeo-apologetic' writings from Alexandria. The 'Alexandrian canon'—if one wishes to speak of one at all—concentrates on the Pentateuch. To be sure, eschatological hope was also alive in the Diaspora, as the Sibylline oracles indicate, but even in the Jewish Sibyllines references to the Pentateuch are only slightly less frequent than to the prophetic books. Furthermore, as Noah's (step-) daughters the Sibyls could not even have known the later Holy Scriptures, Christians considered them pagan prophetesses.[9] In contrast, the didactic poem of Pseudo-Phocylides, dependent entirely on older wisdom literature (see p. 112 n. 26), comprises an exception that proves the rule to a degree.

Nor is it accidental that the Jewish historians who portray the history of their own people—Josephus, Justus of Tiberias, Eupolemos in the Maccabean era, and the somewhat earlier Anonymous Samaritan—were from the motherland, while the Diaspora Jew, Jason of Cyrene, equally linked to the motherland, wrote his history of Judas Maccabeus as an eyewitness of events in Judaea, i.e. as a contemporary chronicle. Primarily Palestinians, including the author of 1 Maccabees, its continuation in the history of John Hyrcanus, and Josephus' priestly source, maintained the ancient tradition of Jewish historiography even in the Hellenistic-Roman period.[10]

---

[8] H. Leisegang, 'Index Locorum Veteris Testamenti', in L. Cohn and P. Wendland, *Philo von Alexandrien* (Opera quae supersunt VII/2; Berlin, 1930), 29–43; cf. also the more recent *Biblia Patristica Supplément: Philon d'Alexandrie* (Paris, 1982), which notes 8462 citations and allusions. The dominance of Pentateuch texts is also dependent on the preserved writings of Philo, which are almost exclusively concerned with commenting on the books of Moses. Notably, of the citations from the Prophets and the Writings, forty-one occur in allegorical exegesis and only the few remaining are found in the other writings, including the *Questiones* on Genesis and Exodus preserved only in Armenian (cf. also H. Burkhard, *Die Inspiration heiliger Schriften bei Philo von Alexandrien* [Giessen and Basel, 1988], 73–4, 129–46).

[9] Cf. Schürer (rev.) III/1, 618–54; M. Hengel, 'Anonymität, Pseudepigraphie und "literarische Fälschung" in der jüdische–hellenistischen Literatur', in *Pseudepigrapha* I, Entretiens sur l'Antiqué Classique XVIII (Vandœuvres and Geneva, 1971/72), 229–329 (286–92) = *Kleine Schriften I* (WUNT 90; Tübingen, 1996), 196–251 (237–41); H. Merkel, JHSRZ V, 8 (Gütersloh, 1998), Sibyllinen (Lit.).

[10] On Jewish-Hellenistic literature in Palestine, see Hengel, *The 'Hellenization' of Judaea* (see above, p. 20 n. 3), 23–5, 45–7.

The significance of the translation of the Torah into the dominant lingua franca was a unique phenomenon in the Greek world and is practically unparalleled. No comparable barbarian 'holy book' was translated into Greek.[11] Although lacking in rhetorical brilliance and quite verbose, it still acquired isolated *interpretationes graecae*, for example, the famed and influential paraphrase of the divine name in Exodus 3:14 with ἐγώ εἰμι ὁ ὤν or of the primal chaos in Genesis 1:2 with ἀόρατος καὶ ἀκατασκεύαστος, reminiscent of the Greek ἄμορφος ὕλη (Wisd. 11:17). Apologetic changes, such as the prohibition against defaming foreign gods in Exodus 22:27, and harmonizations with Ptolemaic law, can also be identified.[12] The religious language of Diaspora Judaism was thereby deeply imprinted; this was consequently also true for the early church, early Christianity, and its theology.

2. *The Translation of Other Writings*

a) Dependence on Palestinian Judaism

The legend of the seventy-two translators, competent in Greek, who came from Judaea to Alexandria as translators, demonstrates, even though it is not historical, that the translation of Hebrew writings into Greek always presumed a narrow connection with Palestinian Judaism. Already in the third century, competence in Hebrew could no longer be assumed for Egyptian Jews. Practically all their synagogue and grave inscriptions, as well as nearly all their names, are Greek.[13] Philo knew little or no Hebrew; he apparently visited Jerusalem only once as a pilgrim.[14] Indeed, the use and translation of Hebrew writings in Greek was an important instrument for the religious propaganda of the motherland among the Diaspora, which intensified after the attainment of independence through the Maccabean struggle for freedom. The (spurious) letter of the

---

[11] There were indeed many claims, but they were all questionable; cf. W. Speyer, 'Angebliche Übersetzungen des heidnischen und christlichen Altertums', *JAC* 11/12 (1968/69), 26–41, now in *idem, Frühes Christentum im Antiken Strahlungsfeld* (WUNT I/ 50; Tübingen, 1989), 70–85.

[12] Cf., for example, E. Bickerman, 'Two Legal Interpretations of the Septuagint', in *idem, Studies in Jewish and Christian History* (AGJU 9/1; Leiden, 1976 = 1956), 201–24; M. Görg, 'Ptolemäische Theologie in der LXX', in H. Mähler and M. Strocka, eds, *Das ptolemäische Ägypten* (Mainz, 1978), 177–85; W. Barnes Tatum, 'The LXX Version of the Second Commandment: A Polemic against Idols, not Images', *JSS* (1986), 177–95.

[13] Cf. the material brought together in Schürer (rev.) III/1, 38–60. See, more recently, W. Horbury and D. Noy, *Jewish Inscriptions of Graeco-Roman Egypt* (Cambridge, 1992), and the catalogue of names in V. A. Tcherikover and A. Fuks, *Corpus Papyrorum Judaicarum* III (Cambridge, Mass., 1964), 167–96. The number of Hebrew/Aramaic inscriptions is extremely small: see Horbury and Noy nos 3–5, 118, 119, 133.

[14] Cf. Schürer (rev.) III/2, 818–19, 973–4; see also III/1, 479 n. 27.

Jerusalemites to the Jews in Egypt in 2 Maccabees 1:10b–2:18 refers near the end to a temple library founded by Nehemiah where he stored 'the books about the kings and prophets and the writings of David and letters of [foreign] kings about votive offerings' (cf. Ezra 1:7–11; 5:13–6:5; 7:19). Judas is supposed to have reassembled what had been scattered by the war. The reference concludes with the clause: 'If, then, you have need of them, send people to get them for you.' 'Book exports' to Alexandria and other places in the Diaspora facilitated the connection with the motherland and, again, especially with the sanctuary on Zion, increasingly the centre of worldwide Judaism, to which thousands of pilgrims from the Diaspora travelled annually.[15] Remarkably, even in the Judaeo-Hellenistic literature of Egypt, the competing sanctuary at Leontopolis, founded by Onias IV c. 160 BCE, plays virtually no role. The exceptional spiritual radiance of Jerusalem in the Diaspora is consistent with the presence of a large number of returning Greek-speakers who made the Greek translation common in the holy city as well as elsewhere. In this context, the LXX was more than merely a translation of the Hebrew Bible: it constituted the leading witness of Judaeo–Hellenistic theology, ethics and exegesis, both in the Diaspora and in the motherland. Even Herod reinforced the political influence of the Palestinian authorities in the life of the Diaspora since they furthered his own political influence on Diaspora Judaism, whose patron he was. For this reason he summoned to Jerusalem leading Diaspora Jews such as the high priest Simon bar Boethus. Apparently, he—and even before him, the Hasmoneans—engaged in intensive exchanges between the Diaspora and the motherland. Acknowledgement of him by Diaspora Judaism strengthened his significance and reputation in Rome and with the Emperor. An essential factor in influence on the Diaspora was Judaeo-Palestinian literature in the Greek language already mentioned. We see it already in the pre-Roman Hellenistic period. The expanded Greek book of Esther contains a colophon referring to the transportation of the book to Alexandria in the 'fourth year of the reign of Ptolemy and Cleopatra'[16] by a priest or Levite, Dositheos, and his son Ptolemy. 'Lysimachus, the son of Ptolemy, a citizen of Jerusalem,' is supposed to have translated it.

[15] For the role and significance of pilgrimage, cf. S. Safrai, *Die Wallfahrt im Zeitalter des Zweiten Tempels* (Neukirchen, 1981); Y. Amir, 'Die Wallfahrt nach Jerusalem aus Philons Sicht', in *idem, Die hellenistische Gestalt des Judentums bei Philon von Alexandrien* (Neukirchen, 1983), 52–64 (originally in Hebrew in FS A. Schalit [Jerusalem, 1980]); Hengel, *Judentum und Hellenismus* (p. 75 n. 1), 30–1, 112, 186–8, 460 = *idem, Judaism and Hellenism*, 17, 60, 100–1, 252; *idem, The 'Hellenization' of Judaea*, 18, 24–6, 37 = *Kleine Schriften I*, 18–20.24; *idem*, 'Der vorchristliche Paulus', 212–14, 224–5, 240–1, 256–8; *idem*, 'Jerusalem als jüdische und hellenistische Stadt Judaica, Hellenistica et Christiana', *Kleine Schriften II* (WUNT 109; 1999), 115–56.

[16] This information may refer to the years 117, 77 or 48 BCE; presumably the intermediate date should be chosen, following E. Bickerman ('The Colophon of the Greek Book of Esther', *JBL* 63 [1944]: 339–62 [= *Studies in Jewish and Christian History*, 225–45]).

Another translator known to us, the grandson of Ben Sirach, also from Palestine, migrated to Egypt in 132 BCE and there translated his grandfather's work.[17] Probably, however, a not insignificant number of the later writings had already been translated in Palestine. This is thought to be true of 1–2 Ezra (Ezra and Nehemiah) and 1 Maccabees, among others.[18] The Greek language was more widespread in the motherland after the third century BCE than generally acknowledged, and Greek authors and translators worked there long before the well-known Judaeo/Judaeo-Christian triad of Theodotion, Aquila and Symmachus in the second century CE.[19] Fragments of LXX texts have been found even at Qumran in the library of the Essenes, who were hostile to all Greek cultural influence.[20] All this indicates, however, that a reciprocal literary exchange and a related translation process existed between the Palestinian motherland and the Greek-speaking Diaspora over a long period in which the motherland tended to give and the Diaspora to receive. One can certainly assume, however, that works such as Wisdom or the writings of Philo were also read in Jerusalem. The LXX had long been at home there.

This relative dependence on Palestinian Judaism and reciprocal literary connection led repeatedly, for example, to new revisions of the Greek texts in the light of the Hebrew text, viewed as authentic, although—except for the Torah, which was the earliest to be established—it was not yet itself clearly determined in the pre-Christian era. We find such a 'revised' text in the Minor Prophets scroll first published by Barthélemy, found in the Judaean wilderness and probably dating

---

[17] Cf. Harl, Dorival and Munnich, 86–9. According to the prologue, in addition to the Torah, the prophets, and at least a portion of the Hagiographa, already existed in Greek when he began his translation.

[18] On the state of the discussion, see Harl, Dorival and Munnich, 101–9. They regard Canticles, Lamentations, Ruth, Esther (because of the colophon, see n. 16 above), and Qoheleth as having certainly been translated in Palestine. For 1 Ezra, see B. Z. Wacholder, *Eupolemos: A Study of Judaeo–Greek Literature* (Cincinnati, 1974), 274–6, 279. On 1 Maccabees, see the unfounded argument of G. Mussies, 'Greek in Palestine and the Diaspora', in *The Jewish People in the First Century*, S. Safrai and M. Stern, eds (CRII/2; Assen and Amsterdam, 1976), 1040–64 (esp. 1054); contrast Harl, Dorival and Munnich, 105. The thesis of the Palestinian origin of the Psalms translation is also represented; cf. A. van der Kooij, 'On the Place of Origin of the Old Greek of Psalms', *VT* 33 (1983), 67–74; H.-J. Venetz, *Die Quinta des Psalteriums: Ein Beitrag zur Septuaginta-und Hexaplaforschung* (Hildesheim, 1974), *contra* Harl, Dorival and Munnich, 104; see also Hengel, *The 'Hellenization' of Judaea* (p. 20 n. 3), 25; cf. J. Schaper, 'Der Septuaginta-Psalter als Dokument jüdischer Eschatologie', in *Die Septuaginta zwischen Judentum und Christentum*, M. Hengel and A. M. Schwemer, eds (WUNT 72; Tübingen, 1994), 38–61, and *idem*, Eschatology in the Greek Psalter (WUNT II/76; 1995), 34–45.

[19] Cf. Mussies (see above, n. 18), 'Greek', and Hengel, *The 'Hellenization' of Judaea*, 7–29, 63–89 (with bibliography) = *Kleine Schriften I*, 12–51, 72–85.

[20] Cf. M. Hengel, 'Qumran und der Hellenismus', in *Qumrân*, M. Delcor, ed. (BEThL 46; Paris and Leuven, 1978), 333–72 (339) = *Kleine Schriften I*, 228–94 (263–4). For the LXX fragments, see above, p. 29 n. 13 and p. 41 n. 54.

from the middle of the first century BCE. It has also been published in a substantial edition by E. Tov (see above, p. 29 n. 13). The text already bears marked elements of the later revisions of the second century, probably due to the influence of Palestinian scholars. D. A. Koch points out that Paul relies on a Hebrew-oriented revision of the Greek translation for his citations from Isaiah, Job and 1 Kings. In my opinion, the possibility cannot be excluded that the Apostle himself undertook such a revision. Even Justin is also fully aware of certain differences between his Christian text and that utilized by the Jews which he considered— incorrectly—to be counterfeit. In the discussion with the Jews he valued citations from the Jewish text.[21]

This tendency to achieve the greatest possible approximation to the original text also continues after the schism between Jews and Christians. On the Jewish side, this took place through significant alterations to the old LXX text in the 'revisions' of Aquila and Theodotion, whose editions could almost be designated new translations. This tendency reached a new zenith in the third and fourth centuries, via the influence of Origen's Hexapla with its critical textual comparison, in the subsequent recensions attributed to Lucian and Hesychius, and in Jerome's Vulgate translation.[22] This influence always exercised a corrective as well as an unsettling, even a confusing, effect. This can be demonstrated in the history of the influence of the Hexapla and in the laborious attempt of modern LXX editors to reconstruct the original LXX behind the various recensions and forms of the text. Even the various attempts to reduce the canon more or less strictly to the books of the Hebrew Bible (or even to reach back to the original wording) are, essentially, a consequence of the influence of the motherland, which existed from the outset. It is hardly accidental that both Origen and Jerome undertook their philological work with the biblical text in Palestine, Caesarea and Bethlehem, and were in contact with Jewish scholars.

b) The Translation and Origin of Individual Writings

The translation into Greek of those documents later assembled in the Hebrew canon may have continued for about three centuries into the middle of the first century, indeed even to the beginning of the second century CE. It starts with the Pentateuch and ends with Qoheleth and 2 Ezra (Ezra and Nehemiah) after the very novelistic version of so-called 1 Ezra was first distributed (see below, pp. 86–7). That is, in various periods and at different places numerous translators worked on 'the' Septuagint. This is especially true if one also includes the revisers of the text.

[21] See above, pp. 28–9. For Paul, see below, pp. 89–90.
[22] Cf. Harl, Dorival and Munnich, 162–73.

Unfortunately, we have only a very few chronological reference points for the historical details of this translation process.[23] It is fundamental that these documents in their Greek form comprise no unity whatsoever; rather, each must be investigated individually, although they all naturally draw on the great linguistic reservoir of the Greek Pentateuch and are, to a significant degree, linguistically shaped by it. Especially interesting is the comparison with the pre-Masoretic and pre-Christian texts from Qumran, some of which diverge substantially on occasion from the rabbinic-Masoretic text transmitted to us. But despite interesting parallels one should not overlook the remark of E. Tov: 'At Qumran only a very small number of texts was found that were closely related to the original text of the LXX (less than five per cent of the biblical texts). The Hebrew scrolls from which the LXX was translated in Egypt have not been found in Qumran.'

We possess in the LXX also two, three, or even more, versions of several books, often starkly divergent. The number of the sometimes substantially divergent forms of the text is greater than in the New Testament. Rahlfs, in his small edition of the LXX, sometimes offers them in synoptic form, as in Joshua 19 (A and B), Judges (A and B), Tobit (B/A and Sin) and Daniel (LXX and [proto-]Theodotion); in addition, there are numerous smaller alterations and awkward transpositions which make reference difficult, as in the Psalms or Jeremiah.[24] As a rule, these alterations can be traced to various forms of the original.

For a few books, the translators had exemplars that diverged significantly from the Masoretic text. A Hebrew text of 4Q for 1 and 2 Samuel, which has a good many agreements with the LXX, discovered almost forty years ago at Qumran and first published (partially) in 1978, exists in three manuscripts. One, written in palaeo-Hebrew script seems, since it dates far into the third century, to be the very oldest biblical text we possess. The author of Chronicles already had this form of the text.[25] Since the Masoretic text is significantly inferior here to the

---

[23] A list with the probable dates of translation appears in Harl, Dorival and Munnich, 96–8.

[24] The differences with respect to the Masoretic text in the individual books are assembled in Swete, 'The Septuaginta as a Version', 314–42. For Qumran and the LXX see E. Tov, *The Greek and Hebrew Bible*, 285–300 (quotation 300).

[25] E. Ulrich *(The Qumran Text of Samuel and Josephus,* HSM 19 [Missoula, 1978]) published the context of the 4QSam[a] scroll and almost all the *variae lectiones* and investigated its relationship to the LXX recensions and Josephus' exemplar. See, however, the review of E. Tov in *The Greek and Hebrew Bible*, 273–83: 'the argument between 4QSam[a] and the LXX is smaller than suggested by Ulrich'. His theses sparked an intense debate and have not gone unchallenged; cf. the overview in van der Woude (see above, p. 46 n. 71), 289–92; Jellicoe, 283–90; Harl, Dorival and Munnich, 175–6. E. Ulrich ('The Biblical Scrolls from Qumran Cave 4: A Progress Report of their Publication', *RQ* 14/2 [1989], 207–28) offers an overview of all the biblical fragments from 4Q. The volume

LXX exemplar, the LXX acquires special significance in relation to some of these fragments from 4Q, especially since the translators worked very precisely.

In contrast, the translation of Isaiah is more context-related. It is to be dated—with Seeligmann[26]—to the early Maccabean period, i.e. in the middle of the second century, after the Jewish high priest Onias IV founded the temple at Leontopolis (c. 160) and also strengthened the political self-consciousness of Jews in Egypt; at a few points the Ptolemaic-Egyptian milieu and the historical situation of its origin becomes evident (cf. Isa. 19:18–21). According to more recent studies, allusions are made even to the Roman conquest of Carthage and the Parthian conquest of Babylon (146 and 141 BCE respectively).[27] It already presumes the translation of the Psalms, the Minor Prophets and Ezekiel.[28] A little later, the Judaeo-Palestinian historian Eupolemos seems to have utilized Chronicles in Greek translation for his work.[29] The possibility cannot be excluded that the Isaiah-LXX involves an updating revision of an older translation. I consider it unlikely that the most important prophetic book would be translated so late. The prologue of Sirach, 2 Maccabees 2:13 and the colophon of Esther demonstrate that the very period, during and after the Maccabean revolt, that led indirectly to a strengthening of Jewry in Egypt, was an epoch of intensive translation activity into Greek, not only in Egypt, but also in the motherland. One can well understand the complaint of the grandson and translator of Ben Sirach in his prologue about the difficulty of such translation from Hebrew into Greek. But apparently in this period many Jews did not flinch from this labour. This series of new translations, which created an entirely new literary corpus, was an intellectual accomplishment of the first order. As indicated by the fragments preserved in Alexander Polyhistor, this translation process was paralleled by a vital

---

(no. 54) contains investigations of 4QJudg[a] and 4QSam[a]; cf. Tov (see above, p. 20 n. 3), *Unpublished Qumran Texts*, 95, and the essays in Brooke and Lindars, *The Septuagint and the Dead Sea Scrolls*, 11–297; cf. *DJD* IX, 161–97.

[26] I. L. Seeligmann, *The Septuagint Version of Isaiah* (Leiden, 1948); Jellicoe, 299–300.

[27] See A. van der Kooij, *Die alten Textzeugen des Jesajabuches* (OBO 35; Freiburg and Göttingen, 1981), 30; Harl, Dorival and Munnich, 97: some time between 170 and 132.

[28] Seeligmann (see above, n. 26), 70–2, 91–3. Cf. also A. van der Kooij, 'The Old Greek of Isaiah in Relation to the Qumran Texts of Isaiah', in Brooke and Lindars, 195–213: 'LXX Isa and 1QIsa[a] reflect a free approach toward their Vorlage' (197).

[29] Harl, Dorival and Munnich, 90: Eupolemos harmonized 1 Kings and 2 Chronicles; for Eupolemos himself, cf. 2 Maccabees 4:11 and 1 Maccabees 8:17; text with commentary: C. R. Holladay, *Fragments from Hellenistic Jewish Authors*, Vol. I: Historians (Chico, California, 1983), 93–158. See also Hengel, *Judentum und Hellenismus*; *Iidem, Kleine Schriften I*, 40–1, 43–4, 202–3; 169–75; Wacholder; Schürer (rev.) III/1, 517–21.

literary productivity dependent on the LXX, in original Greek and in Greek literary forms.

The translation of Jeremiah is severely abbreviated. The LXX offers a text abridged by roughly an eighth, which depends—as demonstrated again by fragments from Qumran—at least in part on an abbreviated Hebrew original.[30] By contrast, in the very free translation of Job, already strongly influenced by Hellenistic thought, the translator probably abbreviated the extremely difficult text by roughly 20 per cent. Consequently the reconstruction of the unabridged Job caused both Origen and Jerome extreme difficulties. The translator of Job added an appendix to the abridged work in which Job was identified with the Edomite king Jobab (Gen. 36:33; cf. 9–13) and at the same time became Esau's grandson and thus Abraham's descendant. A Jewish 'historian', Aristeas, preserved in a fragment of Alexander Polyhistor, seems to have extended this tradition. The later Judaeo-Hellenistic *Testament of Job* even makes Job an Egyptian king. The book of Job, which on the basis of its content seems more like a 'foreign body', is thus linked to biblical history.[31] The translator of Proverbs was even more intensely open to the spirit of the times. He not only inserted purely Greek proverbs, but also experimented with hexameters and iambics. He portrayed the pre-existent wisdom of Proverbs 8:22–24 in a form resembling the Platonic world-soul.[32]

In view of the freedom of translation, it seems to me an open question whether the interpreters of Job and Proverbs already regarded them as sacrosanct 'Holy Scripture' or rather as didactic wisdom books, analogous to the numerous 'international' wisdom books within and beyond Israel. This is especially true since 'Job' involves a presumably non-Israelite 'author'. Indeed, the transmission history of such wisdom writings as Ahiqar, parts of which were included in Aesop's *Vita*, Sirach, Tobit, the *Testaments of the Twelve Patriarchs* and the sayings of Sextus or Menander demonstrate how easily they could be expanded or abridged.

---

[30] Cf. Eissfeldt, 469–70; Jellicoe, 300–1; E. Tov, *The Septuagint Translation of Jeremiah and Baruch: A Discussion of an Early Revision of the LXX of Jeremiah 29–52 and Baruch 1:1–3:8* (HSM 8; Missoula, 1976); Harl, Dorival and Munnich, 180. For the Qumran discoveries, see the summary in van der Woude (se above, p. 46 n. 71), 294–5: '. . . that the fragments of 4QJer^b display a text that corresponds in many respects, not only textually but also structurally . . . to LXX Jer . . .', while 4QJer^a resembles the Masoretic text.

[31] See J. Ziegler, 'Der textkritische Wert der Septuaginta des Buches Job', in *idem*, 9–28 (originally published in 1934); *idem*, *Beiträge zum griechischen Job* (MSU 18; Göttingen, 1985); *idem*, *Job* (Septuaginta: Vetus Testamentum Graecum XI/4; Göttingen, 1982), 9; Swete, 255–6; Harl, Dorival and Munnich, 91, 179; for the historian Aristeas, cf. Schürer (rev.) III/1, 525–6, and C. A. Holladay (see above, p. 85 n. 29), Vol. I, 261–75; for *TestJob*, Schürer, 552–5.

[32] Swete, 255; Harl, Dorival and Munnich, 179; Hengel, *Judentum und Hellenismus* (p. 75 n. 1), 292–5; G. Schimanowski, *Weisheit und Messias* (WUNT II/17; Tübingen, 1985), 35–8.

Free supplementation also occurs, however, in more novelistic fashion, in individual historical books. Most notably here, the so-called 1 (LXX) or 3 (Vulgate-Appendix) Ezra, composed from parts of 2 Chronicles, Ezra and Nehemiah, was expanded by adding the wisdom novella of the contest of the royal pages before Darius in which Zerubbabel prevails (chs 3 and 4). In contrast to the hypothesis that this was an original portion of the chronicler's history, it seems more likely that the translator made a selection leading from Josiah's celebration of Passover, via the destruction of Jerusalem and the return from Exile, to the reading of the law under Nehemiah (7:72–8:13a). He combined them by means of the central account of how Zerubbabel's wisdom gained the permission to return. The translation seems to presume Judah's independence under Simon (141 BCE; 4:49–50). The author was concerned with creating, through selection, expansion and style, a historical account easily read by Greek readers and more interesting for Greek-speaking Diaspora Jewry than the original book of Ezra.[33] His account agreeably bridges the historical gap between Josiah, the last pious king before the Exile and the reform efforts of Ezra and Nehemiah. The older '2 Ezra' (Ezra and Nehemiah) was probably translated only significantly later in the first century CE. Although in his *Antiquities,* written toward the end of the first century, Josephus had already argued for the Palestinian canon (see below, pp. 99–100), he used 1 Ezra as an exemplar, rather than the two 'canonical' books of the Hebrew canon, probably because of the greater readability mentioned above. Here and at countless other points his great literary freedom in relation to the sacred text is evident. To him, making a favourable impression on the reader was more important than 'fidelity to the text' and historico-philological precision. This was true for most Jewish—also for early Christian—literature between the second centuries BCE and CE.

Esther, too, was expanded in a novelistic-didactic manner when translated into Greek by the Jerusalemite Lysimachus, son of Ptolemy, in the second half of the second century: the author added as an introduction to this almost profane novella, in the original form of which religious motifs are subdued, Mordecai's dream and its interpretation; also two royal letters and one prayer each from Mordecai and Esther. The latter give a genuinely religious content to the originally profane work—the Hebrew version does not mention God, for example. In contrast, θεός and κύριος appear about twenty-five times each in the expanded Greek version. It also mitigates the offensive notion that a

---

[33] Jellicoe, 290–4: '. . . the Greek Esdras . . . the first attempt to present the account of the Return in Hellenistic dress' (291); R. Hanhart, *Text und Textgeschichte des 1 Esra-Buches* (MSU 12; Göttingen, 1974), 17–18; in general, Schürer (rev.) III/2, 708–18. J. T. Milik claims to have discovered an Aramaic precursor to the prayer of Esther in 4Q; see 'Les modèles aramées du livre d'Esther dans la Grotte 4 de Qumrân', *RQ* 15 (1991/92), 321–406; but see above, p. 48 n. 75.

Jewess would marry a pagan ruler (ch. 26). Even the political scenario is altered to fit the times: in 10:14 Haman, the Agagite (i.e. Amalekite; cf. 1 Sam. 15:8–9, 32–3), becomes a Macedonian who intends to betray the Persian empire to the Macedonians. Here, too, we have various forms of the text, the LXX proper and a relatively free revision originating in a relatively early period. In the *Antiquities* Josephus utilizes the expanded LXX text in his own revision; yet another forms the exemplar of the Old Latin.[34] One can proceed from the assumption that both 1 Ezra and Esther were not translated as 'Holy Scriptures', but as books of religious instruction that also promised good entertainment. In addition, Esther is intended, as the colophon demonstrates, to encourage the joyous celebration of Purim in Alexandria.

The book of Daniel, including the various 'apocryphal' Daniel fragments from 4Q,[35] permits one to conjecture that the canonized version was composed at the climax of the persecution by Antiochus IV Epiphanes in 165 BCE. In this case the unknown apocalypticist presumably belonged to the circle of the 'Hasidim' mentioned at the end of Daniel 11 as *maśkîlîm*.[36] The translation followed rather early, about one or two generations later. The narrative additions to Daniel (Susanna and Bel and the Dragon) may belong to this wider narrative circle. The Prayer of Azariah and the Song of the Three Young Men are added as liturgical texts. Like the prayers in Esther, they are intended to intensify the didactic character of the 'martyr story' thus emphasized by adding a happy ending to Daniel 3. Once again, there are two versions: (1) the version by Jerome (*Prologus in Danihele Propheta*), incorrectly attributed to Theodotion, but which is nevertheless older than the true Theodotion, which dominates in Christian manuscripts, and (2) the LXX, preserved only in the Syrohexapla, minuscule 88, and, partially, in Papyrus 967, which, in extensive sections, represents more a paraphrase than a translation and which is replaced by the literal (Pseudo-) Theodotionic version. R. Albertz seeks to demonstrate that a 'precursor' of the younger, Aramaic, canonical Daniel narrative underlies the LXX text of Daniel 4–6, which is significantly divergent and, in part, more extensive. He points to an unresolved problem, although his suggestion

---

[34] See R. Hanhart, *Esther* (Septuaginta: Vetus Testamentum Graecum VIII/3; Göttingen, 1966, 2nd edn 1983), 87–9, 96–8; more generally, Schürer (rev.) III/2, 718–22.

[35] Cf. 4QorNab and the Pseudo-Daniel-cycle, 4QpsDan ar[a-c] (see Schürer [rev.] III/1, 440–3; van der Woude (see above, p. 46 n. 71), 'Qumranforschung', 268–9); on the canonical Daniel fragments, see van der Woude, loc. cit., 301–2, and, more recently, Tov, 'Unpublished Qumran Texts', 96–8 (see above, p. 46 n. 71).

[36] For the *ḥasîdîm*, see 1 Macc. 2:42; 7:13; 2 Macc. 14:6. See also Hengel, *Judentum und Hellenismus*, 319–21 = *idem, Judaism and Hellenism*, 175–6; and *idem*, 'Schriftauslegung und Schriftwerdung', in *idem*, 'Judaica, Hellenistica et Christians', *Klein Schriften II* (WUNT 109; 1999), 44–6.

has not itself found widespread agreement.[37] Josephus knew the LXX version of Daniel, although he did not take the additions into account, perhaps because the 'canonical' Daniel, which he valued very much as a work of prophetic oracles, was, for him, in contrast to Ezra and Esther, already 'integral'. According to him, its already fulfilled oracles had convinced Alexander the Great in Jerusalem of its divine origin and refuted the Epicurean denial of God's prescience (*Ant* 10:277). This express estimation of Daniel is consistent with his own report (*Vita* 12) that he had aligned himself with the Pharisees. The problem is only when he did so. This does not preclude the possibility that he also fell back on an Alexandrian legend for his Alexander-Daniel story.

Qoheleth and Canticles were, like 2 Ezra, translated only very late. In Qoheleth, the (rabbinic) translation principles of an Aquila are already evident.[38] Indeed, I doubt whether the translation of Qoheleth was first produced by Aquila, the student of Aqiba, at the beginning of the second century.[39] Had this been so, then it would not have been so readily accepted by the church and already commented upon in the third century (see above, p. 68–9). Its translation may go back to a first-century Pharisaic school of translators, whose tendencies Aquila extended in strengthened form and which had already revised the LXX of the prophets and other documents. Apparently, even Paul utilized a revised text for Isaiah, Job and 1 and 2 Kings, i.e. for relatively freely translated Old Testament texts. I have already said that it is entirely possible that Paul himself took up recensional alterations in the text since, as a Pharisee and scholar who had studied in Jerusalem, he knew the original.[40] After the building of the Herodian temple, Jerusalem became even more than previously the religious centre of world Judaism. The Pharisees, the most influential religious party in Palestine, must have had a particular interest that the form of the text they had established should also gain entry into the Diaspora synagogues and that its gradually forming canon should prevail there too.[41] An example of this

[37] See above, p. 42 n. 57; Harl, Dorival and Munnich, 183–4.

[38] Cf. Jellicoe, 82; G. Bertram, 'Hebräischer und Griechischer Qohelet', *ZAW* 64 (1952), 26–49.

[39] So Barthélemy (see above, p. 29 n. 13), *Les devanciers d'Aquila*, 32–3, 158–9.

[40] See above, pp. 82–3 and below, pp. 108–9. Cf. Deines (see above, p. 43 n. 58), *Jüdische Steingefässe*, 10.

[41] On the problem of a specific Pharisaic canon, cf. Beckwith, 366–9; Barthélemy (see above, p. 44 n. 66), 'L'état de la bible juive,' 22–4. Reports in rabbinic literature that speak of the revision of texts in Jerusalem should be compared; cf. *mMQ* 3:4; *tYoma* 4:18–19; *ySheq* 4:3 (48a); *bYoma* 70a; *bKet* 106a. Cf. Safrai (*Wallfahrt*, 4, 256–7, 262–3) who assumes that the pilgrims brought their own scripture scrolls with them to Jerusalem 'in order to have them corrected in the temple against the "book of the forecourt" found in the care of the temple scribes' (262). The sale of Greek scriptural scrolls to festival pilgrims will also have played a role here. Acts 8:27–8 contains interesting evidence of

influence is the first reference to this very 'canon' of twenty-two writings in Josephus (*Ap* 1:37–42).

They engaged on two fronts: on the one side, they confronted the Essenes (and perhaps also even other Jewish sects), who recognized a much larger number of 'Holy Scriptures'. Among the roughly 800 different scrolls in the library at Qumran of which fragments are preserved, we find all the books of the Hebrew canon except Esther, admittedly in very different numbers. Here, as in early Christianity, the most important book seems to have been the Psalms, with thirty-four exemplars, although the canon of Psalms was not yet fully fixed. It is followed, in both communities, by Isaiah. Alongside these stand, in equally significant numbers, the various sectarian writings, including the *Temple Scroll*, in which God speaks to Moses in the first person, but also other 'apocryphal' and 'pseudepigraphical' books (some of which go back to the third century BCE) such as the *Book of Jubilees*, Enoch documents, patriarchal testaments, Tobit (in four Aramaic examplars and one Hebrew), Sirach, etc.[42] This threatening multitude must be held back with a dam, 'so that', to use a rabbinic formula, 'the divisions in Israel cease' (*bMeg* 3a). On the other side stood the Samaritan heretics, who recognized only the Torah as canonical, and—on this point not so widely removed from them—the Sadducees, who rejected any transcendental-eschatological future hope and consequently could hardly have a very positive relationship to properly prophetic books. They certainly did not recognize the book of Daniel.[43]

---

this. The Ethiopian financial official who came to Jerusalem to worship, i.e. in order to participate in one of the pilgrim festivals, was, as a eunuch, not a proselyte but a God-fearer who had aligned with the Jewish community (cf. M. Hengel, 'Der Historiker Lukas und die Geographie Palästinas in der Apostelgeschichte', *ZDPV* 99 [1983], 147–82 [164–5]). He can hardly have known Hebrew. One must assume therefore that the Isaiah scroll he read on the journey home was written in Greek (the verses cited from Isaiah 53 in vv. 32–3 correspond verbatim to the LXX version, which differs in this passage markedly from the Masoretic text) and that he probably bought it during his stay in the holy city. Luke recounted the story, whose historicity, naturally, cannot be established, but which surely has a historical core, 'in accordance with the situation' (cf. J. Roloff, *Apostelgeschichte* [NTD 5; Göttingen, 1981], 140–1). For the influence of the Pharisees on Palestinian Judaism after Herod, see Deines (see above, p. 43 n. 58), *Jüdische Steingefässe*, 20–2, 244–6, 269–70, 278–83, and *idem*, *Die Pharisäer* (WUNT 101; Tübingen, 1997), 534–55.

[42] Cf. the summaries in van der Woude (see above, p. 46 n. 71), 'Qumranforschung', 274–304; on the problem of the canon, see J. Maier, 'Zur Frage des biblischen Kanons im Frühjudentum im Licht der Qumranfunde', *JBTh* 3 (1988): 135–46; O. Betz, 'Das Problem des "Kanons" in den Texten von Qumran', in G. Maier, ed., *Der Kanon der Bibel* (Giessen and Wuppertal, 1990), 70–82; Tov, 'Unpublished Qumran Texts', 94–103. Cf. above, p. 45 n. 67.

[43] On the relation of the Sadducees to the 'Holy Scriptures', see J. Le Moyne, *Les Sadducéens* (Paris, 1972), 357–9.

c) The Writings Not Found in the Hebrew Canon

There were ten or eleven writings not found in the Pharisaic-rabbinic canon which the church recognized, although only slowly and half-heartedly. These were the additions to Daniel and Esther, Tobit, Judith, Susanna, Baruch, Epistula Jeremiae, Sirach, Wisdom, 1–4 Maccabees; of these 3 and 4 Maccabees were not 'received' in the West at all, and in the East only conditionally. They had a great deal in common.

1. They all belong to the Graeco-Roman period, i.e. they originated between the third century BCE and the first century CE; Tobit, Susanna, other additions to Daniel, and the Epistula Jeremiae may come from the third century, and Sirach from the beginning of the second century. The additions to Esther, Judith and 1 Maccabees belong to the period after the victorious Maccabean rebellion. 2 Maccabees, a pleasantly entertaining and instructive epitome of the five books of Jason of Cyrene, from the time after the death of Judas Maccabeus (161 BCE), and the somewhat later Wisdom originated in the first half of the first century BCE. 3 and 4 Maccabees and Baruch were composed under Roman domination. Assuming the Pharisaic thesis that prophetic inspiration ceased and the period of the scholars began with Ezra (or Nehemiah),[44] their exclusion from the Palestinian 'canon' was thoroughly justified. The inclusion of Qoheleth, Daniel and Esther (and other relatively late writings such as Canticles, the final version of Proverbs, and the books of Chronicles) was based, by contrast, on a 'historical error'. Evidence of awareness that there was a problem can be seen in the fact that, in Palestine in contrast to the Greek Bible (see above, pp. 59–60), Daniel was not counted in the prophetic corpus (this was already closed in the second century), but included among the 'hagiographa'.[45] Qoheleth was still not valued as canonical in the school of Shammai in the first century CE. R. Menasiah (c. 180 CE) could see in it only Solomon's profane wisdom. The earlier doubt of the wise men was later attributed to the fact that 'they found words in it that tended toward heresy (מינות)'.[46] There

[44] See above, pp. 43–4 and p. 44 n. 64. See also Hengel, 'Schriftauslegung' (see above, p. 45 n. 67), 20–8.

[45] In Qumran, however, he was considered a prophet, as 4QFlor 2:3 attests; for Josephus, too, he assumes a leading place. Cf. also Ellis (see above, p. 57 n. 2), *Old Testament*, 41–6, who assumes that Daniel's status was in dispute and that he was reckoned among the prophets in at least some circles. This was especially true for those Diaspora Jews (or Christians) who included Daniel among the prophetic books following Ezekiel.

[46] *mYad* 3:5; *mEd* 5:3; *tEd* 2:7; *tYad* 2:14; *PRK* 8:1; 24:14; *QohR* 1:4; citations in Bill. IV:426–9. The extent to which this debate was serious, however, is disputed. Apparently pedagogical grounds, primarily, led some teacher to conceal the book לגנז, a procedure that attached high esteem to the concealed object (*contra tShab* 13:5: one may burn heretical books and gods, see above, pp. 45–6). ARN 1 recounts that Proverbs, Canticles

was also a certain, less enduring discussion concerning Ezekiel, Canticles and Proverbs. The relatively late origin and acceptance of Esther may have also played a role in the discussion about it, although the command to read 'the Esther scroll' on Purim very quickly made it and the related national festival especially popular.[47] The oldest evidence for the celebration of the festival is 2 Maccabees 15:37 (the 14th Adar as the 'Day of Mordecai'); i.e. the festival was established, at the latest, in the middle of the first century BCE. Canticles, properly a profane love poem, was less discussed. It must have been interpreted allegorically very early. Only in this way can we account for the fact that, with four exemplars recovered—three from Cave 4—it was highly esteemed in the library at Qumran. Aqiba described the fact that its 'canonicity' could be doubted as completely beyond comprehension.[48] Its reception in the church involved similar assumptions: Origen and other Church Fathers commented on it enthusiastically; the sober critic Theodore of Mopsuesta wanted to eliminate it as a profane song. The rejection of the ten or eleven documents, the later 'Christian apocrypha', by the Pharisees and later rabbis, is thus less a question of content than of chronology. Judith (if it was written in Hebrew or Aramaic, which is possible but not certain) and Tobit would fit in the Hebrew canon just as well as Esther and Daniel. As for Sirach, this was the first Judaeo-

---

and Qoheleth were 'concealed' since Solomon's days, before they were interpreted by Hezekiah's men or the men of the Great Assembly, i.e. before their fundamental agreement with the 'canon within the canon', the books of Moses, was demonstrated. The story is recounted as an illustration of the first maxim of the men of the Great Assembly: 'Make decisions cautiously.' Then verses that occasion objections and that can only be satisfactorily interpreted after a certain time are cited (Prov. 7:7–20; Cant. 7:11, 12–13; Qoh. 11:9). Until then, however, the books remain concealed in order to prevent an 'incautious decision' (on this passage, compare also Stemberger [p. 44 n. 66], 'Jabne', 170–2). According to this and other passages, canonicity is demonstrated in relation to the Torah. Concerning the debate over Qoheleth, cf. also Beckwith, 283–88, 297–302, 310–11, 319–21; Barthélemy, 'L'état de la bible juive', 28–30.

[47] For Esther, cf. bMeg 7a; yMeg 1:4 (70d): the nationalistic and xenophobic aspect of the book made it unpopular, especially in the Babylonian Diaspora; on the other hand, the Esther scroll is the only book in the Tanak normally found as a private possession (cf. Barthélemny, loc. cit., on bSanh 100a). The Mishnah tractate Megilla ('scroll') is, correspondingly, devoted to this book and the Purim festival (cf. for the rabbinic passages, Bill. IV:429–32; see also Barthélemy, 'L'état de la bible juive', 38–40; Beckwith, 288–97, 322–3; Harl, Dorival and Munnich (see above, p. 44 n. 66), 325–6; Rüger, 'Werden', 180–1).

[48] On the manuscripts from Qumran, see van der Woude (see above, p. 46 n. 71), 'Qumran-forschung', 300, and Ulrich (see above, p. 84 n. 25), 'Biblical Scrolls from Qumran Cave 4', 226–7: 4QCant[a, b, c]; 6QCant; for the rabbinic discussion, see mYad 3:5 and Bill. IV:432–3; Beckwith, 321–2. The oldest evidence of the allegorical interpretation is 4 Ezra 5:23–30, cf. Eissfeldt, 661; Rüger (see above, p. 44 n. 66), 'Werden', 180. Cf. also 2 John 2,13; Revelation 3:20. Cf. also M. Hengel, Die auserwählte Herrin (see above, p. 69 n. 34).

Palestinian document to know, under Hellenistic influence, the concept of 'intellectual property',[49] so that, although a typical wisdom document, it was named after its author; this very openness led to rejection. Meanwhile, Qoheleth, only one or two generations older and semi-cloaked under a pseudonym, was ultimately accepted. Had Ben Sirach written his work as a pseud-epigraphon of an older biblical author, perhaps as a work of Solomon, it would presumably have become as canonical as the (redacted) book of Daniel, a generation later (165 BCE). Despite the strict prohibition, a portion of these 'outer' documents continued to be read in at least some Jewish circles; others were even later translated into Hebrew and Aramaic so that their influence did not cease even after their exclusion (see above, pp. 45–6).

2. Except for Wisdom and 2–4 Maccabees (and perhaps Susanna) *all of these books probably had Hebrew or Aramaic exemplars* and were translated into Greek, to be sure not yet as 'Holy Scriptures', but in order to edify, educate or entertain. Additionally, some also served a certain propaganda purpose in order to tie Diaspora Judaism even more firmly to the nation's history and to the motherland and thus, at the same time, to covenant, law and sanctuary. Even narrative books such as 2–4 Maccabees, written originally in the Greek language with a degree of rhetorico-literary skill, have these tendencies. Despite their varied form all, without exception, possess a marked 'national-religious' and, therefore, 'theocratic' character. They emphasize, for example, that pagan rulers should refrain from attacking God's people lest they become subject to judgement. The most high God is on the side of Israel or the Jews and does not allow misdeeds committed against his people to go unavenged. In this respect, 2 Maccabees, attributed to Jason of Cyrene and very Hellenistic in character, stands closer to Hasidic-Pharisaic piety than the pro-Hasmonean 1 Maccabees, written originally in Hebrew and more in the style of Chronicles, with Sadducean elements and already possessing almost the character of profane Hellenistic historiography. Typical of this profane quality is the panegyric on Simon Maccabeus in 1 Maccabees 14:4–5 and especially the final chapters of the book, dealing with the period following the installation of Jonathan as high priest by the Seleucid usurper Alexander Balas (10–16). A comparison of this with the Praise of the Fathers in Ben Sirach—about one hundred years earlier—demonstrates the change in the intellectual climate. The fact that religious instruction and pleasant entertainment of the readers are not mutually contradictory is evident from the conclusion given by the unknown epitomizer to his summary of the five-volume older history by Jason of Cyrene:

---

[49] Cf. Hengel, *Judentum und Hellenismus*, 145–6, 214–16 = *idem*, *Judaism and Hellenism*, 78–9, 116–17; *idem*, 'Schriftauslegung' (see above, p. 45 n. 67), 35–44.

For just as it is harmful to drink wine alone, or, again, to drink water alone, while wine mixed with water is sweet and delicious and enhances one's enjoyment, so also the style of the story delights the ears of those who hear the work.[50]

This easy-to-read 'religious entertainment literature' strengthens the national identity of educated Diaspora Judaism and likewise, at a later date, supplies appropriate ethical exhortation and instruction for catechumens and Christian families.

Nor is this national, theocratic character absent from the wisdom documents, Tobit, Sirach, Baruch and Wisdom.[51] A prominent theme in these is the glorification of the Torah; the divine wisdom manifest in it is a prominent additional theme, as is the harsh rejection of foolish and immoral pagan worship. Additional common elements in this literature are the descriptions of the wondrous deliverance of God's people from oppression and the distress of war and—an innovation of the Hellenistic period—the incipient glorification of the martyr prepared to surrender his life for the law and the nation. Only now does the formula of 'dying for' law, God and nation enter Jewish literature.[52] All these features could have made these documents acceptable for Pharisaic-rabbinic Judaism if their late origin had not still been evident in the first century CE. It is all the more puzzling that the Christian church of the second century held to them so that they were finally accepted in the Christian canon, although with a certain persistent second-class character, while the official synagogue in the second century finally distanced itself from them.

3. Notably, too, *apocalyptic-eschatological components are almost totally absent* from the 'apocryphal' writings accepted by the church (e.g. 1 Macc., Jud., Wisd.) or play only a marginal role, limited in a particularistic, Judaic manner.[53] The resurrection of the dead is mentioned only in 2 Maccabees 7:9, 14; 12:43, and the coming of the Messiah is not mentioned at all, with the possible exception of *Psalms of Solomon* 17 and 18, which the church ultimately did not accept.[54]

---

[50] 2 Macc. 15:40; cf. 2:20–33, where the unknown epitomizer explicitly acknowledges his exemplar (Jason of Cyrene) and his own objectives, to teach and to entertain. It is also clear that this author had not the most remote notion of publishing his book as a sacred text. For Jason, cf. Hengel, *Judentum und Hellenismus*, 176–86 = *idem*, *Judaism and Hellenism*, 95–100.

[51] Cf., for example, Sirach 36:1–18; Tobit 13:13–15; 14:5–7; Baruch 4:30–2; Wisdom 13–19; etc.

[52] Cf. the individual contributions in J. W. van Henten, ed., *Die Entstehung der jüdischen Martyrologie* (StPB 38; Leiden, 1989); M. Hengel, *The Atonement* (London and Philadelphia, 1981), 6–8; etc.

[53] Sirach 36:1–19; Tobit 13; Baruch 4:5–5:9. On the other hand, an oppressed church that saw in the Old Testament the distress of the people of God as a type of their own history could pray these eschatological prayers for help and restoration without difficulty.

[54] Cf. Swete, 282–3; Harl, Dorival and Munnich, 327 and above, pp. 58–9.

At the same time, we should not overlook the fact that an entire series of apocalyptic documents (not to mention the Qumran documents) originated in precisely the period that interests us, from the third century BCE to the second century CE. A significant portion of them were translated into Greek: besides the five-part *Enoch* collection, the *Assumption of Moses*, the *Apocalypse of Abraham*, the *Paralipomena Jeremiae*, the *Testament of Levi*, the Syriac *Baruch Apocalypse* and *4 Ezra*, to mention only a selection. Additional texts such as the *Testament of Abraham*, the Greek *Baruch Apocalypse* and the Coptic *Zephaniah Apocalypse*, the Slavonic *Enoch*, and the Jewish *Sibyllines* were probably written in the Diaspora. I limit myself here to the best-known titles. They have all come to us only through church tradition, some in translations from churches outside the mainstream, and often in Christian revisions that at least partially obscure the Jewish core. In fact, in one case or another, the origin continues to be disputed. Characteristically for this 'marginal literature', the 'Jewish' and the 'Christian' can no longer always be clearly distinguished. Of other documents we know only the titles and perhaps a few quotations, because they circulated among the churches for only a limited time before they were suppressed. A whole series of them would have deserved inclusion in the church's Old Testament canon no less than the eleven (themselves only half-heartedly accepted) books of the 'Apocrypha'. The reasons for the rejection of these documents have already been discussed above (pp. 70–3).

The fact that the book of Daniel, which originated only *c.* 165 BCE, was received so quickly and without hesitation seems to be almost a miracle given its late origins (it is younger than substantial portions of the *Enoch* literature). That may depend, in part, on its wisdom-martyrological narratives, especially, however, on its apocalyptic scheme of four empires, the vision of God's dominion in chapters 2 and 7, the coming of the Son of Man to judge the godless powers (7:9–17), and the resurrection of the dead and the judgement in chapter 12. It summarizes Jewish hopes for the future and simultaneously facilitates a comprehensive interpretation of history and the present. Even Josephus—like the nearly contemporaneous *4 Ezra*, the Syriac *Apocalypse of Baruch* (II Baruch) and the Apocalypse of John—relates Daniel's fourth empire to Rome with appropriate caution. Jewish reception of the book was thus also determinative for early Christianity and, because of Daniel 7, was perhaps even more influential there than in Judaism. Thus one of the most messianic texts in the Hebrew Bible, Daniel 7:13, receives remarkably little attention in Jewish exegesis. For Christians, Daniel, alongside the Psalms and Isaiah, therefore became the most important 'prophetic' document. The Apocalypse (as well as Matthew) made extensive use of it and by the beginning of the third century Hippolytus had already commented on it. His commentary on the book of Daniel is the oldest surviving orthodox Bible commentary. This latest work in the 'Hebrew canon' essentially belongs in the vestibule of the New Testament canon.[55]

3. The Canon in the Jewish Diaspora

a) The Prologue of Jesus ben Sirach

In connection with the question of the development of the Jewish canon, reference is repeatedly made to the Prologue by the author's grandson, who was also the translator of Sirach. The author speaks three times of a threefold division of the Jewish Scriptures. The very first sentence reads:

> Whereas many great teachings have been given to us through the law, the prophets, and the other [writings] that followed them . . . (διὰ τοῦ νόμου καὶ τῶν προφητῶν καὶ τῶν ἄλλων τῶν κατ᾽ αὐτοὺς ἠκολουθηκότων).

The next references occur in the description of the activity of his grand-father, who

> devote[d] himself especially to the reading of the law and the prophets and the other books of our fathers (ἐπὶ πλεῖον ἑαυτὸν δοὺς εἴς τε τὴν τοῦ νόμου καὶ τῶν προφητῶν καὶ τῶν ἄλλων πατρίων βιβλίων ἀνάγνωσιν).

The final reference occurs after he has mentioned the difference between the Hebrew original and the imperfect translation:

> Not only this [work], but even the law itself, the prophecies and the rest of the books differ not a little if read in the original (ἀλλὰ καὶ αὐτὸς ὁ νόμος καὶ οἱ προφῆται καὶ τὰ λοιπὰ τῶν βιβλίων).[56]

---

[55] On Josephus, cf. *Ant* 10:186–281, where he retells the whole book of Daniel, but refrains from interpreting the fourth empire because he wants to limit himself in his report to the past and the present and, therefore, passes over 'the future' (τὰ μέλλοντα, 10:210). But, he informs the interested reader, whoever has interest in 'learning hidden things to come' should acquire the book of Daniel, found 'among the Holy Scriptures (ἐν τοῖς ἱεροῖς γράμμασιν)'. Alexander had already found his victory over the Persians predicted in it (cf. *Ant* 11:337). The book of Daniel then came in for intensive use especially in Irenaeus (cf. *Biblia Patristica* I, 211–15) and Hippolytus. The latter's commentary, written *c*. 204 '(is) the oldest commentary on a biblical book preserved for us from the early church' (B. Altaner and A. Stuiber, *Patrologie* [8th edn; Freiburg/Basel/Vienna, 1978], 167), if one brackets out the John commentary of Valentinus' student Heracleon, preserved by Origen only in small fragments, and the *Hypotyposes* of Clement of Alexandria, likewise transmitted only in fragments. Already in *De Antichristo*, a document written somewhat earlier, Hippolytus utilized and cited the book of Daniel extensively (both in *GCS Hippolytus Werke* I). Concerning the exegesis of Daniel in the early church, cf. R. Bodenmann, *Naissance d'une Exégèse* (BGBE 28; Tübingen, 1986).

[56] Reading, with a series of Greek manuscripts and the Latin, Sahidic and Syro-hexaplaric translations οἱ προφῆται, instead of the Christian αἱ προφητεῖαι; cf. the apparatus in J. Ziegler, *Sapientia Iesu Filii Sirach* (Septuaginta: Vetus Testamentum Graecum XII/2; Göttingen, 1965), 125. For the 'canon' of Jesus ben Sirach see above, R. Hanhart, pp. 1–17.

Clearly, the grandson, who himself emigrated from Palestine to Egypt in the year 132, reproduces here the Hebrew concept of canon, although we do not know exactly which books he placed among 'the other books'.

His threefold repetition and the concluding statement that he had published his book for those 'abroad who are eager to learn', who 'desire to lead a life according to the law', suggest that he regarded his grandfather's work no more as 'canonical' but as a type of hortatory introduction to a life according to the 'law, the prophets, and the other books'. He also emphasizes the difference between the original Hebrew and the Greek text and the difficulty of the translation. In his opinion, the pious Jewish lifestyle was apparently no longer to be taken for granted in Jewish Alexandria; therefore he feels the effort of translating the work is necessary. A review of the work, and especially of the writings employed in the Praise of the Fathers in Sirach 44:1–50:24, demonstrates that the grandfather knew or cited all the books of the Hebrew canon except Ruth, Canticles, Esther and Daniel. He could not have known Daniel, because it came into existence only later. Sirach 38:34c–39:1, the self-portrait of the scholar Ben Sirach, already essentially anticipates the division in the prologue:

> . . . he who devotes himself to the study of the *law* of the Most High will seek out the *wisdom* of all the ancients, and will be concerned with *prophecies*; he will preserve the *discourse of notable men* and penetrate the subtleties of parables; he will seek out the hidden meanings of *proverbs* . . . [This is followed in 39:6 by mention of] 'words of wisdom' and 'thanksgiving to the Lord in prayer'.

This statement distinguishes between law, prophets, historical narrative, wisdom books and hymnic poetry.[57] Thus grandfather and grandson already tell us relatively much about the formation of the 'Holy Scriptures' in the motherland during the second century, but nothing about what was recognized as 'canonical' in Alexandria. Instead, the Jews in the Diaspora required special instruction on this point. The 'prophets' in the prologue may—as occurred later in the Hebrew canon—encompass both historical and prophetic books in the sense of the נביאם הראשונים or האחרונים, respectively.[58] References to the 'others that followed'—'other fathers' or 'other books' respectively—betray an uncertainty that makes it clear that this collection of documents was by no means definitely delimited even in the grandson's time.

---

[57] Cf. H. P. Rüger, 'Le Siracide: Un livre à la frontière du Canon,' in Kaestli and Wermelinger, 47–69 (esp. 60–6). Concerning the כתובים, Rüger writes: '. . . the homage to the patriarchs presupposes only knowledge of the *Psalms*, *Job*, *Proverbs*, *Ezra-Nehemiah*, and the two books of *Chronicles*. Taken as a whole, however, *Sirach* permits the addition to this list of *Qoheleth* and *Lamentations* (p. 64).' Unusually, *Sirach* does not mention the name of Ezra in the benediction of the patriarchs.

[58] See Hengel (see above, p. 45 n. 67), 'Schriftauslegung'.

We have already mentioned the spurious letter of the Jerusalemites to the Jews in Egypt (2 Macc. 2:13) with its reference to the 'library' presumably established by Nehemiah in Jerusalem, where 'the books about the kings and prophets, and the writings of David and letters of kings about votive offerings' are listed. The letter also mentions a partial collection of Old Testament Scriptures. This could refer to the historical books beginning with Judges or 1 Samuel, the 'latter prophets', and Ezra and Nehemiah (see above, pp. 80–1).

b) Philo's *Therapeutae*

Roughly 130 years after the grandson of Ben Sirach, Philo's description of the *Therapeutae*, that enigmatic Jewish group who lived close to the Mareotic Lake near Alexandria, offers only a superficial resemblance (*Vit Cont* 25):

> In each of their houses is a holy room into which they bring nothing other than '*laws* and the sacred words of God *proclaimed by prophets*, and *hymns*, *and others* through which knowledge and piety grow and mature (νόμους καὶ λόγια θεσπισθέντα διὰ προφητῶν καὶ ὕμνους καὶ τὰ ἄλλα οἷς ἐπιστήμη καὶ εὐσέβεια συναύξονται καὶ τελειοῦνται)'.

A little later (28) he speaks of their 'Holy Scriptures' and also of 'writings of holy men, who were the founders of the sect, who left behind them numerous (literary) memorials of allegorical nature' (29). They devoted themselves, however, not only to allegorical interpretation of Scripture, 'but include also songs and hymns to God in various metres and melodies'. 'Law and prophecy' may still have involved the traditional Jewish Scriptures, yet it is already questionable whether their hymns are limited to the canonical Psalms.[59] At Qumran, too, we have, besides the—still somewhat variable—Psalms,[60] a number of other

---

[59] That depends on whether Philo reproduces here the terminology of the Therapeutae or his own, since for Philo himself ὕμνοι designates the canonical Psalms. He uses ὕμνος (or ᾠδή) instead of—rather unusual to Greek ears—ψαλμός, which means lyre-playing.

Almost all citations from the Psalms are introduced with ἐν ὕμνοις λέγεται, or a similar expression (*Plant* 29:39; *Conf* 39:52; *Migr* 157; *Fug* 59; *Mut* 115; *Som* I:75; II:245–46), or the Psalmist is designated as ὑμνογράφος (*Gig* 17; *Imm* 74, 77, 82: ὁ ὑμνῳδός; cf. also *Agr* 50; *Her* 290). The citation from the psalm of Hannah (1 Sam. 2:15), which he designates an ᾆσμα, demonstrates that this is no accident. One could perhaps conjecture that the Therapeutae distinguished their own sectarian documents from those generally recognized; compare Rüger (see above, p. 44 n. 66), 'Werden', 117; Ellis (see above, p. 22 n. 10), *Old Testament*, 8–9; Beckwith, 115–18, who overlooks, however, the fact that even at Qumran this boundary was not yet firmly fixed. Significantly, *before* Josephus in *Contra Apionem* we have no detailed, clearly Jewish catalogue of Scriptures. Instead, as a rule, general terms such as γραφή, γραφαί ἅγιαι, etc. were employed.

[60] Especially disputed is 11QPsᵃ, a scroll of Davidic psalms that diverges significantly in character from the Masoretic text and contains a few apocryphal texts and non-canonical psalms. Consequently, the editor, J. A. Sanders (*The Psalm Scroll of Qumrân Cave 11*,

songs and liturgies, even including texts that describe the celestial Sabbath liturgy of the angels before God's throne and that consistently speak of God as 'king' and of his 'kingdom'.[61] Philo explicitly speaks of the Therapeutae as having their own songs. Beyond the traditional core of Law and Prophets, they, like the Essenes, and later the Christians, may have had numerous writings of their own. The attempt has been repeatedly made to assign individual pseudepigrapha, such as the lovely novella of Joseph and Asenath, to the Therapeutae. Yet we cannot get beyond speculation.

c) Josephus: *Ap* 1:37–43

Josephus speaks most clearly of a delimited canon of Jewish Scriptures in *Contra Apionem* 1:37–43 toward the end of the first century CE. At the time, it is apparent from *4 Ezra* 14:45 and the dictum of Simeon b. Azzai (*mYad* 3:5) concerning the decision of the seventy-two at Jabneh ('on the day when they installed R. Eleazar b. Arakh [as chairman]') the dispute in Palestine about the canon was in a final, decisive, phase. Josephus wrote in an apologetic context, defending the absolute reliability of prophetically inspired Jewish historiography from the period from Moses to Artaxerxes: not everyone has the right to write, 'only the prophets, who *received* the most remote and ancient history *communicated from God through inspiration* (κατὰ τὴν ἐπίπνοιαν τὴν ἀπὸ θεοῦ μάθοντες, 1:37)'. Consequently,

> We do not have innumerable writings that disagree and contradict, but only twenty-two books which are truly reliable and contain the account of the whole period [of Jewish history]. Of these, five books of Moses contain

---

DJD IV [Oxford, 1965]) wants to see the scroll as the representative of a proto-masoretic stage of tradition (cf. *idem*, 'Pre-Masoretic Psalter Texts', *CBQ* 27 [1965]: 114–23). The objection is raised against this view that the majority of the Psalm manuscripts from Qumran follow the Masoretic psalter and 11QPs[a] involves a special liturgical text (cf., for example, S. Talmon, 'Pisqa Be'emṣaʿ Pasuq und 11QPs[a]', *Textus* 5 [1966], 11–21; M. H. Goshen-Gottstein, 'The Psalms Scroll [11QPs[a]]: A Problem of Canon and Text', *Textus* 5 [1966], 22–33; R. Beckwith, 'The Courses of the Levites and the Eccentric Psalms Scrolls from Qumran', *RQ* 11 [1982–83]: 499–524; cf. also van der Woude (see above, p. 46 n. 71), 'Qumranforschung', 296–9 [with a list of all the published Psalms manuscripts and their contents]; *idem*, loc. cit., 'Fortsetzung III: Studien zu früher veröffentlichten Handschriften', *ThR* 57 [1992], 1–57 [esp. 45–9]; cf. also Maier (see above, p. 90 n. 42), 'Zur Frage', 144–5).

[61] For the songs and liturgical texts from Qumran, cf. the summary in Schürer (rev.) III/1, 451–64; for the sabbath sacrifice songs, see esp. A. M. Schwemer, 'Gott als König und seine Königsherrschaft in den Sabbatliedern aus Qumran', and H. Löhr, 'Thronversammlung und preisender Tempel: Beobachtungen am himmlischen Heiligtum im Hebräerbrief und in den Sabbatopferliedern aus Qumran', both essays in M. Hengel and A. M. Schwemer, eds, *Königsherrschaft Gottes und himmlischer Kult* (WUNT I/55; Tübingen, 1991), 45–118 and 185–206, respectively.

the laws in addition to the tradition of the origin of humanity up to Moses'
death. This period encompasses almost 3000 years. From Moses' death to
Artaxerxes, the Persian king after Xerxes, the prophets have recorded the
events of their time in thirteen books. The remaining four books contain
hymns to God and didactic poems for human life.

Here we meet for the first time a clearly defined catalogue of inspired
Scriptures, whose significance Josephus further emphasizes by asserting
that in all of Jewish history 'no one dared to add or delete or change
anything'. This contention reflects the old, trusted formula from the
Letter of Aristeas and from Deuteronomy. It was also 'a commonplace
of historiography',[62] however, with which he characterized his own
history in *Ant* 1:17. It has been 'planted' in Jews from their birth 'to
regard [these Scriptures] as God's decrees (θεοῦ δόγματα) and to
persevere in them, indeed, if necessary, to die for them' (*Ap* 1:42). A
courageous statement at a time when Domitian sought to suppress Jews
in Rome and in the Empire by force!

The threefold division is based on the preliminary distinction between
law, prophets and writings already found in Sirach. The thirteen
'prophetic books', said to have treated the entire history of God's people
from Moses' death to Artaxerxes, raise difficulties, however. Josephus
must have also included here books that were assigned in Palestine to
the כְּתוּבִים, 'Writings', perhaps Chronicles, Ezra, Esther and Daniel. The
priest and Pharisee, writing in Rome but coming from Jerusalem, thus
reproduces, for the most part, the Palestinian concept of canon (to which,
however, as author he does not strictly adhere, see above pp. 86–7; the
goodwill of the educated ancient reader was more important to him on
this point). Supremely significant for him is the cessation of prophetic
inspiration at the time of Artaxerxes I, the time of the last prophets,
Haggai, Zechariah, Malachi and the first '*sofer*', Ezra. This concept
corresponds completely to the rabbinic view.[63] This view of history was
prefigured long before by the concept of the end of prophecy already
apparent in Psalm 74:9; Lamentations 2:9; Zechariah 13:2; cf. Daniel
3:38; it had already become a fixed theory in the Maccabean period (1
Macc. 4:46; 9:27; 14:41). Eschatological movements such as Essenism,
the 'zealot' prophets of the first century described by Josephus, and early
Christianity must count against this theory of the end of prophetic
inspiration. Pharisaism and the rabbinate held it because, from this

---

[62] L. Feldman, *Josephus and Modern Scholarship (1937–1980)* (Berlin and New York,
1984), 135; see also above, p. 77 n. 5.

[63] Cf. above, p. 45 n. 67 and R. Meyer, 'Bemerkungen zum literaturgeschichtlichen
Hintergrund der Kanontheorie des Josephus', in *Josephus-Studien (FS O. Michel)*,
O. Betz, K. Haacker and M. Hengel, eds (Göttingen, 1974), 285–99 (= *idem, Zur
Geschichte und Theologie des Judentums in hellenistisch-römischer Zeit*, W. Bernhardt,
ed. (Neukirchen, 1989), 196–207.

viewpoint, scholars had taken the place of prophets since the legendary 'men of the Great Assembly' (*mAv* 1:1).[64] The political misuse of prophecy in Jewish Palestine during the decades before the Jewish War and its importance for early Christianity, as an eschatological-prophetic and universal movement motivated by the eschatological gift of the Spirit, may have further consolidated this position.[65]

The number of only twenty-two documents raises difficulties since Palestinian Judaism speaks of twenty-four. They were later supposed to have already been available to the 'men of the Great Assembly' (*bBB* 14b). Either Josephus, like the Church Fathers later, counted Ruth with Judges and Lamentations with Jeremiah, or, as seems more likely to me, he operated with a smaller canon. Perhaps it did not include Canticles and Qoheleth, which were translated into Greek very late and were still controversial among the rabbis in the second century.[66] The account of Ruth in *Ant* 5:318–37 has a thoroughly independent character between Judges and 1 Samuel. It would be dubious to attempt, with earlier scholarship, to point to the twenty-two books of Josephus as an 'Alexandrian canon', which would then have been smaller than the Hebrew Bible. As a historian and 'Jewish' theologian, Josephus is more strongly oriented toward Palestinian Judaism, from which he came, than toward the Diaspora in Alexandria. That also applies generally to the Jewish community in Rome where he lived.

The Jewish historian, who wrote, in addition to the *Bellum Judaicum*, the *Antiquitates Judaicae*, a history of the Jewish people from the creation to the outbreak of the Jewish War in twenty books, follows the description of the historical record in the canonical books, which ends in the *Antiquitates* with the Esther narrative (11:184–296), by assuring readers that in addition 'the whole history (ἕκαστα) from

[64] See Hengel (see above, p. 45 n. 67), 'Schriftauslegung', 24–8.

[65] For the zealot prophets, cf. M. Hengel, *Die Zeloten* (AGJU 1; 2nd edn; Leiden, 1976), 235–51 = *idem, The Zealots* (Edinburgh, 1989), 229–45; regarding early Christianity as a prophetic movement, see, among others, G. Theissen, 'Die Tempelweissagung Jesu. Prophetie im Spannungsfeld von Stadt und Land', *ThZ* 32 (1976), 144–58 (= *idem, Studien zur Soziologie des Urchristentums* [WUNT I/19; 3rd edn; Tübingen, 1989], 142–59); M. Sato, *Q und Prophetie* (WUNT II/43; Tübingen, 1989); D. E. Aune, *Prophecy in Early Christianity and the Ancient Mediterranean World* (Grand Rapids, 1983); U. B. Müller, *Prophetie und Predigt im Neuen Testament* (StNT 10; Gütersloh, 1975); K. O. Sandnes, *Paul—One of the Prophets?* (WUNT II/43; Tübingen, 1991). In principle, no one could have hindered Josephus from assigning 1 Maccabees, which, like 1 Ezra, Chronicles and Kings, was an important source for him, to the Holy Scriptures and regarding it as an inspired history. But this was no longer possible for him because of the influence of the formation of the Pharisaic 'canon'.

[66] See above, pp. 44–6. Contrast Meyer, 'Bemerkungen', 197: 'Nevertheless, this contrast [between 22 or 24 books, *M. Hengel*] is only apparent; it simply rests on the fact that Josephus still knew an arrangement of the Holy Scriptures such as the one on which the LXX was already based.' The number 22, which is, in fact, related to the number of letters in the Hebrew alphabet, points to Palestine. That is also clear in Melito.

Artaxerxes to the present [had] been recorded'. These later sources, however, are not considered as reliable as those preceding them 'because *the precise succession of the prophets* no longer existed (διὰ τὸ μὴ γενέσθαι τὴν τῶν προφητῶν ἀκριβῆ διαδοχήν)'.[67] Nevertheless, Josephus, who utilized both the Hebrew Bible and the LXX for his history (tending to employ the first up to the time of Joshua and the Judges and the latter from the books of Samuel onward), can also copy from later Jewish sources without reservation. Like individual Christian authors who were familiar with the Hebrew original (Paul, Mark, Matthew, John), he increasingly employed the Greek translation for the sake of his readers. Nor did he shrink—despite a strict 'prohibition against alteration'—from repeated paraphrases and expansions of the biblical report directed at the Greek reader, similar to the rabbis in narrative midrash or Luke in his history. In the context of his portrayal of the Jewish 'constitution', i.e. the Mosaic law (πολιτεία: *Ant* 4:196), he explicitly justified his method of selecting and arranging the material.

For the earlier history, he cites only isolated pagan sources in order to demonstrate for apologetic purposes the reliability of the biblical report from an outside perspective, but following the Persian period Jewish sources and pagan historians appear alongside one another with a certain equal validation, although he never names the former. He writes, after all, primarily for non-Jews and wants to overcome the mistrust of predominantly anti-Jewish educated readers by referring to well-known pagan historians. Thus he utilizes 1 Maccabees while he disdains or does not know Tobit, Judith, the additions to Daniel and the most linguistically Hellenistic 2 and 3 Maccabees.

It should no longer be doubted that when Josephus refers to the twenty-two biblical books originating between Moses and Artaxerxes (*Ap* 1:37–43), the ἰδία γράμματα (42), he is describing the 'pharisaic' Jewish 'canon' originating in Palestine. This is evident from their incontrovertibility, witness the fact that only the divinely inspired prophets were justified in recording the sacred history; the reference to the 'exact succession' of these inspired historians; the prohibition against 'adding, removing, or altering'; and the willingness, if necessary, to die for those that contain 'God's directives (θεοῦ δόγματα)'. For the subsequent history, beginning with Artaxerxes II in the *Antiquitates* (11:297–99), he also tries to give a continuous historical account based largely on different Jewish sources, although these were no longer Holy Scriptures for him and were consequently not of the same importance. Furthermore, and notably, Josephus' 'Holy Scriptures' are portrayed here

---

[67] *Ap* 1:41. For Josephus as a historian and his treatment of the sources, cf. H. Lindner, *Die Geschichtsauffassung des Flavius Josephus im Bellum Judaicum* (AGJU 12; Leiden, 1972); P. Vallalba i Varneda, *The Historical Method of Flavius Josephus* (ALGHL 19; Leiden, 1986), 266–72; etc.

as the exclusively reliable sources of the earlier fundamental Israelite-Jewish history, whose authors represent an unbroken chain of prophets. This recalls *Mishnah Avot* 1:1, on the one hand, and, on the other, the view of history of later Christian authors.

Basically, the last and greatest Jewish historian of antiquity already stands near in conception to the Christian apologists and chronologists who were interested in demonstrating both the great antiquity and the reliability of biblical tradition, as well as extending 'salvation history' into the moment of the appearance of Christ. The rabbis, by contrast, consciously chose to become 'ahistorical'. For them historiography broke off with the last prophets. N. N. Glatzer's statement applies to them:

> Jewish historiography was not extinguished by a 'lack of strength', as many historians assume, but by the acknowledgment that Jewish 'history' in the proper sense of the word no longer existed. From the Jewish perspective there was only a history of 'the others', which overshadowed the life of the Jewish community and created the circumstances under which its external life must be realized. The Jew no longer made history, but endured it.[68]

---

[68] *Geschichte der talmudischen Zeit* (Berlin, 1937), 11 (republished with the author's bibliographical supplement by P. von der Osten-Sacken [2nd edn; Neukirchen, 1981]); cf. also *idem, Untersuchungen zur Geschichtslehre der Tannaiten* (Berlin, 1933).

V

THE ORIGIN OF THE 'CHRISTIAN SEPTUAGINT' AND ITS ADDITIONAL WRITINGS

1. Early Christianity

If we consider the use of Old Testament Scriptures by the earliest Christian authors in the New Testament itself, it becomes evident how remote they are from any question about the canon and its limits. 'The Scriptures' (αἱ γραφαί) are mentioned quite self-evidently and without further qualification. While Matthew employs the plural exclusively, John prefers the singular, ἡ γραφή, and Luke and Paul use both. Only once, in the majestic introduction to Romans (1:2), does Paul mention that God promised the gospel in advance through his prophets ἐν γραφαῖς ἁγίαις. Substantially rarer is the double formula, 'the law and the prophets', which can vary in a number of ways. Since, from the very beginning, early Christianity saw the Scriptures in a new light as fulfilled or fulfilling eschatological-messianic promises', the entire Scriptures can also be encompassed in the term 'prophets',[1] just as, conversely, Paul and John can, under certain circumstances, cite a passage from a prophet or the psalms as 'law'. According to the sources preserved for us, the question of a delimited canon was not a problem considered or discussed. It was believed to be self-evident that one could know what were 'Holy Scriptures' and that one could refrain from making any definitive distinction.[2] This was first undertaken—surely with a sidelong glance at that dangerous 'heretical' messianic splinter group, the Christians—by the rabbinical teachers of Jabneh.

The threefold division of the Jewish canon is seen—in incipient form—only once, in Luke 24:44, where the resurrected Jesus instructs his disciples 'that everything must be fulfilled that stands written concerning me in the law of Moses, the prophets, and the Psalms'. The

---

[1] Cf. Luke 1:70; 13:28; 18:31; 24:25 (cf. 27); Acts 3:18–24; 10:43; 13:27; 26:27 (cf. 22); Rom. 1:12; Heb. 1:1; 1 Peter 1:10; cf. also Matt. 13:35 (Pss. 78:2: διὰ τοῦ προφήτου); Acts 2:29–30 (David as a prophet, the Psalms as his prophecy). Cf. Hengel, 'Schriftauslegung des 4. Evangeliums', 249–51, 261–3, 268–70; Campenhausen (see above, p. 20 n. 4), 'Entstehung', 28–30. See also Justin, above, pp. 26–9.

[2] J. Barton ('"The Law and the Prophets", Who are the Prophets?', OTS 23 [1984], 1–18) comes to the conclusion that: 'In New Testament times, to describe a book as one of the prophets, or as written by a prophet, is to say that it is authoritative and inspired, although not part of the Torah' (p. 15), see above, p. 68 n. 30.

question arises, however, whether Luke uses 'Psalms' as *pars pro toto*—the part for the whole—to refer to the Hagiographa. In my opinion, it is more likely that he mentions them—although they (like all 'Scriptures') are a prophetic work—alongside the 'prophets' because, for him, as for all early Christianity, indeed for the early church, they represent the most important, most utilized book of the Old Testament. Luke is the only New Testament author who explicitly mentions the book of Psalms four times, otherwise they are simply subsumed under 'the prophets' (indeed, in Paul and John sometimes under ὁ νόμος) and introduced with one of the usual citation formulae.[3] This particular importance of the Psalter in early Christianity is related to christological scriptural evidence. A substantial portion of its texts were familiar to every Jew through the temple liturgy, singing at the great festivals, and use of the Psalms in private prayer. In my opinion, the christological hymnody of early Christianity is also based on messianic psalms such as Psalms 2; 8; 22; 45; 69; 89; 118, etc. Psalm 110:1 is the most quoted Old Testament text in the New Testament and a basic proof for the development of earliest Christology. The potent influence of the Psalter is further evident in *1 Clement*, in the Apologists, and in the papyri from the second century.[4] Alongside Isaiah, it is basically the most important 'Christian Scripture' in the first and second centuries. Only in the second half of the second century did Matthew and John overtake it.

Isaiah and then Deuteronomy follow close behind. A list of the literal citations supplied with introductory formulae, according to the index of Old Testament citations in the 25th edition of Nestle produces the following picture:

Psalms, 55;

Isaiah, 45;

Deuteronomy, 41 (14, however, are from the Decalogue and the love commandment);

Exodus, 23 (10 from the Decalogue);

---

[3] Luke 20:42, Δαυὶδ λέγει ἐν βιβλίῳ ψαλμῶν; 24:44, ἐν τῷ νόμῳ Μωϋσέως καὶ τοῖς προφήταις καὶ ψαλμοῖς; Acts 1:20, γέγραπται γὰρ ἐν βιβλίῳ ψαλμῶν; 13:33, ... ὡς καὶ ἐν τῷ ψαλμῷ γέγραπται τῷ δευτέρῳ; Codex D and the old Latin Codex Gigas from the thirteenth century, which seems to preserve a very old form of the text, read here—'in the first Psalm'. Correspondingly, Justin (*Apol* I 40:8–10) cites the first and second Psalms as a unit. Origen knew of two different Hebrew manuscripts. In one the first Psalm was linked to the second (cf. also Bill. II:772: Similarly, *bBer* 9b does not distinguish between the two Psalms). The reading 'in the first Psalm', very often attested in the Church Fathers in contrast to the manuscript tradition, depends on Origen (cf. the extensive treatment in Metzger, *Textual Commentary*, 412–14).

[4] Cf. M. Hengel, 'Hymnus und Christologie', in *Wort in der Zeit* (FS K. H. Rengstorf), W. Haubeck and M. Bachmann, eds (Leiden, 1980), 1–23; *idem*, 'Christuslied' (above p. 65 n. 19). On Psalm 110 see *idem*, 'Sit at my Right Hand', in *Studies in Early Christology* (Edinburgh, 1995), 119–225.

Minor Prophets, 21;

Genesis, 16;

Leviticus, 14 (7 of 19:18);

Jeremiah, 9;

Proverbs 4;

Ezekiel, Daniel, Numbers and 2 Samuel, 2 each;

Job, Joshua, 1 Kings, 1 each.

Thus approximately 60 per cent of all the direct citations of the Old Testament come from three books: Psalms, Isaiah and Deuteronomy.

In Paul, the picture shifts in favour of Isaiah. According to D. A. Koch, Paul has sixty-six scripture citations introduced with a formula from seventy-five passages. Of these, twenty-one are from Isaiah, sixteen from the Psalms, and eleven each from Deuteronomy and Genesis (promises to Abraham). Thus fifty-nine passages, approaching 80 per cent, are taken from only four books, five each from the Minor Prophets and Exodus, two each from Leviticus and Kings, and one from Job.[5] In contrast, Revelation, with its numerous allusions and paraphrases without citation formulae falls outside this framework. Here, the prophetic books, including Ezekiel and Daniel, naturally dominate much more. Notably, Daniel, which is, after all, much shorter than the major prophets, appears primarily in allusions. By contrast, the historical books recede noticeably in the New Testament—Chronicles, Ezra, Esther, as well as Canticles, Lamentations and Qoheleth are entirely absent. The same is true of the extra books of the Christian LXX. The new Nestle-Aland (26th edn), however, offers many more texts, since it also sometimes lists remote allusions, and, in contrast to the 25th edition, adds the 'apocrypha' and 'pseudepigrapha', for which, however, especially in Paul, unambiguously identifiable citations introduced with formulae are absent. This could be accidental, for there is no question that he knew apocryphal scriptures. A few enigmatic citations may derive from them (see below, pp. 109–10). Apparently, the problem of the delimitation of the holy, and thus inspired 'Scriptures', what may and may not have been γραφὴ θεόπνευστος (2 Tim. 3:16), and who the 'men' and their scriptures were who 'moved by the Holy Spirit spoke from God' (2 Pet. 1:21), was at first hardly controversial. At least we hear nothing of such controversies.[6] At first the danger did not consist, as later in the dispute with the Gnostics, in the introduction of new, counterfeited 'scriptures', but more in the 'idiosyncratic interpretation' of those which were universally recognized (2 Pet. 1:20), or in

---

[5] Koch (see above, p. 22 n. 11), 'Schrift als Zeuge', 21–3.

[6] Cf. also P. Stuhlmacher, 'Die Bedeutung der Apokryphen und Pseudepigraphen des Alten Testaments für das Verständnis Jesu und der Christologie', in *Apokryphenfrage* (see above, p. 66 n. 22), Mererer, ed., 13–25.

corrections and expansions of the text. Nevertheless, the problem is implied in 2 Peter, the latest New Testament document (about 130). The unknown author strikes from the letter of Jude, a text he used, the reference to the book of *Enoch* and the dispute over the body of Moses that probably comes from the *Assumption of Moses*.[7] In view of the use of the Old Testament in early Christianity, one could speak, if one wished, of a—tacitly assumed—eschatologically determined 'centre of the Scriptures' (*Mitte der Schrift*), that of fulfilment in the gospel. One could also say that it was determined by Christology, soteriology and the new righteousness or—in a phrase—by the 'justification of the ungodly' (Rom. 4:5; 5:6), and that it thus essentially excluded the possibility of an external delimitation of 'the truth of the gospel' (Gal. 2:5–14) through a firmly defined collection of 'canonical' Scriptures, although one primarily concentrated on relatively few, very specific well-known Scriptures.

The text employed was, as a rule, that of the LXX. As I have already said, it was read and exegeted even in the synagogues of the Hellenists in Jerusalem. As a student in Jerusalem, Paul may have worked with both the Hebrew and the Greek texts in accordance with the bilingual milieu in the Jewish capital, where the Hellenists had their own synagogues.[8] Even those New Testament authors who presumably understood Hebrew (or Aramaic) generally cited the text familiar to Greek-speaking readers, admittedly with certain limitations. The use of the LXX and its language in a document does not, therefore, supply adequate evidence that the author(s) did not come from Jewish Palestine nor even that they were necessarily Gentile Christians. Paul, for example, uses the LXX of Isaiah—the most important Scripture for him—in a form that 'had already undergone a Hebraizing revision'.[9] The same is true for the few citations from Job and Kings. This circumstance hardly results from the fact that Paul accidentally came into possession of such texts and was not even conscious of the peculiarity of this version, as Koch suspects.[10]

---

[7] Jude 14–15, cf. 2 Pet. 2:17–18; Jude 9, cf. 2 Pet. 2:11; see above, pp. 54–6, 70–4.

[8] Acts 6:9. The Greek Theodotos synagogue inscription also refers to a Greek-speaking synagogue culture in Jerusalem. The two Greek warning inscriptions in the temple that prohibited any non-Jew from entering the inner court of the temple also indicate, similarly, that the city represented a religious attraction for the entire Roman Empire. For this international character, compare also the account in Acts 2:9–11. See also above, pp. 80–3 and Hengel, *'Hellenization'* (see above, p. 20 n. 3), 11, 13–15; *idem*, 'Der vorchristliche Paulus', 256–66: 'Das griechischprechende Jerusalem und die griechische synagogale Bildung'. M. Hengel and A. M. Schwemer, *Paulus zwischen Damaskus und Antiochien* (WUNT 108, Tübingen, 1998), 56ff. That Paul spoke Aramaic can be presupposed because of his stay in Nabatean Arabia and his long time in Syria where in rural regions the Aramaic language still prevailed.

[9] Koch, 'Schrift als Zeuge', 78.

[10] Koch, 'Schrift als Zeuge', 81. Cf. in contrast, Hengel, 'Der vorchristliche Paulus', 234 and n. 191.

According to Koch, of the total of ninety-five texts that Paul adduces, sometimes without citation formula, he altered fifty-two and left only thirty-seven untouched, while in four cases no clear judgement can be reached;[11] this may be related to his 'spirit-guided apostolic freedom'. In this respect he differs substantially from contemporary Jewish exegetical practice. One should not overlook the fact that he was a Pharisee and, according to Galatians 1:13–14, very likely also a scholar. During his time, one could only study pharisaical scholarship properly in the Holy Land and best in Jerusalem.[12]

The Apocalypse also presents a special case in this connection. Like Josephus, it utilized both the Hebrew text and the LXX (including the Proto-Theodotion of Daniel) and, furthermore—for an apocalyptic work nothing else was even possible—voluminous apocalyptic-pseudepigraphic traditions.[13] Nor should one overlook a series of texts introduced in the New Testament as scriptural citations but unidentifiable in the Old Testament in this form: for example, 1 Corinthians 2:9, where Koch suspects an oral logion dependent on Isaiah 64:3, while H. Gese points to the agreement between the third phrase and Sirach 1:10b.[14] A written pseudepigraphical source cannot be completely ruled out, however. Origen referred to an unknown Elijah Apocryphon that was apparently available to him.[15] Similarly inexplicable is the verse in 1 Corinthians 9:10 adduced by Paul as a Scripture citation. Here, too, it seems to me, an unknown pseudepigrapha is conceivable.[16] The fragment of a christological hymn in Ephesians 5:14 is cited as Scripture. Severianus of Gabala in Syria (d. post 408) already pointed out that this is probably an inspired Christian 'psalm',

---

[11] Koch, 'Schrift als Zeuge', 186.

[12] Cf. Hengel, 'Der vorchristliche Paulus', 222–32, 239–42.

[13] Cf. the introduction to R. H. Charles, *A Critical and Exegetical Commentary on the Revelation of St. John*, Vol. I (ICC; Edinburgh, 1920), lxxii–lxxiii; *idem, Enoch*, xcvi–ci. Cf. also J. Frey in, *Die johanneische Frage*, M. Hengel, ed. (WUNT I/67; Tübingen, 1993), 326–429.

[14] Koch, 'Schrift als Zeuge' (see above, p. 22 n. 11), 16–41. Thus, already Jerome, who writes, in fact, in his exegesis of Isaiah 64:3, '*Ascensio enim Esaiae et Apokalypsis Eliae hoc habent testimonium*', but still seeks to trace the citation to the Isaiah passage ('Commentariorum in Esaiam zu Jes 64:3', CChr. SL 73A: Hieronymus I/2A, M. Adriaen and G. Morin, eds [Turnhout, 1963], 735); cf. also Rüger (see above, p. 44 n. 66), 'Werden', 178 n. 4, who argues that Jerome could be absolutely correct on this point. The citation was introduced into the Latin version of *Ascension of Isaiah* as a later interpolation. For H. Gese, see *Alttestamentliche Studien* (Tübingen, 1991), 25, 259, 268 n. 9. 1 Cor. 2:6–10 also concerns the revelation of God's true wisdom in the cross of Jesus Christ.

[15] Matthew commentary on 27:9 (see above, p. 71 n. 41), 250: '. . . et apostolus scripturas quasdam secretorum profert, sicut dicit alicubi "quod oculus non vidit nec auris audivit"; in nullo enim regulari libro hoc positum invenitur, nisi in secretis Eliae prophetae'. On the Elijah Apocalypse in general, see Schürer (rev.) III/2, 799–803.

[16] So also H. Lietzmann and W. G. Kümmel, *An die Korinther*, I/II (HNT 9; 5th edn; Tübingen, 1969), 41, etc.

such as that which Paul presupposes in 1 Corinthians 14:26.[17] An additional enigmatic, unidentifiable 'Scripture citation' appears in James 4:5–6. If one disregards the verbal citations, quite a plethora of tradition-historical linkages and dependencies can be established. Among the many possibilities, H. Gese refers to a fundamental example: 'One simply cannot—to name only one example—understand John 1 without Sir 24.'[18] This series of citations and allusions continues seamlessly in the Apostolic Fathers, for example, *Barn* 6:13; *2 Clement* 4:5; 11:2–4 (ὁ προφητικὸς λόγος); 13:2b.[19] If such statements were attributed to the Lord, it can no longer be determined whether they are 'Old' or 'New Testament agrapha'. Attention has already been called to the occasional use of known pseudepigrapha, especially of *Enoch*, but also of the *Assumption of Moses, Eldad and Modad, Jannes and Jambres*, etc. (see above, pp. 70–4). This state of affairs changes only with the Apologists after Justin, with Irenaeus and Tertullian, that is with more highly educated authors influenced by the dispute with the 'restrictive canon' of Palestinian Judaism, among other things. From now on, it is with only a few exceptions, 'acknowledged Scriptures' that are cited. Thus a more pronounced consciousness of the gradually developing 'canonical' authority of the Scriptures cited becomes evident. But even such a learned teacher of the church as Clement of Alexandria is still relatively generous on this point and does not permit his 'use of Scripture' simply to be externally prescribed.

This picture of the New Testament and early Christian use of the Greek Bible, sketched with over-simplifying brevity, indicates a thoroughly bipartite reality: on the one hand, the concentration on a relatively tight circle of frequently cited scriptures in which 'the Scriptures' were primarily seen from the perspective of the fulfilled prophetic promise. Thus, the νόμος was no longer placed at the centre, but the 'prophetic word' fulfilled in Christ, with a clear preference for quotations from the Psalms and Isaiah. In contrast, a quite free, inspired treatment of the text could adduce as 'Scripture' even individual apocrypha and pseudepigrapha, some known to us and some no longer known, or oral statements 'of the Lord'. The question of the external compass of the scriptural canon is not yet clearly posed. At any rate, a

---

[17] K. Staab, *Pauluskommentare aus der griechischen Kirche* (NTA 15; Münster, 1933; 2nd edn 1984), 311. In his Daniel commentary (p. 328, on Dan. 4:56), Hippolytus cites Isaiah as the source, while Epiphanius once again mentions the Elijah Apocalypse as the source (*Adv Haer* 42:12:5), which is unlikely. Otherwise Origen, who still knew this document, would also probably have referred to it. Finally, Euthalius (fourth century) refers to a Jeremiah Apocryphon as the source (BVP Vol. 10, A. Galland, ed. [2nd edn; Venice, 1788], 260); cf. Schürer (rev.) III/2, 800. For Ephesians 5:14 see also M. Hengel in *Studies in Early Christology*, 281–5.

[18] H. Gese, *Alttestamentliche Studien*, 27.

[19] Cf. also Oepke (n. 108), 'Βίβλοι ἀπόκρυφοι', 988–90.

certain dependence on Judaeo-Palestinian tradition is unremarkable for a movement that originated there. All the more noteworthy is the relative distance from contemporary scriptural interpretation, whether the psychologized, allegorical exegesis of Philo, or the literal, but equally associative Torah interpretation of the rabbis. One developed one's own christologico-eschatological exegesis oriented toward contemporary fulfilment in a way that, with all its differences, most closely parallels the prophetic *pesher* interpretation of the Essenes at Qumran.[20]

The question of the origin of the *larger* canon of the early church, which so occupies us today, was apparently not yet in view. On the basis of the New Testament's use of Scripture, one would actually expect a *smaller* canon. Apparently the contents of the bookcases of the Christian community in the first and at the beginning of the second century were, to a degree, quite divergent and, in poorer communities, also still relatively modest. The essential books of Psalms, Isaiah, Jeremiah, the Twelve Prophets, the Pentateuch and Daniel predominated. But the fact that we have no associated citations does not preclude the notion that occasionally other Scriptures were eagerly read and studied. Thus Paul very likely knew Wisdom and probably also Sirach. There are also remarkable parallels to later texts such as *4 Ezra* and the Syriac *Apocalypse of Baruch*.[21] Here he must have known older apocalyptic traditions that point back to Palestine. Luke, who so exquisitely imitates the style of the LXX, probably knew several of the so-called Apocrypha, especially the Maccabean history and, once again, especially 2 Maccabees. Furthermore, he seems to have been familiar with haggadic historiography in the style of the *Liber antiquitatum biblicarum*.[22] The author of Hebrews, also a scholar, was familiar with the martyr tradition of the *Vitae prophetarum*.[23] James and Matthew knew the wisdom tradition of Sirach.[24] But we have no indication that these (and other 'pseudepigraphical') books were read essentially as 'Holy

---

[20] On Jewish exegesis before 70, see D. I. Brewer, *Techniques and Assumptions in Jewish Exegesis before 70 CE* (TSAJ 30; Tübingen, 1992), and Hengel, 'Schriftauslegung', 61–3. On scriptural quotations in the first half of the second century in the name of the Lord and the use of Apocrypha see *idem, The Four Gospels and the One Gospel of Jesus Christ* (London, 2000).

[21] Cf. Hengel, 'Der vorchristliche Paulus' (see above, p. 22 n. 10), 251; Stuhlmacher, 'Bedeutung' (see above, p. 107 n. 6), 20. About the early Christian bookcases see M. Hengel, *The Four Gospels and the One Gospel of Jesus Christ* (London, 2000), 121ff., 136–40.

[22] See E. Reinmuth, *Pseudo-Philo und Lukas: Studien zum Liber Antiquitatum Biblicarum und seiner Bedeutung für die Interpretation des lukanischen Doppelwerks* (WUNT 74; Tübingen, 1994). On Luke as a Hellenistic historian, see C.-J. Thornton, *Der Zeuge des Zeugen: Lukas als Historiker der Paulusreisen* (WUNT I/56; Tübingen, 1991).

[23] Hebrews 11:35–7; see below, pp. 118–19.

[24] Cf., for example, James 1:19 and Sirach 5:11; Matthew 11:28–30 and Sirach 24:19; 51:23, 26–27; 6:28–29.

Scripture'. In any case, they were not cited as such. Jude 14, where
Enoch is introduced as a 'prophet (ἐπεπροφήτευσεν)', constitutes an
exception. Apparently, both among Jews and Christians, opinions
concerning the complex and widely known literature still differed
significantly in the first century.[25] In various localities, a variety of
Scriptures, sometimes quite divergent, will have been read and treasured
in synagogues and churches, although a recognized 'basic canon' of
major Scriptures, such as was already familiar to the grandson of Jesus
ben Sirach, existed in larger communities. Furthermore, one must take
into account the fact that wisdom sayings from Sirach, Tobit, Baruch,
etc. were also dispersed through oral tradition and catechetical
introductions in the style of the 'Two-Way Catechism'. This dispersal
may have been analogous to that of the prophetic testimonia collections
which are presumed to have existed quite early among Christians and
whose explanatory expansions of the text, as Justin and later Christian
authors demonstrate, have at least superficially influenced the text of the
Christian LXX (see above, pp. 28–9). Familiarity with these scriptures
still outside the 'core canon' was related to the personal interests or
learning of individual teachers and authors and, at the same time, to the
library holdings of the churches in question.[26]

2. *The Problem of the Inclusion of the Writings*
Not Contained in the 'Hebrew Canon'

The question of *why* the Old Testament attained in the church precisely
the form present—still not completely uniformly—in the great codices
of the fourth and fifth centuries is essentially insoluble. On the basis of

---

[25] Cf., however, Titus 1:12, where the Cretan priest, Epimenides, one of the seven wise
men of the world, is cited affirmatively as a *prophet*, with the modifying clause (v. 13), ἡ
μαρτυρία αὕτη ἐστὶν ἀληθής. The acknowledgement of a truth attested 'only' extra-
biblically was no problem for the authors of the New Testament (cf. Acts 17:28 and John
11:50–1). The term may, however, have been intended ironically here.

[26] Cf., for example, *Pseudo-Phocylides*, which probably originated in Alexandria at the
beginning of the first century and represents a kind of ethical compendium. Among Old
Testament passages treated, wisdom literature dominates. Sirach is 'cited' (i.e. trans-
formed here into hexameter) most often (75×), followed by Proverbs (52×), Leviticus
(48×), Deuteronomy (44×) and Exodus (31×). Qoheleth (10×), Tobit (8×), Job and
Wisdom (7× each) are cited more often than Genesis (6×) or the prophets, which occur
collectively only eighteen times (divided among eight prophets). The Psalter, too, with
only six instances, plays no great role. Cf. K.-W. Niebuhr, *Gesetz und Paränese* (WUNT
II/28; Tübingen, 1987), 9–10. Otherwise the use of the Pentateuch dominates as a rule
(see above pp. 79–80). Herein is evident the degree to which the literary form and the
setting in life influences the type and origin of the citation. This must be said especially in
view of the distinctive teaching personalities since the second half of the second century,
who, like the extremely learned and independent Clement of Alexandria, undertook to
work systematically through Jewish as well as pagan literature in order to trace the
praeparatio evangelica. At the same time, the search for traces of the *logos spermatikos*
is undertaken here for apologetic and missionary reasons.

New Testament use of Scripture, it seems likely that the scope of the Christian Old Testament would have been smaller than the Hebrew Bible. Indeed, the church could have disregarded Qoheleth, Canticles, 2 Ezra or Esther without difficulty. Here the model of the Hebrew canon is evident; the 'canon lists' of a Melito and later of Origen demonstrate that Christians wished to possess those Scriptures in their entirety. Because of its offensive content, Esther had difficulty gaining acceptance despite its place in the Hebrew canon. Ultimately the question of how Judith, Tobit, Sirach, Wisdom and the books of Maccabees came to be included, and not others such as *Enoch* or the *Testament of the Twelve Patriarchs*, remains a mystery. It may, as mentioned above, be related to the (Jewish) rejection of authors before Moses (see above, pp. 72–3).

a) Writings Outside the 'Hebrew Canon'

The situation is simplest with the texts already present in expanded form in the LXX. Even Josephus utilizes the expanded Esther and the novellistically amplified 1/(3) Ezra. From the Jewish scrolls the first Christian scribes adopted without reserve the expanded Daniel with Susanna, Bel and the Dragon, the Prayer of Azariah and the Song of the Three Young Men. The various Jewish recensions from the pre-Christian period moved seamlessly into the church. The so-called Theodotion version of Daniel (which predates Theodotion) can be identified in Hebrews 11:33, in Josephus, in the *Shepherd of Hermas* (Rome) and in the Apocalypse of John (Asia Minor).[27] Somewhat later Irenaeus not only repeatedly cites the additions to Daniel,[28] but also twice, explicitly, passages in Baruch, once as an oracle of the 'prophet Jeremiah'[29] and once (Bar. 3:29–4:1) with the introduction, 'This is why Jeremiah also speaks on his subject.'[30] In his codex of the prophets, Jeremiah and Baruch were already linked, a combination that probably goes back to

---

[27] Daniel 6:23 = Hermas 23:4 (*Vis* 4:2:4), cf. J. Ziegler, *Susanna, Daniel, Bel et Draco* (Septuaginta: Vetus Testamentum Graecum XVI/2; Göttingen, 1954), 61–2; N. Brox, *Der Hirt des Hermas* (KAV 7; Göttingen, 1991), 24–5, 174; (Pseudo-)Theodotion's version of Daniel may be a very early revision of the LXX text that almost completely supplanted its less exact predecessor; see J. Schüpphaus, 'Das Verhältnis von LXX- und Theodotion-Text in den apokryphen Zusätzen zum Danielbuch', *ZAW* 83 (1971), 49–72; Schürer (rev.) III/2, 727–8. See also above, p. 42 n. 57 (R. Albertz).

[28] *Adv Haer* 4:26:3 = Susanna: Daniel 13:20, 52–3; *Adv Haer* 3:25:6 = Daniel 13:55, 59; *Adv Haer* 4:5:2 = Bel: Daniel 14:4–5, 25. An overview of the use of the apocryphal additions to Daniel in the early church appears in C. Julius, *Die griechischen Danielzusätze und ihre kanonische Bedeutung* (BSt[F] VI/3–4; Freiburg, 1901), 107–21; on the canonicity of the Susanna story, see Engel (see above, p. 48 n. 75), *Susanna-Erzählung*, 17–29.

[29] *Adv Haer* 5:35:1 cites Baruch 4:36–5:9.

[30] *Demonstrationes* 97, L. M. Froidevaux, ed. (SC 62; Paris, 1959), 166. Furthermore, *Adv Haer* 4:20:4 alludes to Baruch 3:38.

Jewish LXX scrolls.[31] Tertullian, too, cites the letter of Baruch 6:3–5 as 'Jeremiae scribentis' (*Scorpiace* 8:5). Similarly, Athenagoras attributes Baruch 3:36 to the Φωναὶ τῶν προφητῶν, presumably because he regards it as part of the book of Jeremiah. He follows it with Exodus 20:2–3; Isaiah 44:6; 43:10–11; and 66:1. Under the name of Jeremiah, then, Lamentations, Baruch and the Letter became one prophetic book.[32] Baruch 3:38, attested unanimously in the manuscripts, on the other hand, is probably a Christian addition that refers to the 'incarnation' of 'Wisdom' and shows how even Jewish 'prophetic texts' were 'supplemented' very early by Christians. Numerous examples of such 'supplementations' occur already in Justin (see above, pp. 31–3).

b) Independent Documents outside the 'Hebrew Canon'

The following discussion concerns only the *independent* documents mentioned above. The great unknown is the content of the 'community archives' or 'libraries' in the period of the church's consolidation under the leadership of the—largely unknown—men of the second and third generations who became the most important New Testament authors between 70 and 110. As already stated, it was certainly quite varied to a degree and probably often consisted not only of generally acknowledged 'Holy Scriptures' in the strict sense but also of a multi-

---

[31] Cf. Beckwith, 341–2: the fact that in Lamentations there is already one 'canonical' addition to Jeremiah greatly facilitates additional appendices that supply edifying reading, but these originally did not necessarily enjoy the same status as the prophetic book itself. The difference was obscured when Judaeo-Hellenistic and later Christian readers attributed everything to the prophet Jeremiah himself. The significance of the book of Baruch in Judaism has not been fully clarified, for Baruch is reported to have been read together with Lamentations once a year in the synagogue (*Apost Const* 5:20; cf. Schürer [rev.] III/2, 739; Sundberg, 74–7; this report could, however, be based on a confusion or be an—ahistorical—inference drawn from Baruch 1:14. This passage requires that the book be read on the Feast of Booths; see Rüger [p. 44 n. 66], 'Werden', 180). Barthélemy (*Les devanciers d'Aquila* [see above, p. 29 n. 13], 159) postulates a reading during this festival in the synagogues of the Diaspora. According to Tov (*Jeremiah and Baruch* [p. 86 n. 30], 209–12, 215), the revision of the second half of Jeremiah and of Baruch 1:1–3:8 was undertaken by the same hand (50 BCE or earlier), which demonstrates how closely the books were linked, if not seen as one work, in fact. The Hebrew text of the book of Jeremiah cites a word of encouragement to Baruch toward the end (45:1–5). The book of Baruch probably seeks to establish a connection to it.

[32] Athenagoras, *Legatio* 9:1, 38 (ll. 2 and 9) does not mention Baruch, but lists only 'Moses, Isaiah, Jeremiah, and the other prophets'. The quotation from Baruch 3:36, 'The Lord is our God and no one can be compared to him' (Κύριος ὁ θεὸς ἡμῶν· οὐ λογισθήσεται ἕτερος πρὸς αὐτόν) is very general and fuses smoothly into the following quotations. These may derive from a Testimonia collection. Cf. also Rüger, 'Apokryphen I' (see above, p. 56 n. 96), 291, 307–8, and for the other, numerous references to Baruch in the early church, see Swete, 274–6; Schürer (rev.) III/2, 740–1.

faceted 'instructional literature' of lesser significance. Certain large and therefore leading communities (e.g. Rome, Alexandria, Ephesus and Antioch) may have been better equipped than others. Unfortunately, we have no information about Alexandria from this early period. The catastrophe of 115–17 must have also harshly impacted the church, of which we are ignorant, but which must have been significantly shaped by Jewish Christianity. The great Jewish community in Alexandria was probably nearly entirely destroyed by the two 'Jewish Wars' in Egypt (115–17) and Judaea (132–5). The only *direct* second-century witnesses are the earliest Christian papyri with their concentration in the Old Testament on the Psalms (besides three papyri of John, two or three of Matthew and some fragments of apocryphal gospels). At the end of the second century we find in Clement an Alexandrian teacher who enjoyed access to a superior library and who cites, or at least knows, most of the apocrypha, among other texts like Philo and Josephus.[33]

In my opinion, substantial library holdings in the early period can also be identified in Rome, as early indeed as the earliest document not included in the New Testament canon, the letter of the Roman community to the Corinthians (*1 Clem.*—after 96 CE).[34] Here we find a few citations or allusions that presuppose acquaintance with our documents. After a series of examples of self-sacrifice among pagans and Christians, the author mentions the 'blessed Judith', who 'placed herself in danger ... out of love for her paternal city', and 'Esther, perfect in her faith' (ἡ τέλεια κατὰ πίστιν) who, through 'her fasting and self-abasement', persuaded God to save his people (*1 Clem.* 55:4–6). This shows that these women were used in Rome as sermon illustrations and that Esther was actually cited according to the didactically expanded Greek text used by Josephus also at almost the same time and in the same place. In his letter Clement of Rome assumes that these brave women were also known in Corinth. Roughly a hundred years later, the two appear again in Clement of Alexandria, who extensively repeats Clement of Rome's paraphrase and adds Susanna and Miriam, Moses' sister.[35] The book of Esther also appears, for example, in a Chester Beatty uncial papyrus from the third century CE in Egypt.[36] Clement of Rome probably also knew

---

[33] See above, p. 21 n. 5. For the apocryphal material in Clement of Alexandria and the problem of his canon see the investigations of J. Ruwet, *Bib* 25 (1944), 134–66, 311–34; 29 (1948), 77–99, 240–68, 391–408.

[34] On the dating 'in the last decade of the first century', cf. A. Lindemann, *Die Clemensbriefe* (HNT 17; Tübingen, 1992), 12–13.

[35] *Strom* 4:118:4–4:119:3; cf. also 1:123:2. For Clement, cf. Lindemann (see above, n. 34), 156.

[36] Aland, *Repertorium* (see above, p. 41 n. 53), 30–3 (no. 010, Rahlfs no. 967). The Codex also contains significant portions of Ezekiel and the expanded Daniel; see above, p. 42 n. 57. There is an earlier Jewish text of Esther (late first or early second century) on a scroll published by K. Luchner, P Oxy 65 (1998), 4–8.

Wisdom.³⁷ Admittedly, Wisdom is never cited as 'Scripture'. The matter involves brief citations or allusions that are never specially indicated as such. *1 Clement* 34:1 probably alludes to Sirach 4:29b.³⁸ On the other hand, similarities in the context of the great concluding prayer³⁹ can be explained in relation to common Jewish liturgical diction. *1 Clement* demonstrates more clearly than any other document from the New Testament period how the piety, ethos and liturgy of Diaspora Judaism could be adopted almost seamlessly by Christian communities. Knowledge of the Maccabean martyr tradition and the *Martyrdom of Isaiah* could also contribute to the letter to the Hebrews, which, in my opinion, is also related to Rome, and which is already utilized in *1 Clement*.⁴⁰

It also seems noteworthy that traces of the documents with which we are concerned occur primarily in the West, but are scarcely transmitted in the East until Clement of Alexandria.

Tobit also seems to have been known very early in the Christian communities, even if the citation in the letter of Bishop Polycarp of Smyrna to the church in Philippi (*eleemosyna de morte liberat* [10:2], comes from Tobit 4:10/12:9) need not depend on the reading of the book of Tobit, being a basic moral injunction.⁴¹ The exhortation in *2 Clement* 16:4 may be more likely to presuppose the text of Tobit 12:8–9 since parallels are quite numerous.⁴² It seems relatively likely

---

³⁷ Cf. *1 Clement* 3:4 and Wisdom 21:24; *1 Clement* 27:5 and Wisdom 12:12 or 11:21–22; see also *1 Clement* 7:5 and Wisdom 12:10 (and Heb. 12:17); *1 Clement* 60:1 and Wisdom 7:17–18. Here, too, we do not know the origin of Clement's information. Knowledge of the book in the Christian community from the outset can, however, be demonstrated; cf. C. Larcher, *Études sur le livre de la Sagesse* (EtB; Paris, 1969), 11–84 (esp. 36–37); Stuhlmacher (see above, p. 107 n. 6), 'Bedeutung', 14–16, 20. Regarding additional passages, see Schürer (rev.) III/1, 573–6.

³⁸ *1 Clement*: ὁ νωθρὸς καὶ παρειμένος οὐκ ἀντοφθαλμεῖ τῷ ἐργοπαρέκτῃ αὐτοῦ; Sir: μὴ γίνου . . . νωθρὸς καὶ παρειμένος ἐν τοῖς ἔργοις σου. Cf. Rüger, 'Apokryphen I', 291.

³⁹ Cf., for example, *1 Clement* 59:3 and Sirach 16:18–19; Judith 9:11; 2 Maccabees 7:35; *1 Clement* 60:1; 61:2 and Sirach 2:11; 43:29–30; Tobit 3:2; 13:7, 11; *1 Clement* 63:1 and Sirach 51:26. Lindemann, *Clemensbriefe*, 168: 'Echoes of biblical (LXX) diction and also, especially, certain analogies to the Jewish Eighteen Benedictions are obvious.' See his exegesis, pp. 162–75.

⁴⁰ Cf. H.-F. Weiss, *Der Brief an die Hebräer* (KEK 13; 15th edn; Göttingen, 1991 [= the first edition of the revision]), 619–20, 621–2. For the parallels between *1 Clement* and Hebrews, cf. 76–8 (written to Rome) and 115–16; Lindemann, *Clemensbriefe*, 19–20.

⁴¹ Cf. Gamberoni (see above, p. 68 n. 33), *Die Auslegung Tobias*, 19–20.

⁴² *2 Clement*: καλὸν οὖν ἐλεημοσύνη ὡς μετάνοια ἁμαρτίας· κρείσσων νηστεία προσευχῆς, ἐλεημοσύνη δὲ ἀμφοτέρων· ἀγάπη δὲ καλύπτει πλῆθος ἁμαρτιῶν, προσευχὴ δὲ ἐκ καλῆς συνειδήσεως ἐκ θανάτου ῥύεται . . . ἐλεημοσύνη γὰρ κούφισμα ἁμαρτίας γίνεται; Tobit (Codices B + A): ἀγαθὸν προσευχὴ μετὰ νηστείας καὶ ἐλεημοσύνης καὶ δικαιοσύνης· ἀγαθὸν τὸ ὀλίγον μετὰ δικαιοσύνης ἢ πολὺ μετὰ ἀδικίας· καλὸν ποιῆσαι ἐλεημοσύνην ἢ θησαυρίσαι χρυσίον. ἐλεημοσύνη γὰρ ἐκ θανάτου ῥύεται, καὶ αὐτὴ ἀποκαθαριεῖ πᾶσαν ἁμαρτίαν. Cf. Lindemann, *Clemensbriefe*, 248.

that *2 Clement* is a Roman sermon from the first half of the second century.[43] Then at the beginning of the third century, Hippolytus of Rome, in his commentary on Daniel, compares God's help for Susanna with that experienced by Tobias and Sarah.[44] Whereas, *contra* Gamberoni, no use of Tobit in Tertullian can be demonstrated, this little book is cited relatively often in Cyprian's ethical exhortation and is introduced as 'scriptura divina' or even 'Dominus'.[45] On the other hand, Irenaeus knows Tobit and Haggai only as the names of Old Testament prophets among the Ophites.[46] This may have already been older community tradition. Clement of Alexandria mentions the Tobit story in his outline of the 'salvation history' from Moses to Malachi (*Stromateis* 1:123:5). He cites (2:139:2) the golden rule from Tobit 4:15 as ἡ γραφή and, similarly (*Stromateis* 6:102:2), the piety rule from Tobit 1:28 as ἀγαθὸν προσευχὴ μετὰ νηστείας, although in the transposed form, ἀγαθὸν νηστεία μετὰ προσευχῆς (cf. *2 Clem.* 16:4).[47]

In all, up to the beginning of the third century, there is a rather timid use of the book, through which, thanks to its catechetico-paraenetic interests, an element of Jewish piety in the best sense also pervaded the church. The catechetico-paraenetic use of such texts indicates the extent to which the self-understanding and lived piety of early Christian communities essentially resembled those of the synagogue elites.

Tertullian is the second witness for Judith after Clement of Rome— once again in the West. The Montanist rigorist praises her after Isaac and John, the 'spado Christi', for the uniqueness of her marriage and 'tot alia exampla sanctorum'.[48] In *Adversus Marcionem* 1:7:2 we find reference to Holofernes after Alexander and Darius. As with the two Clements, of Rome and of Alexandria, the book does not stand so much in the foreground as does the person as a moral example. The Alexandrian is the first to cite (*Strom* 2:35:4) from the work itself the conclusion of the heroine's exhortation (8:27b), although with no formal introduction. Only Origen deals with the document rather more frequently.[49] In his homily

---

[43] Despite Lindemann's reservations (see above, p. 115 n. 34; p. 89 n. 37) about Rome as the origin, this solution seems more likely to me because of parallels with *1 Clem.*; so also A. v. Harnack, *Geschichte der altchristlichen Literatur bis Eusebius, II/1: Die Chronologie der Literatur bis Irenäus nebst einleitenden Untersuchungen* (2nd edn; Leipzig, 1958), 442–6.

[44] Op. cit. (see above, p. 96 n. 55), 40 (1:28:6).

[45] *De Biblia Patristica* II, 207 counts eighteen citations, some of which are extensive (from seven documents), two others occur in the *Vita Cypriani*. Of the second- and third-century authors, Cyprian cites it most often after Origen.

[46] *Adv Haer* 1:30:11; see above, p. 68 n. 33.

[47] The references can be found in Schürer (rev.) III/1, 227; *Biblia Patristica* I (see above, p. 67 n. 23), 217–18 (seven passages); cf. also Swete, 273–4.

[48] *De Monogamia* 17:1.

[49] For the references, cf., besides Swete, 272–3, and Schürer (rev.) III/1, 220, also A.-M. Dubarle, *Judith, Formes et sens des diverses traditions I* (AnBib 24; Rome, 1966), 110–25, 172–4, and *idem*, 'La mention de Judith dans la littérature ancienne juive

on Numbers 27:1, he refers to the moral instruction of the catechumen through reading Esther, Tobit, Judith and the commandments of Wisdom;[50] in *De Oratione* 29:3, he praises her along with Esther and others as the model supplicant, although, referring to Ephesians 4:25, he reproaches her skill—also that of Jacob—in deception.[51] In the Jeremiah homilies[52] he offers, in reference to Judith 12:6–7, 14, an example ἀπὸ τῆς γραφῆς of how a 'righteous person' can break an agreement. Despite certain ethical reservations, the book found ultimate recognition from him, while his contemporary Cyprian completely ignored it, probably because of his objections to its content.

With respect to the books of Maccabees, one can assume that Hebrews 11:35 (presumably in Rome once again)—ἄλλοι δὲ ἐτυμπανίσθησαν οὐ προσδεξάμενοι τὴν ἀπολύτρωσιν ἵνα κρείττονος ἀναστάσεως τύχωσιν—shows knowledge of the martyr legends in 2 Maccabees 6:18–7:42. Hebrews 11:3–4 could be based on 2 Maccabees 5:27 (cf. 6:30).[53] The motif of the creation of the world from nothing (ὅτι οὐκ ἐξ ὄντων ἐποίησεν αὐτά [sc. heaven and earth] ὁ θεός—2 Macc. 7:28) appears again in Hermas 26:1 (= *Mandata* 1:1—ὁ θεός, ὁ . . . ποίησας ἐκ τοῦ μὴ ὄντος εἰς τὸ εἶναι τὰ πάντα). Since at this point Hermas is quoting part of a Jewish confession of faith, literary dependence remains uncertain. We find such dependence, however, in the *Letter of the*

---

et chrétienne', *RB* 66 (1959), 514–49. On the Greek text, see R. Hanhart, *Text und Textgeschichte des Buches Judith* (MSU 14; Göttingen, 1979); for the problem of the Aramaic or Hebrew exemplar and the confusion already of the texts available to Jerome, see pp. 8–10.

[50] Origen, 'In Numeros Homilia XXVII', *GCS Origenes* 7, W. A. Baehrens, ed. (Leipzig, 1921), 255–80 (256): 'His ergo cum recitatur talis aliqua divinorum voluminum lectio, in qua non videatur aliquid obscurum, libenter accipiunt, verbi causa, ut est libellus Hester aut Iudith vel etiam Tobiae aut mandata Sapientiae.' The reason is 'because it contains a simple moral instruction, without obscurity, immediately accessible to the reader' (so Harl, Dorival and Munnich, 323). According to Origen, the opposite of these books is Leviticus, from which the beginner would turn immediately away because he cannot recognize its hidden meaning, which is the main thing in this case. We may set aside the question of whether this betrays an anti-Jewish polemic against the use of Leviticus as a reading primer for children (so Rüger, 'Werden', 187 n. 11; cf. also Hengel, *Judentum und Hellenismus*, 151 = *idem*, *Judaism and Hellenism*, 82–3), or whether this advice is simply the product of long teaching experience. In any case, it is certain that the use of Judith, Tobit, Sapientia Salomonis and Sirach by minors and catechumens indicates the protreptic character of these documents. In the longer term, however, it provides for their 'secondary' canonization since they were gradually sanctioned by expanding use in the church. This development is more pronounced in the West than in the East (see above, pp. 63, 66–9).

[51] Origen, 'De oratione', *GCS Origenes 2*, P. Koetschau, ed. (Leipzig, 1898), 295–403 (citation, p. 382).

[52] Origen, 'Homile 20 zu Jer 20:7–12', *GCS Origenes 3*, E. Klostermann, ed. (Leipzig, 1901), 176–94 (187–8).

[53] See above, p. 116 n. 40.

Martyrs of Lyon (177 CE)[54] where the slave Blandina is compared to the heroic martyr mother who exhorted her sons and was the last to die.

Since Clement of Alexandria mentions the 'book of the deeds of the Maccabees', in the same breath as Esther (*Strom* 1:123:2), he presumably means the second book, since, just before (1:123:1), he refers to Nehemiah as the builder of the temple. This idea is found only in the story in 2 Maccabees 1:19–36. In *Strom* 5:97:7 he refers directly to 2 Maccabees 1:10.[55]

1 Maccabees, utilized extensively by Josephus in Rome (who disregards 2 Maccabees), is first mentioned by Tertullian in *Adversos Judaeos* 4:10 (*temporibus Maccabaeorum*), where he describes the victorious battle against the enemy on the Sabbath (1 Macc. 2:38, 40–41, 48). At almost the same time, Hippolytus of Rome utilized it frequently in his Daniel commentary to demonstrate the fulfilment of Daniel's prophecies in the period of the Diadochi and the persecution under Antiochus IV. Later, Porphyrius showed Daniel to be a *vaticinium ex eventu* during the Maccabean struggle, i.e. he too must have known the Jewish sources well. The fact that, in addition to Origen, Hippolytus already knew several books of Maccabees can be deduced from the fact that in his commentary on Daniel 3 he refers to 1 Maccabees 1:5–9 with the formula ἐν τῇ πρώτῃ βίβλῳ τῶν Μακκαβαϊκῶν ἀναγέγραπται.[56] In contrast, he seems to have regarded the second book as having only marginal status. At about the same time as Hippolytus, the Christian Julius Africanus, the librarian of Caesar Severus Alexander (222–35), attests to knowledge of 1 Maccabees in his chronography.[57]

Cyprian also cites 1 Maccabees repeatedly, and even more often the story of the martyrs in 2 Maccabees 6 and 7. This acquaintance continues in the West with Victorinus of Pettau (d. 304).[58] Furthermore, Lactantius could use 2 Maccabees as something of a literary model for his work, *De mortibus persecutorum*.[59] Notably, here, too, the first two books of Maccabees were apparently less valued in the East: Clement of Alexandria mentions them only in passing and they appear more often only in the great work of Origen, primarily here too the martyrology of

---

[54] Cf. Eusebius, *Hist Eccl* 5:1:55 with 2 Maccabees 7:21–3, 27–9.

[55] Cf. Schürer (rev.) III/1, 534.

[56] Hippolytus (see above, p. 96 n. 55), 194. For the references, cf. Schürer (rev.) III/1, 183.

[57] Cf. *Biblia Patristica* II (see above, p. 67 n. 23), 228 (1 Macc. 16:1–2, 21–4). The scanty remains of this first Christian chronicle of the world are published in M. Routh, *Reliquiae Sacrae* II (Oxford, 1846), 238–309 (290).

[58] *De Fabrica Mundi* 6, CSEL 49, J. Haussleiter, ed., 1–9 (6), an allusion to the events reported in 1 Maccabees 2:24–25 and 2:40–41. In his commentaries, Victorinus depends on Papias, Irenaeus, Hippolytus and, especially, Origen.

[59] Cf. Lactantius, *De Mortibus Persecutorum*, J. L. Creed, ed. (Oxford, 1984), xxxviii–xxxix.

2 Maccabees 6 and 7. Interest is concentrated on a few passages.[60] This more prominent use of the books of Maccabees in the West may be related, among other factors, to the typical Roman regard for anything military. We already encounter this attitude in *1 Clement* 21:4; 28:2; 36:6–37:4; 41:1—also even in Tertullian, generally so rigorous, but a centurion's son.

One might anticipate better attestation for Wisdom, theologically multi-faceted and often very similar to New Testament literature, than for the works mentioned so far. But as C. Larcher's extensive overview demonstrates,[61] this is true only to a degree. Apart from *1 Clement*, already cited, clear allusions are missing in the Apostolic Fathers and in the majority of the Apologists. Perhaps one may assume that Tatian, Justin's student in Rome, summarized the statement in Wisdom 2:23 in his *Oratio ad Graecos* 7:1. Melito, too, may assume knowledge of Wisdom in his Passover Homily, although, in my opinion, Larcher over-estimates the significance of the similarities. These can be explained equally well through the terminology of Judaeo-Hellenistic passover preaching Melito employs.

Irenaeus, by contrast, does mention the document—again in the West. According to Eusebius (*Hist Eccl* 5:26), Irenaeus refers to the Letter to the Hebrews and the 'so-called Wisdom of Solomon' in a lost book of 'various conversations' (διαλέξεων διαφόρων), probably a collection of sermons and also cites the latter. To be sure, we find a few points of contact in *Adversus Haereses*, but only one 'citation', and this without direct introduction.[62]

A little later, Tertullian (*Adversus Valentinianos* 2:2) alludes to the beginning of the work (Wisd. 1:1–2): 'Porro facies dei spectatur in simplicitate quaerendi, ut docet ipsa Sophia, non quidem Valentini, sed Salomonis.'[63] He also adduces Wisdom 2:12. There are a few additional citations and points of contact. Thus, Wisdom was unambiguous Holy Scripture for neither Irenaeus nor Tertullian. The relative confusion concerning this book is also reflected in the contemporary Muratorian Canon—also of Roman origin, perhaps in the time of Hippolytus—where it turns up among New Testament writings between the two letters of John and the apocalypses of John and Peter. In the Greek original, the unknown author may have even claimed Philo as the author (see above, pp. 69–70). Clement of Alexandria was the first to be fully satisfied with the book and to cite it as Solomon's work. Cyprian also makes frequent

---

[60] See *Biblia Patristica* III (see above, p. 67 n. 23), 220–1; cf. also Swete, 276–8.

[61] Larcher (see above, p. 115 n. 37), 36–46.

[62] *Adv Haer* 4:38:3, 'incorruptela vero proximum facit esse Deo', derives from Wisdom 6:19, ἀφθαρσία δὲ ἐγγὺς εἶναι ποιεῖ θεοῦ.

[63] Tertullian, *Adv Valentinianos*, CChr.SL 2, 751–78, here, 754; cf. also *De Praescriptione Haereticorum* 7:10; *Adversus Marcionem* 3:22:5 and Fragment IV, where Wisdom 3:1 is cited (loc. cit. 1335).

use of it under the name Sapientia Salomonis and sometimes introduces it as 'scriptura divina', 'scriptura sancta', or 'scriptum est', etc.[64] Origen, who occasionally cites it, although very much less often than Proverbs or Job, is aware of the canonical problem and has reservations about its Solomonic authorship (see above, p. 69 n. 38). Methodius of Olympus in Asia Minor (d. 311) was the first to show a pronounced preference for it.[65] Yet a certain reticence could never be completely eliminated in the Eastern church.

The proverbial wisdom of Sirach, too, exercised no major influence in the second century so far as is known. *Didache* 4:5 and the identical *Barnabas* 19:9 correspond in substance to Sirach 4:31, but what we find here is a common exhortation from the doctrine of the two ways. No use can be demonstrated in the Apologists, not even in Irenaeus and Tertullian. It is in the *Paidagogos* of Clement of Alexandria that the relatively frequent catechetical use, already mentioned, first becomes apparent. He also repeatedly cites Sirach as γραφή or with ἡ σοφία λέγει and related formulae, and in certain circumstances as sayings of Christ, the true παιδαγωγός.[66] The designation, σοφία 'Ιησοῦ appears twice.[67] Four times in the *Stromateis* Clement also names Solomon as the author, presumably because at these points he is quoting from memory.[68] In the *Paidagogos*, where, understandably, most of the references occur, he seems to have had the book to hand and avoids such errors. In one case, however, he declares the maxims of Sirach 34(31):29 to be older than the tragedies of Sophocles, presumably because he attributed it to Solomon.[69]

The pseudo-cyprianic document, *De Aleatoribus* chap. 2, which may date back to the beginning of the third century, cites Sirach for the first time in the West with the formula 'et alia scriptura dicit'. Cyprian values Sirach much as did Clement, but consistently introduces it as a work of Solomon (!).[70] This practice spreads in the West and Jerome polemicizes

---

[64] The passages in Clement of Alexandria or Cyprian can be found in Schürer (rev.) III/1, 574 or 575, respectively.

[65] For the Septuagint passages in his work, cf. the index in *Le Banquet*, H. Musurillo and V.-H. Debidour, eds (SC 95; Paris, 1963), 336 (nine passages).

[66] γραφή: *Paid* I:8:62, 68; II:2:34; 5:46; 8:69; 8:76; 10:98–9; III:3:17, 23; 4:29; 11:58, 83; ἡ σοφία λέγει: *Paid* I:8:69, 72; 9:75; 13:102; II:1:8; 2:24; 7:54, 58–9; *Strom* 5:3:18; παιδαγωγός: *Paid* II:10:99, cf. 101, 109.

[67] *Strom* 1:4:27; 10:47. The title of the book in the Greek manuscripts is Σοφία 'Ιησοῦ υἱοῦ Σιράχ.

[68] *Strom* 2:5:24 (2×); 6:16:146; 7:16:105.

[69] *Paid* II:2:24; regarding the entire subject, see O. Stählin, *Clemens Alexandrinus und die Septuaginta* (Nürnberg, 1901), 46–58; Schürer (rev.) III/1, 207.

[70] For *De Aleatoribus*, cf. CSEL 3/3, 94; the passages in Cyprian are in Schürer (rev.) III/1, 208. The Latin designation Ecclesiasticus also stems from Cyprian: 'The later name . . . marks the book as the most important or the most popular of the *libri ecclesiastici*— the books which the Church used for the purpose of instruction, although they were not included in the Jewish canon' (Swete, 270).

against it in his commentary on Daniel 9:24, where he alludes to the high priest Simon—'quo regente populum, Iesus filius Sirach scripsit librum qui graeca Πανάρετος appellatur et a plerisque Salomonis falso dicitur'.[71] For this reason, Western canon lists often list five Solomonic documents as a wisdom 'Pentateuch'.[72] Despite its profitable content, Sirach had difficulty in gaining acceptance in the church, as among the rabbis, because it was too recent. Only 'intellectual kinship' to the biblical author Solomon strengthened its authority, primarily in the West, very much as the anonymous letter to the Hebrews earlier found acceptance in the East as a purportedly Pauline document. In the East, the designation πανάρετος σοφία, first used in reference to Proverbs,[73] was also applied to it.[74]

c) The Dissemination and Prevalence of These Writings in the Church

Why did these writings, although absent from the Hebrew Bible (which, despite all reservations, still finally remained the model) ultimately prevail in church use, immediately in the West, more slowly and half-heartedly in the East? Basically, Luther's well-known assessment is sufficient here. They were 'useful and good to read' for the church, which was gaining stability and moving into broader layers of society toward the end of the second and the beginning of the third century. The ethos represented in them—except for the readiness for martyrdom—rejected all extremes. At the same time, they were clearly monotheistic and humanitarian, with an orientation towards God's commandments. Their effect was didactic, and truly furthered discipline (παιδεία); thus they essentially bound together church and synagogue, which stood nearer to one another at this point than both wished to acknowledge. They represented a practical civic humanity and piety which was just, upright, even heroic in conflicts of faith, and thus constituted a genuine 'praeparatio evangelica'. Admittedly, there remained a thorn that may have even become more pointed as scholarship developed: these words were still 'not considered of equal value with the Holy Scriptures'—

---

[71] CChr. SL 75 A: *Hieronymus* I/5, *Commentariorum in Danielem III zu Dan 9:24*, F. Glorie, ed. (Turnhout, 1965), 860–912 (873), with reference to Eusebius, *Dem Ev* 8:2:71 (see below, n. 74).

[72] Schürer (rev.) III/1, 208; cf. E. Nestle, 'Miscellen 8. Fünf Bücher Salomos', *ZAW* 27 (1907): 294–7.

[73] Cf. *1 Clem.* 57:3–5: the citation from Proverbs 1:23–25 is introduced with οὕτως γὰρ λέγει ἡ πανάρετος σοφία; cf. also Clement of Alexandria, *Strom* 2:136:3 (Prov. 1:32); and Hegesippus in Eusebius, *Hist Eccl* 4:22:9. Cf. G. W. H. Lampe, *A Patristic Greek Lexicon*, 1961, 1001: 'Title of Wisdom Books (as enshrining revelation of divine wisdom)'.

[74] First by Eusebius in his history, then also in his *Dem Ev* 8:2:71, see *GCS Eusebius* 6, I. A. Heikel, ed. (Leipzig, 1913), 380: '... Ιησοῦς ὁ τοῦ Σιρὰχ ... ὁ τὴν καλουμένην πανάρετον Σοφίαν', cf. Schürer (rev.) III/1, 207.

especially not in the East. Their moral-pedagogical effect, to which Clement and Origen called attention, was helpful primarily for the instruction of catechumens. For this reason, especially, these writings were not overlooked. A solid literature, suitable for edification and instruction, venerable because of its age, was needed; but at the same time, a literature that expressed the continuity of the church with the teachers and pious heroes of ancient Israel, God's chosen people. It may be that Tobit, Judith, Sirach and Wisdom already had an analogous function in the instruction of proselytes in a number of synagogues of the Diaspora. This remains mere speculation, however; it is mentioned by neither Philo nor Josephus.

The question of *how* they prevailed is to be separated from the question of *why*. What I offer in conclusion is necessarily no more than a hypothesis. The cause may lie in the community archive or library of the Roman mega-church at the time of Clement. After 70, Rome—unlike Alexandria and Antioch, which had both suffered heavily because of the Jewish War of 66–73—still had an intact, large and prosperous Jewish community with a considerable 'aura', despite all efforts, such as Domitian's, to suppress it. Christians participated in it. In Alexandria, the two Jewish rebellions in the first half of the second century will presumably have also involved the (predominantly Judaeo-)Christian community in severe suffering. This would explain the lack of information before the end of the second century. The dispute about the conversion—to Judaism or Christianity?—of Titus Flavius Clemens and his wife Domitilla typifies the situation in Rome toward the end of the first century.[75] The great Christian community was, as shown presumably in Hebrews and clearly in *1 Clement*, harshly impacted by this Judaeo-Hellenistic milieu in the Roman capital. What was valued there as instructional reading was also interesting for the Christians. Thus, the books named were also available to them: 'not equally valued . . . but useful and good to read'. In this light, the starting point for Clement of Rome and the wider attestation in the West becomes comprehensible. So does the early translation of the Old Latin, around or soon after 200, from the Greek, including the books under discussion, sometimes in a unique old form of the text. So the Old Latin text of Sirach has additions which must go back to a Greek original that has not been preserved. It is perhaps the most important witness for the significance of this 'edifying-instructional' literature, borrowed from the synagogue. During the first three centuries no community attracted so many Christian travellers of all kinds, bishops and intellectuals from all parts of the Empire, as the capital city. Its archive was also interesting to

---

[75] Dio Cassius 67:14:2. *Contra* Schürer (rev.) III/1, 79 n. 97 and 168–9 n. 57, the question of the conversion to Judaism or Christianity is *not* to be decided definitively in favour of the first possibility; cf. Hengel (see above, p. 48 n. 75), 'Schürer', 39–40.

visitors, as Hegesippus and Irenaeus testify. The list of bishops as well as the catalogue of Gospels and their authors in Irenaeus originated there, in my opinion.[76] Occasionally the community itself published books; in *Hermas* 8:3 (*Vis* 2:4:3), Clement is given the responsibility of sending the heavenly letter received by the prophet Hermas to 'cities abroad'. Thus the distribution of documents, in addition to letters, also served propaganda purposes to some extent. Such need not have been the case with our texts; the interest of visitors who made copies is sufficient to explain this. Thus the books came to Lyon, Carthage, even finally in the third century to Pettau in Styria, and, naturally, also to the East. There was an old connection between Rome and Alexandria. The Mark legend in Eusebius (and in the letter fragment of Clement of Alexandria, the authenticity of which is very disputed) was not created entirely from thin air.[77] Naturally, some of these documents also circulated in the East, but they were less highly esteemed there. But the mere fact that they were read and utilized in instruction in Rome and then also in Alexandria (*1 Clement*, Clement of Alexandria) made them interesting elsewhere as well, especially since they were completely non-speculative and gave rise to no 'gnostic dangers'. *1 Clement*, Hermas and *2 Clement*, and the leader of the catechetical school in Alexandria attest to a 'Christian civic spirit' that might seem to be in sympathy with the tone of those apocryphal Jewish writings.

This does not rule out the possibility that some documents were also transmitted in other places. *3* and *4 Maccabees*, originating considerably later in the first century CE, and attested only since Eusebius,[78] seem to have 'caught on' in the East. The same is true of the *Psalms of Solomon* which only rarely found their way on to church book-shelves.

The strict authority of the community, which did not have monarchical leadership until well into the middle of the second century but was divided into several 'house churches', was not decisive for dependence on Rome as the motivation for adopting these simpler works, but rather the curiosity and practicality of visitors interested in books 'useful and good to read'. Initially, they were rarely employed in

---

[76] I follow here the convincing thesis of Thornton (see above, p. 111 n. 22), 48–53, who has extensively investigated these witnesses; see also Hengel, *Evangelienüberschriften* (see above, p. 22 n. 12), 37–40. On Sirach see W. Thiele, 'Die lateinischen Sirachtexte als Zeugnis der griechischen Sirachüberlieferung', in *Evangelium-Schriftauslegung-Kirche: FS P. Stuhlmacher zum 65: Geburtstag*, ed. J. Ådna et alii (Göttingen, 1997), 394–402.

[77] Eusebius (*Hist Eccl* 2:24) names the evangelist Mark as the first bishop of Alexandria, active until the eighth year of Nero's reign; cf. however, the contradictions in *Hist Eccl* 4:11:6. For the purported letter of Clement, which cites the 'Secret Gospel according to Mark', cf. H. Merkel, 'Anhang: Das "geheime Evangelium" nach Markus: Fragmente des "geheimen Evangeliums" nach Markus', in *NTApo* I (5th edn), 89–92 (bibliography). I personally believe it is unauthentic.

[78] Cf. Schürer (rev.) III/1, 540, 591.

worship and theological debate. The marked reticence of the Apologists and the relative reticence of an Irenaeus or a Tertullian speak against such usage. The fact that this church, which was rich and situated in the capital of the empire and which, after the destruction of Jerusalem, became the most important, could 'teach' otherwise is evident, not only in *1 Clement* and the *Shepherd of Hermas*, but also in opinions such as those expressed in Ignatius, *Letter to the Romans* 3:1, and later in Irenaeus, *Adversus Haereses* 3:3:1–3.[79]

The practical sensibility they address, a sensibility related to the shaping of life and the significance of examples, unites two otherwise very distinct figures: Clement of Alexandria and Cyprian both held these documents in high esteem for ethical instruction and—not least— for their exhortation to martyrdom. They contain impressive examples and practical-moral wisdom for the Christian citizenry that, since the time of Commodus himself, was spreading even into senatorial circles. Clement, probably born in Athens and widely travelled—from lower Italy (probably even Rome) to Syria or Palestine—helped them, then, to gain acceptance even in the East, although only with partial success. The greater confidence in their use in the West could be an additional indication of their Roman origin.

Despite this pragmatic attitude, East and West could not fully agree on the question of the Old Testament canon. This is not the place to trace the disputes that continued in the fourth and fifth centuries; we have already referred briefly to them above (pp. 63–4). Only the West was truly 'consistent'. In contrast, Athanasius' bipartite division prevailed in the East. According to the testimony of the Interorthodox Commission, it is still valid today. Its assessment of the second group, the Ἀναγινωσκόμενα, comes astonishingly close to Luther's: 'that these texts are to be distinguished from the canonical and inspired books as regards the authority of their divine inspiration, but that they are to be considered nevertheless as part of Holy Scripture, and *useful and profitable to the faithful*'.[80]

As a New Testament scholar and Christian theologian, I would like to pose a question in view of the problem emerging here. Does the church

---

[79] Cf. Lampe (see above, p. 22 n. 9), *Christen*, 70–1, 341–3, 433, index, s.v. 'Lehrer'; Thornton (see above, p. 111 n. 22), *Zeuge des Zeugen*, 31–47. See also for the Gospel collection M. Hengel, *The Four Gospels and the One Gospel of Jesus Christ* (London, 2000). The bookshelves of the Roman community were the most important after 70 and until the end of the second century.

[80] 'Divine Revelation and the Way It Expresses Itself for the Salvation of Man: Towards the Great Council' (1973), 4. Thus was rescinded a decision of the Synod of Jerusalem (1672), in which Tobit, Sirach, Judith and Wisdom had been declared canonical; cf. Rüger, 'Apokryphen I', 138–40; E. Oikonomos, 'Die Bedeutung der deuterokanonischen Schriften in der orthodoxen Kirche', in *Apokryphenfrage* (see above, p. 66 n. 22), Meurer, ed., 26–40.

still need a clearly demarcated, strictly closed Old Testament canon, since the New Testament is, after all, the 'conclusion', the goal and the fulfilment of the Old? Indeed, does one not face an essential contradiction if one, in an unhistorical biblicism, clings to a limited 'Hebrew', or better pharisaical, 'canon' from Jabneh? Must not the Old Testament remain to a degree open to the New? Is not a figure like the eschatological prophet John the Baptist the most important example—in the New Testament itself—of this openness of the Old for the New, the final? 'The Law and the Prophets are until John', says Jesus in Luke 16:16 (cf. Matt. 11:13). We simply cannot go any further back. Even the varying, relatively open margins of the Greek Old Testament in the early church, where the book of *Enoch* was discussed with equal intensity, can be regarded as a sign that 'the Law and the Prophets' were not simply closed with 'Ezra' or Esther, but only find their goal and fulfilment in the messianic work of Jesus of Nazareth. Only through this understanding of the Old Testament 'canon' does the religious wealth of late Old Testament and early Jewish literature from the time before the closing of the Hebrew-Pharisaic canon (*c.* 100 CE) become truly visible. The origin of Christianity as well as of rabbinic Judaism after 70 CE becomes at all historically interesting and comprehensible only through this literature, which includes in a wider dimension also Josephus, Philo and the Pseudepigrapha. One portion of this literature was preserved, sometimes unwillingly, by Christian tradition; the other comes to light now in the Qumran texts. The great interest that this rich 'post-biblical' Jewish text tradition finds among Jews and Christians could perhaps be assessed as a sign of the relative openness of the 'canon' in both directions, given the fact that Jews and Christians parted ways conclusively only after the destruction of Jerusalem toward the end of the first century CE.

I would, therefore, like to end with some fundamental reflections of Harmut Gese:[81]

A Christian theologian may never approve of the masoretic canon. The continuity with the New Testament is in significant measure broken here. It seems to me that, among the effects of humanism on the Reformation, the most fateful was that the reduced pharisaic canon and the masoretic textual tradition which was appealed to as a 'humanistic' source were confused with one another and the apocrypha were set aside. With the thesis of the essential

---

[81] H. Gese, 'Erwägungen zur Einheit der biblischen Theologie', in *Vom Sinai zum Zion* (BevTh 64; Munich, 1974; 3rd edn 1990), 11–30 (16–17); the essay appeared first in *ZThK* 67 (1970), 417–36; see also, *idem, Zur biblischen Theologie* (BevTh 78; Munich 1977 = 3rd edn; Tübingen, 1989), 13: 'Since the historical discoveries of the nineteenth century and especially after those at Qumran, we no longer have scientific grounds for separating the apocrypha. But precisely since this time, the Bible societies seem to have sworn to protect us from the apocrypha.' See also *idem, Alttestamentliche Studien*, 25–8.

unity of the Old and New Testaments, of the one biblical tradition, the precarious question of the Christian interpretation of the Old Testament was settled . . . The New Testament brought the formation of Old Testament tradition to an end, a final conclusion. The formation of biblical tradition is thus, as a whole, concluded and thus, for the first time, in a deeper sense, canonical.

INDEX OF BIBLICAL AND EXTRA-BIBLICAL CITATIONS

Citations in square brackets refer to alternative versification in the LXX;
italicized page numbers refer to footnotes.

I. Old Testament

Genesis	78, *107*, *112*
1:2	80
36:33	86
49:10 (LXX)	33
Exodus	78, 106–7, *112*
3:14	80
7:8–10	71
20:2–3	114
22:27	80
Leviticus	107, *112*, *118*
Numbers	42, 107
11:24, 26	*26*
11:26f.	71
Deuteronomy	42, 100, 106–7, *112*
4:2	77
10:15	36
12:32	77
29:19, 26	77
34:10	27
Joshua	78, 107
19	84
Judges	78, 84, 98, 101
1 Samuel [1 Kings]	98, 101, 107
2:15	*98*
15:8–9, 32–33	88
2 Samuel [2 Kings]	107
22:3, 47	16
23:3	16
1 Kings [3 Kings]	107
2 Kings [4 Kings]	107
17:9	*16*
18:8	*16*

Isaiah	30, 42, 46, 83, 85, 89, 95, 106–7, 111
3:10	33
7:10	31
7:14	9, 29–30, 33
7:14 (LXX)	29–30, 33
10:17 (LXX)	*70*
19:18–21	85
26:3	*16*
25:(6,) 8	7
43:10–11	114
44:6	114
53:7–8 (LXX)	*90*
64:3	*109*
66:1	114
Jeremiah	42, 84–5, 101, 107, 113, *114*
11:19 (LXX)	32
45:1–5	*114*
Ezekiel	42, 85, 92, 107
19:9	*16*
Hosea	
13:10	7
Jonah	
2:10	54
3:4	53
Micah	
4:3–7	*29*
Habakkuk	
3	59
Haggai	45, 100, 117
Zechariah	45, 100
11	4
11:11	4
12:10	7

13:2	100
13:7	4
Malachi	45, 100
Psalms see also Subject Index	
2	106
8	106
22	106
31:3 [30:3]	15–16
45	106
49:14 [48:14]	15
69	106
74:9	100
78:2	*105*
80:14 [79:14]	1
81:6f. [82:6f.]	33
89	106
96:10 [95:10]	32
118	106
151 (LXX)	57, 65
Job	28, 72, 79, 83, 86, 89, 107–8, *112*
42:17b–e (LXX)	86
Proverbs	78, 91–2, 107, 112, 121–2
1:23ff.	*122*
1:32	*122*
4:13	*16*
7:7–20	*92*
8:22–24	86
20:28	*16*
Ruth	46, 62, *82*, 97, 101
Canticles	28, 46, 62–3, 68–9, *82*, 89, 91–2, 97, 101, 107, 113
7:11, 12–13	*92*
Qoheleth	28, 46, 62, 68–9, *82*, 83, 89, 91, 93, 101, 107, 113
11:9	*92*
Lamentations	28, 46, 62, *82*, 97, 101, 107, 114
2:9	100
Esther	28, 42, 46, 62, 68–9, 73–4, 87–92, 97, 100–1, 107, 113, 115, 119, 126
10:3l (LXX)	81, 85

Daniel	42, 84, 90–3, 95, 97, 100, 107, 111, 119
2	95
3	88
3:38	100
4–6 (LXX)	88
6:23	*113*
7	95
7:9–17	95
7:13	95
9:27	*67*
11	88
11:31	*67*
12	95
12:1 (Prototheod.)	*32*
12:11	*67*
Ezra [= 2 Ezra]	28, 32, 73, 82, 83, 87, 89, 98, 100, 107, 126
1:7–11	81
5:13–6:5	81
6:19–21 (LXX)	*32*
7:19	81
Nehemiah	45, 82, 83, 87, 89, 98
7:71–8:13a	87
1 Chronicles	84, 91
2 Chronicles	42, 84, 87, 91

II. Additional Scriptures of the Septuagint and the Old Testament Apocrypha and Pseudepigrapha

a) LXX Scriptures

3 Ezra [1 Ezra]	32, 82, 87, *101*, 113
1:1–2	*32*
3–4	87
4:49f.	87
7:10–12	*32*
Judith	11, 46, *50*, 68, 70, 74, 91–92, 102, 113, 118, 123, *125*
8:27b	117
9:11	*116*
12:6–7, 14	118

Tobit	46, 50, 68, 70–1, 84, 87, 90–2, 102, 112–13, 117–18, 123, *125*
1:28	117
3:2	*116*
4:10	116
4:15	117
12:8–9	116
12:9	116
13	*94*
13:7, 11	*116*
13:13–15	*94*
14:5–7	*94*
1 Maccabees	3, 46, 69, 70, 74, 79, 82, 91, 93, 101–2, 113, 119–20
1:5–9	119
2:38, 40–41, 48	119
2:42	*88*
4:46	*45*, 100
7:13	*88*
8:17	85
9:27	*45*, 100
10–16	93–4
14:4–15	93
14:41	*45*, 100
16:1–2, 21–24	*119*
2 Maccabees	3, 8, 68–71, 74, 91, 93, 102, 111, 113, 119–20
1:10	119
1:10b–2:18	81
1:18–19	119
2:13	85, 98
4:11	*85*
5:27	118
6–7	119
6:30	118
6:18–7:42	118
7:9, 14	*94*
7:21–23	*119*
7:27–29	*119*
7:28	118
7:35	*116*
12:43	*94*
14:6	*88*
15:37	92
15:40	*94*
3 Maccabees	69, 70–1, 91, 113, 118, 124

4 Maccabees	69, 70–1, 91, 113, 118, 124
Oratio Manassis	58
Wisdom of Solomon	8, 11, *50*, 70–1, 73–4, 82, 91, 93–4, 111–13, 116, 120–1, 123, *125*
1:1–1	120
2:12	120
2:23	120
2:24	*116*
3:1	*120*
6:19	*120*
7:17	*116*
11:17	*70*, 80
11:21–22	*116*
12:10	*116*
12:12	*116*
14:11	*67*
Jesus ben Sirach	3, 11, 44–6, *50*, 70–1, 73–4, 86, 90–1, 93–4, 100, 111–12, 121, 123, *125*
Prolog	4, 85, 96–8
Prolog 1	2
Prolog 10	2
Prolog 10–11	2
Prolog 22	2
Prolog 25	2
Prolog 26	2
Prolog 44–50	2
1:10b	109
2:11	*116*
4:29b	116
4:31	121
5:11	*111*
6:28–29	*111*
16:18–19	*116*
24	110
24:19	*111*
31:29	121
36:1–19	*94*
36:1–18	*94*
38:4c–39:1	97
43:29–30	*116*
44–50:24	97
46:1	*27*
49:10	2
49:13–15	*45*
51:23, 26–27	*111*
51:26	*116*

Baruch   55–6, 70, 73, 91,
                  94, 112–14
1:1–3:8   *114*
1:14   *114*
3:29–4:1   113
3:36   *114*
3:38   114
4:5–5:9   *94*
4:30–32   *94*
4:36–5:9   *113*
6:3–5   114

Letter of Jeremiah   91, 114

Greek Additions to Daniel see also
Subject Index

Susannah
14   *47*
20:52–53
  [13:20, 52–53] *113*
55:59 [13:55, 59] *113*

Bel and the Dragon
4–5, 25 [14:4–5, 25] *113*

b) Old Testament Apocrypha and
Pseudepigrapha

*Apocalpyse
of Abraham*   72, 95

*Apocalypse
of Baruch (Syr)* 72, 95, 111
20:3   *73*

*Apocalpyse of
Elijah*   *109*

*Apocalypse of
Zephaniah (Copt)* 95

*Ascension
of Isaiah*   29, 71–2, *109*,
                  116

*Assumption
of Moses*   71, 95, 108, 110

Eldad and Modad 71, 110

4 Ezra   72, 95, 111
5:23–30   *92*
12:37   *73*

14:6   *73*
14:18–20   *45*
14:37–46   *39*
14:44–46   73
14:45   62, 99

Joseph's Prayer 71

Ethiopic Enoch (= 1 Enoch) see also
Subject Index
1:9 (Eth)   *55*
1:1–32:6   *55*
5:4   *67*
6:6   *67*
8:1   *67*
8:3   *67*
9:8   *67*
10:2   *67*
10:6   *55*
10:13–14   *67*
12:4   *55*
15:8   *67*
18:5   *55*
19:1   *67*
19:3–21:9   *55*
37–71   *55*
75–87   *55*
89:16–64 (Eth)   *67*
90:17–18 (Eth)   *67*
91:13 (Eth)   *67*
97:6–107:3   *55*
99:7   *67*

Slavic Enoch   72, 95

Joseph and Aseneth 99

Book of Jubilees 72, 90
2:22   62
2:22–23   62

*Liber antiquitatum
biblicarum*   111

*Paralipomena
Jeremiae*   95

Psalms of Solomon 58–9, 124
17 + 18   *94*

Sibyllines   79, 95

*Testament of
Abraham*   95

Testament of Job   86

Testament of the
Twelve Patriarchs   72, 86, 90, 113

Levi   95

Vita prophetarum   111

III. Documents from Qumran
and the Judean Desert

4QJudg[a] *(4Q 49)*   85

4QSam[a] *(4Q 51)*   84

4QJer[a] *(4Q 70)*   86

4Q Jer[b] *(4Q 71)*   86

4Q Cant[a, b, c]
(4Q 106–108)   92

4Q LXX Lev[a + b]
(4Q 119 +120)   41

4Q LXX Num
(4Q 121)   41

4Q LXX Deut
(4Q 122)   41

4Q OrNab *(4Q 242)*   88

4Q psDan ar[a–c]
(4Q 243–245)   88

4Q MMT C
(4Q 394–399)
10–11   45

4Q Flor
2:3   91

6Q Cant   92

7Q1 LXX Ex   41

7Q2 EpistJer   41

11Q Ps[a]Zion   98–9

11QT
(Temple Scroll)   90

11Qtg Job
(Job Targum)   47

CD *(Damascus Scroll)*
5:18   71
15:1 (Rost ed.)   8
19:1 (Rost ed.)   8
19 (Text B):7–9   4

8HevXII Gr.   *41*, 82–3

IV. Judeo-Hellenistic Literature

Letter of Aristeas see also Subject Index
32   78
302   78
310–311   76–7
311   35

Aristobulus *see also* Subject Index
   Fragment 1   75
   Fragment 3   75
   Fragment 4   75

Eupolemos   79, 85

Flavius Josephus *see also* Subject Index

   Antiquities
   of the Jews   88

   1:17   100
   4:196   77, 102
   5:318–337   101
   10:79   *55*
   10:186–281   *96*
   10:210   *96*
   10:277   89
   11:184–296   101
   11:297–299   102
   11:337   *96*
   12:12–118   77
   12:56   *26*
   12:57   *26*
   12:107   *26*
   12:109   77
   13:297–298, 408   77
   18:15   77

   Contra Apionem   98
   1:36–42   3
   1:37–43   90, 99–103
   1:37   99
   1:38–41   61
   1:40–41   *45*
   1:41   102
   1:42   100, 102

Jewish Wars	101
6	73
Vita	
12	89
Philo *see also* Subject Index	
De Agricultura	
50	*98*
Confusione Linguarum	
39, 52	*98*
Quod Deus sit Immutabilis	
74, 77, 82	*98*
De Fuga et Inventione	
59	*98*
De Gigantibus	
17	*98*
Quis Rerum Divinarum Heres sit	
290	*98*
De Migratione Abrahamo	
157	*98*
De Mutatione Nominum	
115	*98*
De Plantatione	
29, 39	*98*
De Praemiis	
et Poenis	78
Questiones in Genesin	
4:152	*79*
De Somniis	
I:75	*98*
II:245	*98*
De Vita	
Contemplativa	70
25	*98*
28	*98*
29	*98*
De Vita Mosis	
2:32	26
2:33–44	78
2:37, 40	26

Pseudo-Phokylides	
Sententiae	79, *112*

V. New Testament

Matthew	95, 102, 105–6
11:13	126
11:28–30	*111*
12:40	54
13:35	*195*
Mark	102
Luke	102, 111
1:70	*105*
10:1	*26*
13:28	*105*
16:16	126
18:31	*105*
20:42	*106*
23:18	*34*
24:25	*105*
24:27	*105*
24:44	*28*, 105
John	102, 105
1	110
10:42	*27*
11:50–51	*112*
19:15	*34*
19:37	7
Acts	
1:3	54
1:20	*106*
2:9–11	*108*
2:29	*105*
3:18–24	*105*
6:1–15	22
6:9	*108*
8:27–28	89
8:32–33	90
10:43	*105*
13:27	*105*
13:33	*106*
17:28	*112*
18:25	21
26:22	*105*
26:27	*105*
Romans	
1:2	*27, 105*
3:19	*27*
4:5	108
5:6	108

1 Corinthians
2:6–10   *109*
2:9   109
5:7   32
9:10   109
14:21   *27*
14:26   110
15:54–55   7

Galatians
1:13–14   109

2 Timothy
3:8   71
3:16   107

Titus
1:12   *112*
1:13   *112*

Hebrews   111, 116, 120,
                122–3
1:1   *27, 105*
11:3–4   118
11:33   113
11:35–37   *111*
11:35   118
11:37   *29, 71*
12:17   *116*

James
4:5f.   110

1 Peter
1:10   *27, 105*

2 Peter   *55, 68*, 108
1:20   107
1:21   107
2:11   *108*
2:17–18   *108*

2 John   *69*, 120
2:13   *92*

Jude   *54–55, 68, 71*, 108
6   *55*
9   *108*
14   *55, 67, 112*
14–15   *108*
16   *55*

Revelation   *62, 95–6*, 107, 115,
                120
1:7   7

3:20   *92*
22:18, 26   77

VI. New Testament Apocrypha

Apocalypse of Peter 55, 120

Gospel of Peter   5

*Secret Gospel
According to Mark*   *124*

VII. Apostolic Fathers

Letter of Barnabas   58–9
4:3   67
6:13   110
8:5   *32*
16:5   67
19:9   121

1 Clement   58–9, 106, 116,
                123–5
3:4   *116*
7:5   *116*
21:4   120
27:5   *116*
28:2   120
34:1   116
36:6–37:4   120
41:1   120
55:4–6   116
57:3–5   *122*
59:3   *116*
60:1   *116*
61:2   *116*
63:1   *116*

2 Clement   58–9, 124
4:5   110
11:2–4   110
13:2b   110
16:4   116–17

*Constitutiones
Apostolorum*   58
5:20   *114*

Didache   64
4:5   121

*Shepherd of
Hermas*   *43*, 58, 64, 125

Vis 2:3:4 (7:4)   71
Vis 2:4:3 (8:3)   124
Vis 4:2:4 (23:4)   *113*
Man 1:1 (26:1)   118

**VIII. Church Fathers and
Later Christian Authors**

Ambrosius
  De Tobia   *68*

Aristo of Pella
  *Disputatio Iasonis
  et Papisci*   34

Athanasius *see also* Subject Index
  Epistulae Festales
    39   *56*, 63–4

Ps-Athanasius
  *Synopsis scripturae
  sacrae*   58

Athenagoras
  *Supplicatio (Legatio/
  Libellus) pro Christianis*
    9:1   114
    24:1   *67*

Augustine *see also* Subject Index

  De Civitate Dei   51
    18:42   *26*, 51–2
    18:43   51–2
    18:44   53

Muratorian Canon   120
    69–71   70

Clement of Alexandria *see also* Subject
Index

  Paedagogus
    I:8:62   *121*
    I:8:68   *121*
    I:8:69   *121*
    I:8:72   *121*
    I:9:75   *121*
    I:13:102   *121*
    II:1:8   *121*
    II:2:24   *121*
    II:2:34   *121*
    II:5:46   *121*
    II:7:54   *121*

    II:7:58–59   *121*
    II:8:69   *121*
    II:8:76   *121*
    II:10:98–99   *121*
    II:10:99   *121*
    II:10:101   *121*
    II:10:109   *121*
    III:3:17   *121*
    III:3:23   *121*
    III:4:29   *121*
    III:11:58, 83   *121*

  Stromata
    1:4:27   *121*
    1:10:47   *121*
    1:28:1   *61*
    1:123:1   119
    1:123:2   *115*, 119
    1:123:5   117
    1:149:2   *38*
    1:149:3   40
    2:5:24   *121*
    2:35:4   117
    2:136:2   *122*
    2:139:2   117
    3:4:29   *56*
    4:118:4–4:
      119:3   *115*
    5:3:3   *61*
    5:3:18   *121*
    5:85:1   *61*
    5:97:7   119
    6:16:146   *121*
    6:102:2   117
    7:16:105   *121*

  Hypotyposes   96

Ps-Clementina
  Homiliae 3:47–49   35

Ps-Cyprianus
  De aleatoribus 2   121
  *De montibus
  Sina et Sion* 9   *32*

Cyrill of Jerusalem
  Catecheses
    IV:33–36   65

Dialogus Timothei
et Aquilae   35

Didascalia
Apostolorum   58

Epiphanius of Salamis *see also* Subject Index

Panarion
(Adversus haereses)
42:12:5   *110*

De mensuris et ponderibus
5+6   *26, 37*
14–15   *43*

Eusebius of Caesarea *see also* Subject Index

Demonstratio evangelica
8:2:71   *122*

Praeparatio evangelica
13:12:1–2   *75*

Historia Ecclesiastica
2:16–17   70
2:24   *124*
3:10:6   *69*
4:11:6   *124*
4:22:9   *61, 122*
4:26:13–14   *61*
5:8:10   *43*
5:8:11–14   *39*
5:8:12   *38*
5:8:13   *38*
5:8:15   *39*
5:26   120
6:14–15   45
6:16   *12–13*
6:25–26   *63*
6:25:1   *62*
6:25:2   11
6:52:2   *61*
7:32:16   *75*
8:9:3   15

Pseudo-Gregentius
Disputatio cum
Herbane Judaeo   35

Heracleon
Commentarii
in Iohannem   *96*

Jerome *see also* Subject Index
Liber quaestionum
Hebraicarum in Genesim

Introduction
(Lagarde p. 2)   *49*

Commentariorum
in Esaiam

in Es XVII
(on Isa 64:3)   *109*

Commentariorum in
Hiezechielem
II (on Ez 5:12)   *49*

Commentariorum
in Danielum
III (on Dan 9:24)   *122*

Commentariorum in
Michaeam Prophetam
I (on Mic 1:9–10) *49*

Apologia contra Rufinum
II 25   *38*

Dialogi contra
Pelagioanos libri III
2:6   *69*

De viris inlustribus
11   70
13   *69*

Praefatio de translatione
graeca in libris
Salomonis
(Weber II 957)   *69*

Praefatio in librum
Paralipomenon juxta
LXX interpretes 49

Prologus in Pentateucho
(Weber I 3:3f)   *38*

Prologus in
libro Regum
(Weber I 365)   *50, 62*

Prologus Tobiae   *46*, 50

Prologus Iudith   *46*

Prologus in
Danihele
Propheta   88

Hilarius of Poitiers
  Instructio Psalmorum
  15   62

Hippolytus *see also* Subject Index
  De Christo et
    Antichristo   96

  Commentarii
    in Danielem   96
  on Dan 1:14
    (Prototheod.)   47
  on Dan 1:28
    (Prototheod.)   117
  on Dan 3   119
  on Dan 4:56   110

  Refutatio omnium
  haeresium
  7:20:1   72

Hrabanus Maurus   69

Commentaria in
  libros
Machabaeorum   69

Irenaeus of Lyon *see also* Subject
Index
  Adversus
    Haereses   120
    1:10:1   67
    1:15:6   67
    1:20:1   56, 72
    1:30:11   68, 117
    3:1:1 (= Gospels
      list)   124
    3:3:1–3   125
    3:20:4   32
    3:21:1   30, 43
    3:21:2   39, 50
    3:21:3   39
    3:21:3–4   39
    3:25:6   113
    4:5:2   113
    4:20:4   113
    4:22:1   32
    4:26:3   113
    4:33:1   32
    4:33:12   32
    4:36:4   67
    4:38:3   120
    5:28:2   67
    5:31:1   32
    5:35:1   113

  Epideixis (=demonstratio)
  Praedicationis apostolicae
  78   32
  97   113

Pseudo-Johannes
Chrysostomus
  In sanctum
  pascha sermo VII 35

Julius Africanus *see also* Subject Index

  Chronographiae   119

  Epistula ad
  Origenem   36, 48

Justin Martyr *see also* Subject Index

  Apologia   26–8
  I:31:1–5   27
  I:32:4   27
  I:33:1, 4–6   30
  I:40:8–10   106
  I:41:4   32
  I:67:3   61

  Dialogus cum
  Tryphone Iudaeo
  17:2   33
  30:1–2   28
  43:3–8   30
  43:8   9
  48:4   30
  49:1   30
  66:2–4   30
  67:1   30
  67:2   30
  68:5   30
  68:6–8   30
  68:7   27, 30
  71:1   27, 31
  71:2   29, 31–2
  71:3   30, 31
  72:1   28, 32
  72:2   32
  72:4   32
  73:1   32
  73:3–4   32
  73:5   33
  73:6   43–4
  77:3   30
  84:1   30
  84:2   32
  84:3   30, 31

91:4   27
120:3–4   33
120:4   27
120:5   28, 29, 71
124:2–3   33
124:3   27
131:1   27
133:2   33
136:2   33
137:3   27, 33

Ps-Justin
  Cohortatio
  ad Graecos   37, 44
  13   37
  13:3   37

Justinian
  Novelle 146
  'Peri Hebraion'
  I   50

Lactanz
  De mortibus
  persecutorum   119

Luther *see also* Subject Index

  WADB 12   74

Prolog to Wisdom
(WADB
12:50:25–28)   70

Melito of Sardes
  Easter Homily 55, 120

Nicephoros of Constantinople
  Chronographia brevis
  Stichometry   58, 71

Origen *see also* Subject Index

  In Numeros homiliae
  XXVII (on Num
  27:1)   117–18

  Libri X in Canticum
  Canticorum
  Prolog   69

  Homiliae in
  Ieremiam (graecae)

Homily 20
(on Jer 20:7–12)   *118*

Commentarii
in Matthaeum
XV:14
(on Mt 19:16–30) 10
on Mt 23:37–39
(com. Ser. 28)   71
on Mt 27:9
(com. Ser. 117)   71, 109

Contra Celsum
5:54   68

De oratione
29:3   118–19

De principiis
IV 2:5 (12)   61–2
IV 4:6   69–70

Epistula ad
Iulium Africanum   47–8
8   10
9   10, 71
13   46

Polycarp of Smyrna
  Epistula ad Philippenses
  10:2   116

Rufinus Tyrannus
  Apologia contra
  Hieronymum
  II:36–41   49

Synode of Laodicea
  Canon 60   65

Tatian
  Oratio ad Graecos
  7:1   120
  8:1   67
  20:4   67

Tertullian *see also* Subject Index
  Apologeticum
  19:5–9   40

  De praescriptione
  haereticorum
  7:10   120

De patientia
14:1   71

De cultu feminarum
3:1–3   54

Adversus Marcionem
1:7:2   117
3:19:1   32
3:22:5   120

Adversus Valentinianos
2:2   120

Scorpiace
8:3   71
8:5   114

De idolatria
4:2   54
15:6   54

De monogamia
17:1   117

Adversus Judaeos
4:10   119
10:11–12   32
13:11   32

Fragm. IV   120

Ps-Tertullian
  Carmen adversus
  Marcionem
  4:198–210   62

Victorinus of Pettau
  Commentarii in
  Apocalypsim Ioannis
  4:3:5   62

  Tractatus de
  fabrica mundi
  6   119

IX. Rabbinic Literature

Mishnah
mMeg   92
mMQ 3:4   89
mSan 10:1   45–6
mEd 5:3   91

mAv 1:1   36, 101, 103
mYad 3:5   44, 92, 99
mYad 3:6   44

Tosefta
tShab 13:5   45, 91
tYoma 4:18–19   89
tEd 2:7   91
tYad 2:13   45
tYad 2:14   91

Babylonian Talmud
bBer 9b   106
bShab 115a   47
bShab 116a/b   45
bYoma 70a   89
bMeg 3a   90
bMeg 7a   92
bMeg 9a-b   44
bKet 106a   89
bGit 45b   45
bBB 14   72
bBB 14b   45
bSan 100a   92
bSan 100b   46

Jerusalem Talmud
ySheq 4:3 (48a)   89
yMeg 1:4 (70d)   92

Soferim
1:6   44
1:7   44
1:8   44

Qohelet Rabba
1:4   91

Pesiqta deRav
Kahana
8:1   91
24:14   91

XI. Ancient Pagan Literature

Cassius Dio
67:14:2   123

XII. Inscriptions and Papyri

Chester Beatty
Papyrus 12   55

Chester Beatty
Papyrus 967   42

CIJ I² II
No. 693a   76

No. 1440/1532a   76

PCair 10759   55
PFoud inv. 266   41
POxy 1166   *41*
POxy 2069   55
PRyl 1458   41

INDEX OF AUTHORS

Adams, A. W. 41, 43, 57, 60
Aland, K. 41–2, 55, 115
Albertz, R. 43, 113
Altaner, B. 96
Amir, Y. 81
Aune, D. E. 101

Bammel, C. 36, 49
Barthelemy, D. 6, 29, 44–5, 50, 72, 77,
    89, 92, 114
Barton, J. 105
Baudissin, W. W. Graf von 8
Beckwith, R. 45, 63, 68, 72, 89, 92,
    98–9, 114
Bedouelle, G. 57
Berger, K. 62
Bertram, G. 89
Betz, O. 90
Bi(c)kerman(n), E. (J.) 4, 80–1
Bidez, J. 37
Black, M. 55
Bodenmann, R. 96
Böttrich, Ch. 72
Bogaert, P.-M. 42
Bornkamm, H. 65
Berger, P.-R. 43
Brewer, D. I. 111
Brock, S. P. 29, 77
Brooke, P. J. 85
Brox, N. 113
Bruneau, P. 76
Burkhardt, H. 79

Campenhausen, H. von 20, 27, 105
Charles, R. H. 29, 67, 109
Collins, L. 19
Crown, A. 76–7

Deines, R. 43, 89
Deissmann, A. 76
Dorival, G. 20, 26, 43, 59, 68, 78, 82–5,
    89, 92, 94, 118
Dubarle, A. M. 117

Eißfeld, O. 42, 86, 92
Ellis, E. E. 57, 68, 72, 91
Engel, H. 48, 113

Feldman, L. H. 100
Fischer, U. 78
Frey, J. 109
Fricke, K. D. 65
Frisch, C. T. 29, 44
Froidevaux, L. 113
Fuks, A. 80

Gamberoni, J. 68, 116
Geissen, A. 42–3
Gese, H. 109–10, 126
Glatzer, N. 103
Görg, M. 80
Goodspeed, E. J. 67
Goshen-Gottstein, M. H. 98–9

Haelst, J. van 41, 55
Hahn, R. R. 58
Hamm, W. 42
Hanhart, R. 4, 11, 87–8, 118
Harl, M. 20, 26, 43, 59, 68, 78, 82–5,
    89, 92, 94, 118
Harnack, A. von 117
Hengel, M. 20–2, 28–9, 31–5, 37,
    40, 48, 54, 61, 63, 67, 69, 71, 76,
    79–81, 82, 85–6, 90–1, 93–4, 97,
    101, 105–6, 108–9, 111, 118,
    123–5
Henten, J. W. van 94
Holm-Nielsen, S. 58
Horbury, W. 80
Hyrvärinen, K. 43

Jellicoe, S. 37, 43, 77, 84, 87, 89
Jellinek, A. 46
Joannou, P. P. 65
Julius, C. 113
Junod, E. 60, 64, 68, 70

Kaestli, J.-D. 73
Kamesar, A. 30
Kasher, A. 21
Katz, P. 29
Kenyon, F. G. 41, 43, 57, 60
Koch, D.-A. 22, 107–9
Kooij, A. van der 82, 85
Krauss, S. 43
Kümmel, W. G. 109
Kuhn, K. G. 44–5

Lampe, G. W. H. 56, 122, 125
Lampe, P. 22
Larcher, C. 116, 120
Lehnardt, A. 72
Leisegang, H. 79
Leon, H. J. 22
Lietzmann, H. 109
Lindars, B. 85
Lindemann, A. 115–16
Lindner, H. 102
Lohse, B. 66, 70, 73
Lohse, E. 8
Luchner, K. 42, 115
Luri, B. Z. 44
Lutz, R. T. 71

Maier, J. 90, 98–9
Markschies, Ch. 21
Martin, E. G. 71
Medina-Lechtenberg, R. 43
Merkel, H. 124
Metzger, B. M. 21, 65, 106
Meyer, R. 100–1
Milik, J. T. 48, 54–5, 67, 87
Mittmann, S. 69
Moyne, J. le 90
Müller, U. B. 101
Munnich, O. 20, 26, 43, 59, 68, 78,
    82–5, 89, 92, 94, 118
Mussies, G. 82

Nardi, C. 65
Nautin, P. 14, 36, 48
Nestle, E. 122
Neuser, W. 65
Niebuhr, K.-W. 112
Noja, S. 75

Oepke, A. 56, 110
Oikonomos, E. 125

Pearson, B. A. 21, 72
Pelletier, A. 19, 26, 41, 49
Pietersma, A. 71

Ploeg, J. P. M. van der 47
Preuschen, E. 57, 60, 64–5, 71
Prigent, P. 28, 32

Quack, J. 66

Rahlfs, A. 32, 55, 58–9, 68–9
Reinmuth, E. 111
Resch, A. 32
Roberts, C. H. 21
Rösel, M. 30
Rost, L. 8
Roloff, J. 90
Rubinkiewicz, R. 72
Rüger, H.-P. 44, 56, 66, 72, 92, 97–8,
    109, 114–16, 118, 125
Ruwet, J. 21, 115

Safrai, S. 81, 89
Salvesen, A. 36
Salzmann, J. 61
Sanders, J. A. 98
Sanderson, J. E. 42
Sandnes, K. O. 101
Schäfer, P. 45
Schenker, A. 12
Schild, M. E. 48–9
Schimanowski, G. 86
Schneider, H. 59
Schreckenberg, H. 35, 50, 73
Schüpphaus, J. 113
Schürer, E. (rev.) 43, 46–7, 58, 62,
    68, 71, 75–6, 79–80, 85–6, 88, 99,
    109–10, 113–14, 116–17, 119,
    121–4
Schwartz, E. 13, 67
Schwemer, A. M. 45, 69, 99
Seeligmann, I. L. 85
Shekan, P. W. 42
Shutt, P.-J. 26
Skarsaune, O. 28–9, 32–3, 43
Smith, J. Z. 71
Smitmans, A. 62
Speyer, W. 80
Staab, K. 110
Stählin, O. 121
Steck, O. H. 45
Stemberger, G. 44, 46, 92
Strack, H. L. 46
Stuhlmacher, P. 107, 111, 116
Stuiber, A. 96
Sundberg, A. C. 20, 45, 60, 113
Swete, H. B. 32, 43, 57–8, 63, 75,
    84, 86, 94, 114, 117, 119, 121

Talmon, Sh. 98–9
Tatum, W. B. 80
Tcherikover, V. (A.) 77, 80
Theißen, G. 101
Thiele, W. 124
Thornton, R. J. 111, 124–5
Tov, E. 29, 42, 46, 55, 69, 76, 84, 90, 114

Ulrich, E. (C.) 42, 84, 92
Unnik, W. C. van 77

Veltri, G. 26, 37, 44, 50
Venetz, H.-J. 82
Villalba I Varneda, P. 102
Volz, H. 65

Wacholder, B. Z. 82, 85
Walter, N. 76
Waszink, J. H. 54
Weiss, H.-F. 116
Wendland, P. 36, 41, 49
Wengst, K. 67
Werbeck, W. 69
Wermelinger, O. 48–9, 65
Winden, J. C. M. van 54
Woude, A. S. van der 47–8, 84, 86, 88, 90, 92, 98–9

Zahn, Th. 54, 61, 65
Ziegler, J. 60, 86, 97, 113
Zuntz, G. 37, 68

INDEX OF SUBJECTS

Abraham 86, 107
Adam and Eve 33
Ahaz 31
Alexander Balas 93
Alexander the Great 89, 117
Alexander Polyhistor 85–6
Alexandria/Alexandrian 19–23, 25–6,
  38, 40, 64, 75–6, 81, 97–8, 101, *112*,
  115, 123–4
Alexandrian catechetical schools 124
Alexandrinus, Codex 57–9
allegory/allegorical 54, 68–9, *79*, 92,
  98, 111
Amoraim *45*
Amphilochus of Iconium 65
Anatolios, Bishop of Caesarea *75*
angel 99
anthropomorphism 16
anti-Judaism 48
Antioch 115, 123
Antiochus IV Epiphanes *43*, 88, 119
Antoninus, son of Severus 13
apocalypticism/apocalyptic 2, 73, 95
apocrypha/apocryphal 2–3, 11, 20, 29,
  32, 45–6, *50*, *56*, 64–5, *68*, 70, *73*,
  90, 92, 94, 107, 110, 115, 124, 126,
  79
Apollinarius 16
apologetics/apologetical 2, 6–7, 9, 11,
  66, 80, 99, 102–3, 105, 110, *112*,
  120–1, 125
apostle/apostolic 17, 38–9, 49, 54, 61, 64
Apostolic Fathers 26, 64, 66, 120
Aqiba, Rabbi 45–6, 92
Aquila 6, 9, 13–14, 31, 34–5, 39, 43–4,
  50–1, 53, 60
  translation
  principles 89
Aramaic 46, 92–3
Aristeas, Jewish historian 86
Aristeas (Letter of) 1, 4, 11–12, 19, 25,
  38, *39*, 50–1, 76, 100
Aristotle 79

Artaxerxes I 3, 73, 99–100
Artaxerxes II 102
Asia Minor 113
asterisk 52
Athanasius, lists of 65–6, 73
  division of canon by 125
Athens 125
Augustine *36*, *39*, 49, 51–4, 63, 78
authors, biblical 45, *49*, 102, 114
authority, biblical 51
  of the Hebrew Bible 74
  of the Septuagint 50–3
Azariah, Prayer of 88

Babylon/Babylonia 85
Basiliano-Venetus, Codex 59
Bede 68
Benedictus 59
Berenice, wife of Ptolemy 76
Bethlehem 83
Bible, Hebrew 22, 50, 56–7, 64–5,
  69–70, 83, 95, 101–2, 113, 122
Bible manuscripts 59
Books *see also* Hagiographa
  biblical 126
  canonical/non-/deuterocanonical *50*,
    56, 64–5, 69
  Christian 61
  distribution of 281
Caesarea 83
Cairo Geniza *see* Geniza
canon/canonical/extra-/canonicity 2,
  3–4, 6, 10–11, 19, 21–2, 28–9,
  60–1, 83, 97, 105, 125–6
  Alexandrian 3, 8, 17, 19–20, *79*, 101
  Christian 68, 94–5, 111
  delimited/fixed 44, 55, 57, 99, 105,
    126
  Ethiopian *72*
  Hebrew 19–20, 22, 36, 40, 54–5, *56*,
    60–1, 64–6, 70–74, 83, *88*, 90, 92,
    96–7, 102, 113

canon (*cont.*)
New Testament 70, 115–16
openness of 126
origination of 97, *101*
Pharisaic-Palestinian 3–4, 17, 44, 87,
91, 99, 111, 126
scope of 36, 62–65, 99, 101
Septuagint 3, 19, 25, 40
sequence of writings in 59–60
tripartite *28*, 96, 100, 105
Canon question *50*, 64, *99*
canonical authority 110
canonization 10, *118*
canon lists/catalogues 11, 20, 28,
50, 52, 58–61, 63–5, *98*, 100,
122, cf. Melito of Sardis and
Origen
canonical formula 100
Caracalla 14
Caraite/caraitic *37*
Carthage 85, 124
Carthage, Synod of 57, 66, 68
catechites/catechetic 64, 66, 94, 112,
117–18, 121, 123
catenae (tradition) 16–17
Celsus 68
Christians/Christianity/Christian 21,
35–6, 39, 42, *45*, 47, 54–5, 66,
70–2, 99, 102–3, 112, 115,
126
Christology/Christologica 27, 29–31,
49, 54, 69, 106, 108
Christological hymn 109
chronographies,
Christian 103
church 10–11, 15, 22–3, 35, 39, 49,
51–2, *56*, 64–5, 89, 91, 94, 112–13,
117, 122, 124, cf. Early church
adherence to the OT 41
church doctrine 55
praxis 55, 65
Clement of Alexandria 12, 21, 56, 61,
67, *76*, 110, *112*, 115–17, 119–21,
124–5
Clement of Rome 28, 66, 115, 117,
123–4
codex/ices 41–2, 55, 60
commandments 122
Commodian 67
Commodus 125
communities, Christian 2, 4–5, 9, 47,
74, 111, 114–17
Roman 28, 56, 115, 123
Alexandrian
Judeo-Christian 56, 123

communities, Jewish 22, 76, *90*, 112
Roman 34, 123
confessions of faith, Jewish 118
congregational archives 114–15
Corbeiensis, Codex 67
Corinth 115
Creator/creation 118
criticism, historico-philological 53
culture, Greek/Hellenistic 82
Cyprus 21
Cyprian 67, 117, 119–21, 125

Damasus, Bishop of Rome 49
Daniel narratives, early 88
Daniel fragments, Apocryphal 88
Daniel, additions to 47, 63, 70, 88, 91,
93, 113, 115
Darius 87, 117
Decalog 106
Delos 75
Demetrius, Jewish historian 76
Demetrius of Phaleron *39*
Diaspora/diaspora/Judaism 20–2, 43–4,
75, 79–83, 85, 93–4, 97, 101, 116
Egyptian 75, 85
Samaritan 75
Diaspora synagogues 44, 89, *114*, 123
Didymus the Blind 68
Dionysius of Alexandria 68
disciples 105
Dodekapropheton 63, 85, 111
see also 'Minor Prophets Scroll'
Domitian 100, 123
Domitilla, Flavia 123

Early Christianity/Early Christian 9, 90,
100, 105–6, 108
Early church 22, 41, *50*, 56, 60, 63, 65,
105–8, 112, 126
Christian interpretation of 127
Christological
exegesis of 27
prophetic understanding of 27
Ebionites 30, *45*
Egypt/Egyptians 26, 41, 82, 85, 97,
115
Eighteen Benedictions *116*
Elders, the seventy on Sinai 36
Eleazar, high priest 51
Elijah Apocryphon 109
Enoch, as prophet 112
Enoch literature 29, 40, 54–6, 64, 71–2,
95, 108, 110, 113, 126
Ephesus 20, 22, 115
Epimenides *112*

Epiphanius 48, 50, 65
eschatology/eschatological 22, 79, 90,
    94–5, 100–1, 105, 108
Essenes 82, 91, 99–100, 111
Esther, Colophon of 81, 85
ethics/ethical/ethos 71, 81, 116, 122
Eucharist 61
Eusebius of Caesarea 12–16, 63, 73, 76,
    124
Euthalius *110*
exegesis/exegetical 33, 38, 109, 111
    Christologico-eschatological 111
    rabbinic 111
exile 87
Ezekiel Apocryphon 55
Ezra 45, 54, 91

faith, Christian 10
Feast of Booths *114*
Flood, the 54
Florilegia 34
Four Empires Scheme 95

Gamaliel 47
Geniza, Cairo 44, 47
Gentile Christians 108
gilyonim 44–5
Gloria in excelsis 59
gnosis/Gnostic 21, 42, 55–6, 72, 107,
    124
God, kingdom of 95, 99
    name(s) of 7–9, 16, 45, 80
    throne of 99
golden rule, negative 117–19
golden calf 33, 144
Gospel(s) 44, 63, 105, 108
grave inscriptions 80
Gregorius Thaumaturgus 68
Gregory of Nazianzus 65
Greek 19, 35, 76, 80–2

Haggadah/haggadic 68
hagiographa 20, 47, 62, *82*, 91, 106
hallel 47
Haman the Agagite 88
hasidim 88
Hebrew 35, 46, 51–3, 92–3, 109
Hebraica Veritas 49, 66
Hegesippus 124
Hellenists 22
hellenistic 70, 81, 86, 90, 92
Heracleon *96*
heresy/heretic/heretical 44–5, 56, 64,
    67, 72, 91, 105
Hermas, Letter from Heaven 124

Herod 26, 81
Hesiod 79
Hesychius 83
    see also Septuagint, recensions of
Hexapla of Origen 5, 9, 12–13, 15–17,
    34, 36, 48–9, 52, 63, 83
Hezekiah 30
high priest 93
Hippolytus 67–8, 70, 95, *96*, 119
historical books 19–20, 98, 107
history, biblical 86
    Jewish 100
historiography/er, Jewish 79, 99, 103
    profane Hellenistic 92, 102
Holofernes 117
Holy Scripture(s) 1–4, 6, 8–11, 22, 28,
    44, 47, 50, 54, 69, *71*, 73, 78–9, 88,
    90, 93, 98, *101*, 102, 105, 111, 114,
    122, 125
    inspired 20, 44, 50, 107
    Israel's/of the Jews 35, 61
    profaning the hands 44
    public reading in synagogues 50
Holy Spirit 48–49, 52, 78, 101
Holy Land 6, 109
Homer 78
Homily(ies)/sermon(s) 61, 68
humanism/humanist/humanistic 53,
    126
hymn writing
    early Christian 106

idolatry 94
inspiration/inspired 12, 16, 45, 53, 125
    end of prophecy 91, 99–100
inspiration legend (the Seventy) 12, 16,
    36
inspiration miracle 35–6, 39, 49, 78
instructional literature 115, 123
interpretationes
    graecae 80
Irenaeus 28, 51, 66, *96*, 110, 113, 120,
    124–5
Isaiah, translation of 85–6
Isaiah legends *71*
Islamic *37*
Israel 44, 90, 93–4, 123

Jabneh 99, 105, 126
Jacob's blessing 33
Jason of Cyrene 79
Jehuda (ben'Ilai), Rabbi 44
Jeremiah, translation of 86
Jeremiah Apocalypse 32
Jeremiah Apocryphon *110*

Jerome *33*, 37–9, 41, 46, 48, 50–4, *56*, 61–2, 66, 70, *71*, 86, *109*
Bible translation 49, 53, 83–4
criticism of the Septuagint 52–3
Jerusalem 20, 80–2, 89, 98, 108–9, 125
destruction of 39, 73, 87, 125–6
Jericho 14–15
Jesus/Jesus Christ 8, 27, *28*, 29–31, 38, 50, 54, 73, 103, 105, *109*, 126
appearance of 50, 103
Jesus Sirach 92–3, 97, 112
grandson, translator of 82, 85, 96–7, 112
Prolog of 96–8
Jews/Jewish 19–22, 27–8, 37, 40, 50–1, 54–5, 60–2, *71*, 76, 83, 87, 93, 95, 105, 110, 112, 116
Jewish Christians 40, 45, 60
Jewish Wars 35, 101, 115
Job 86
Job Targum 47
Jobab 86
John the Baptist 126
Johannes Hyrcanus I 79
Jonathan (Maccabee) 93
Joseph, father of Jesus 30
Josephus Flavius 25, 38, 62, *69*, 77, 79, 87, 99–103, 113, 119
Josiah 87
Judaism 34, 46, 68, 73, 95, *114*
Alexandrian 20–1
ancient 6
Hellenistic 2, 6, 8–9
Palestinian 6, 80, 82, 101, 111
(Pharisaic-)rabbinical 94, 126
Judas (Maccabee) 79, 91
Judea/Judean 21, 27, 75, 80, 87, 115
judgment 93, 95
Judith 115
Julius Africanus 17, 47, 63, 67, 70, 119
justification of the ungodly 108
Justin Martyr 26, 35, 47, 66, 78, 83, 110, 112, 114
Justinian 50
Justus of Tiberias 79

Laodicea, (Particular) Synod of 65
law 19–20, 22, 87, 93–4, 96–8, 100
lectionary 68
Leontopolis, Temple of 81, 85
libraries, ancient 27, 38, 72, 81, 90, 92, 98, 114–15, 123
literature
early Christian *56*, 70, 87
heathen/pagan *112*

literature (*cont.*)
Jewish 55, 76, 81, 87, 94, *112*
rabbinic *71*, *89*
liturgy/liturgical 46, 88, 99, 116
logos spermatikos *112*
Lord 110
Lucian 83
see also Septuagint, recensions of
Luther *66*, 122
Lyon 124
Lysimachos, son of Ptolemy 81, 87

Magnificat 59
martyrs/martyrdom 94, 116, 118, 122, 125
Maccabees/Hasmoneans/Hasmonean 81, 116
Maccabeean rebellion 80, 91
Malachios Monachos 69
Manicheeans *55*
Marchalianus, Codex 16
Marcion 30, 61
Masada 46
Masoretes/masoretic 3–4, 7
Masoretic text 7–8, 84–5, *90*
Megillot, the five 46
Melchizedek 72
Melito of Sardis 29, 60–1, 120
canon list 113
'Men of the Great Assembly' *92*, 101
Menasiah, Rabbi 91
Menedemus of Eritrea 40
messianic/Messiah/messianism 29–30, 78, 94–5
Methodios of Olympos 121
midrash/midrashic 102
Minor Prophets book/scroll 6, 9, 11, *29*, 34, 82
Minucius Felix 67
Miriam, Moses' sister 115
mission/missionary *112*
monotheism/monotheistic 122
Montanist 117
Mordecai 87
Moses 35, 72–3, 76, 100, 108, 113
Murabba'at, Wadi *see* Naḥal Ḥever

Naḥal Ḥever 6
Nag Hammadi 72
Nebuchadnezzar 73
Nehemiah 3, 81, 91, 119
New Testament/New Testamental 19, 22, 26, 37, 42, 61, 63–4, 70, *71*, 96, 105, 107, 126–7
Nicopolis (near Actium) 13, 15

Noah 54, 79
nomina sacra 14, 41
Norea 72
nunc dimittis 59

obelos 10, 52
odes 58–9
Old Testament 28, 41, *49*, 55, *56*, 60,
   62, 65–6, 105–8, 112–13, 126–7
Onias IV 81, 85
Onkelos *43*
Ophites 117
Origen 1, 5, 6, 9–17 (*passim*), 36, 46,
   49, 52–3, 61–3, 67–8, *71*, 73, 83, 86,
   92, *106*, 109, 117–19, 121, 123
   canon list of 113
   original text, Hebrew 12–13, 29, 31, 36,
      47, 49–50, 53, 63, 78, 82, 84–5, 89,
      96–7, 102

pagan 26, 37, 67, 76, 88, 102, 115
Palestine/Palestinian 20, 25, 29, 43–4,
   65, 76–7, 89, 97, 99, 108, 110,
   125
Pamphilus 16
papyri, Christian 115
Parthians 85
Passion Narratives 34
Passover *28*
patriarchs 72
Paul 22, 83, 89–90, 102, 108–12
Pentateuch 79, 83–4, 111
   translation of 19, 27–28, 44, 49, 52,
   76
pesher interpretation 111
Peter 70
Pharisees/pharisaic 20, 43, 73, 77, 89,
   92, 100
Pharos 78
Philippi 116
Philo/philonic 8, 11, 25, 70, 78–9, 82,
   98–9, 120
philosophers/philosophy 79
piety 116–17, 122
pilgrim 81, *89*
Pindar 79
Plato *75*, 79
platonic world-soul 86
polemic/polemical/polemicize 64, *118*
   between Jews
   and Christians 48, 64–5
Polycarp of Smyrna 116
Porphyrius 119
praeparatio evangelica *112*, 122
prediction 54, 89

priests 76–7
profane 91–2
promise 105, 107, 110
propaganda, religious 80, 124
prophets/prophecy/prophetic 38–9,
   46, 49, 53–5, 60, 78, 95–7, 100–1,
   103
prophecy, the end of 100
prophetic books 20, 22, *28*, *82*, 90
proselyte *90*, 123
Proto-Theodotion 42, 109, 113
Proverbs
   translator of 86
   Greek 86
providentia dei 40
Psalms/psalter *28*, 42, 46–7, 65–6, 78,
   82, 85, 90, 95, 105–6, 111, *112*
   Hebrew *98–9*
   messianic 106
Psalm manuscripts
   Greek 59
Psalm canon 90, 98
pseudepigrapha/pseudepigraphical 20,
   29, *56*, 66, 72, 90, 93, 99, 107,
   109–10
Ptolemies/Ptolemaic 38–9, 75–6, 80
Ptolemy II Philadelphos 19, 25–8,
   37–8, 40, 44, 56, 74–5
Purim festival 88, 92
Pythagoras *75*

Quinta (column of the Hexapla) 14–16
Qumran 41, 46–7, 55, *69*, 82, 84, 86, 90,
   92, 95, 98, 111, 126
Qumran, Psalm manuscripts *98–9*

rabbis/rabbinic 44, *56*, 62, 69, 90, 92,
   100, 102–3, 122
reading, worship 66
   see also Holy Scripture(s)
recensions *see* Septuagint, recensions
Reformation/reformers/reformational
   66, 74, 126
Resurrection 94
Reuchlin 53
revelation 52
revision(s) *89*
Romans/roman 20–1, 89, 91, *108*
Rome 20, 22, 77–8, 81, 95, 100–1, 115,
   123–5
Rufinus 14, 49, 63

Sadducees/sadducean *4*, 90, 93
Salvation history 103, 117
Samaritan *37*, 79

Samuel, Hebrew
  LXX Vorlage of 84
Scriptural evidence 7, 27, 29, 106
scripture citations 56
scripture
  collections of 19, 56–7, 73–4, 95
  falsification of 31–4, 43, 47–8
  NT use of 111–12
scripture scholars
  Jewish/Palestinian 29, 83, 91, 101
scrolls, Jewish 41, 60, 89–90
Septima (column of the Hexapapla) 14
Septuagint 1–2, 5–8, 19–20, 22–3, 34,
    50–1, 54, 59, 73–4, 83–4, 88–9, 102,
    108–9, 126
  Christian appropriation of 41, 43, 50,
    61
  Christian 7, 47, 56, 59, 112
  criticism of 48
  division of the tradition 33
  forms of the text 34, 83, 88
  history of the text 1–17 (passim)
  inspiration of 39, 49–50, 78
  in Judaism 8
  Jewish-Christian consensus 30
  Jewish manuscripts 33, 113
  Jewish use of 36
  new translations of 43–4
  original/ancient tradition 10, 11–12,
    16
  problematic of 35, 38
  recensions 29, 33, 53, 56, 83, 113
  reputation/authority of 20, 36
  revisions of the text 43–4, 47, 52,
    82–3
Seth 72
Seventy/seventy-two, The 19, 25–6,
    30–1, 34–5, 37–8, 43, 48–51, 53–4,
    75, 78, 80
  authority of 27–8, 30, 36
  divinely inspired 11, 17, 35, 38–9, 47,
    74
  isolation of 27, 30, 53–5
  prophets 50–4
Severianus of Gabala 109
Severus Alexander 47, 119
Sexta (column of the Hexapla) 14–15
Shammai, school of 91
Shem 72
Simon II, high priest 3
Simon (Maccabee) 87, 93
Simon, son of Boethos 81
Sinai 36
Sinaiticus, Codex 16, 57–60
Solomon 69–70, 120–1

Son of Man 54
  coming of 95
Sophocles, tragedies of 121
soteriology 108
Spirit of God 17, 45
  see also 'Holy Spirit'
Stoa/Stoics 79
Symmachus 5, 13–14, 16, 43, 51, 53,
    60, 82
synagogue/synagogal 21–2, 29, 32, 35,
    37, 44, 50, 73, 94, 108, 112, 117,
    122–3
synagogue inscriptions 76, 80, 108
synagogue, Samaritan 75
Syria/Syrian 125
Syrohexapla 16, 88

Targum 47
temple 108
  cult 47
  destruction of 21, 73
  Jerusalem 20–1, 81, 89
  liturgy 106
  worship 46–7
Tertullian 54, 61, 66–7, 110, 117, 120,
    125
Testimonia collections 28, 67, 112, 114
tetragrammaton 7, 14, 41
tetrapla 9, 13, 16
text comparison, philological 63, 82
text, fidelity to 87
Theodore of Mopsuestia 92
Theodotion 4, 10, 13–14, 39, 43, 51, 53,
    60, 82, 88
  see also Proto-Theodotion
Theodotus synagogue inscription 108
  see also synagogue inscriptions
theology/theological 80–1
Theophilus of Antioch 66
therapeutoi 98–9
Thessalonica 75
Titus Flavius Clemens 123
Tobit, Aramaic version of 46
Torah 4, 36, 44, 46, 82, 90, 94
  oral 78
Torah shrine 54, 60
Translation 77
  Greek 22
  Jewish 9, 10, 12, 14, 16
  Literality/fidelity 52–3
  unalterability 77
Translation legend
  Christian 26–8, 30, 36–8, 40–1, 48–9,
    51, 56, 65, 78
  Jewish 17, 25, 34, 43–4, 77–8, 80

Translators, Jewish 5, 10, 16
Trent, Council of 57
Truth 73
  evidence of 37, 73
Trypho 30–1, 33, 43, 78

Valentinans *69*
Vaticanus, Codex 57–60, 64, 73
Vetus Latina 17, 88, 123
Virgin birth 29, 38
Vulgate *50*

wisdom 2, 114, 118
  divine 85, *109*
  Incarnation of 114
  preexistence of 86
Wise men, the seventy-two *see*
  Seventy, The
worship
  Christian 21–2, 52, 61, 65, 125
  Jewish 22, 44, *77*

Zerubbabel 87